GO SPY
THE LAND

George Alexander Hill MC DSO

GEORGE ALEXANDER HILL

GO SPY
THE LAND

BEING THE ADVENTURES OF IK8 OF THE BRITISH SECRET SERVICE

Biteback Publishing

First published in Great Britain in 1932 by Cassell and Company, Limited
This edition published in 2014 by
Biteback Publishing Ltd
Westminster Tower
3 Albert Embankment
London SE1 7SP
Copyright © George A. Hill 1932

ISBN 978-1-84954-652-2

10 9 8 7 6 5 4 3 2 1

A CIP catalogue record for this book is available from the British Library.

Set in Garamond

Printed and bound in Great Britain by
CPI Group (UK) Ltd, Croydon CR0 4YY

Contents

Introduction

The adventures of some of the early members of Britain's secret service inside Bolshevik Russia were so full of derring-do that they seem incredible to a modern audience, with historians often mistakenly dismissing them as fantasy. Sidney Reilly, the so-called 'Ace of Spies', who features heavily in this book, has suffered more than most, largely because of a series of fictitious stories written about him long after his death. Yet the real Reilly was regarded, and is still regarded, within MI6 as 'a very able agent and a far more serious operator than the impression given by the myth'.

The other British secret service officer to suffer from this misconception that espionage is necessarily a dull occupation more worthy of the prose of le Carré than that of Fleming, was the author of this book, Reilly's close friend and fellow spy, George Hill, whose adventures included using a swordstick in action against two German spies in the Russian town of Mogilev. Hill hurried back to his hotel to examine the blade, 'anxious to know what it looked like after its adventure. I had never run a man through before. It was not a gory sight. There was only a slight film of blood halfway up the blade and a dark stain at the tip.' He sounded distinctly disappointed.

Hill was born in Estonia, and grew up speaking a variety of languages fluently, including Russian. He was in Canada when war broke out and joined a Canadian infantry regiment, serving on the western front, where he was seriously wounded and, as a result of his linguistic ability, transferred into Military Intelligence, taking the unusual designation IK8.

When Bulgaria entered the war on Germany's side, in October 1915, Hill was given a crash course in Bulgarian and taught to fly and then sent to Greece, from where he flew agents across the Bulgarian lines. Later, in Russia, he and Reilly went underground, assisted by a network of female agents they had hand-picked to run their safe houses, a group of train-watchers reporting on troop movements, a large network of couriers recruited by Hill to take the intelligence north to the British forces, and a special operations 'wrecking gang' to sabotage Bolshevik lines of communication.

Hill's sexist description of his recruitment of his female agents might have embarrassed even James Bond. His main base was a house in Ulitsa Pyatnitskaya, Moscow's pre-revolution equivalent of Knightsbridge, and his main assistant a half-English, half-Russian musician

> who could turn her hand to anything which required skill ... It was essential that the people about us should be entirely trust-worthy. Evelyn and I discussed the matter and decided to ask two friends of ours, girls of English birth but Russian upbringing, to join our organisation ... Sally was one of the most beautiful girls I have ever seen. She had raven-black hair, a peach-like complexion and the most sensitive, pale, transparent hands. Annie, her sister, was not so good-looking but was a plump, merry, good-natured soul ... We wanted another ally to run messages for me ... After a great deal of thought we decided to enrol a young Russian girl we knew, an orphan who had just reached the mature age of seventeen. Vi was a tall blonde with blue eyes, and the most appealing ways, and time proved she was also full of pluck.

The couriers, who included the centre-half of a leading Russian football side, rested up between missions in the flat owned by a high-class prostitute. 'What was more natural? ... Our weary couriers could rest in safety in one of the rooms there.'

Reilly and Hill eventually got out of Russia using false passports, and were both awarded the Military Cross, with Hill also receiving the Distinguished Service Order. The citation read:

> He has since early December 1917, been constantly working between the north of Russia and Romania and southern Russia. He has attended Bolshevik meetings at night when street fighting was at its height, passing back and forth through the Bolshevik fighting lines, and has been almost daily under fire without protection. He has conducted himself with courage and coolness and rendered valuable service.

That goes some way to adding credence to the story told here, as – despite some discrepancies – does Hill's official report for the War Office and intelligence chiefs, reproduced in full at the end of this book, which tells the truth of the so-called Lockhart Plot to remove the Bolshevik leadership and Reilly's involvement.

Go Spy the Land is an exciting tale of gung-ho derring-do that features a host of fascinating characters, including not just Hill and Reilly themselves but Leon Trotsky, the Bolshevik Commissar of War, Robert Bruce Lockhart, joint architect with Reilly of the Lockhart Plot, and Arthur Ransome, the author of *Swallows and Amazons*, another of Britain's top spies in post-revolutionary Russia.

Michael Smith, Editor of Dialogue Espionage Classics
December 2013

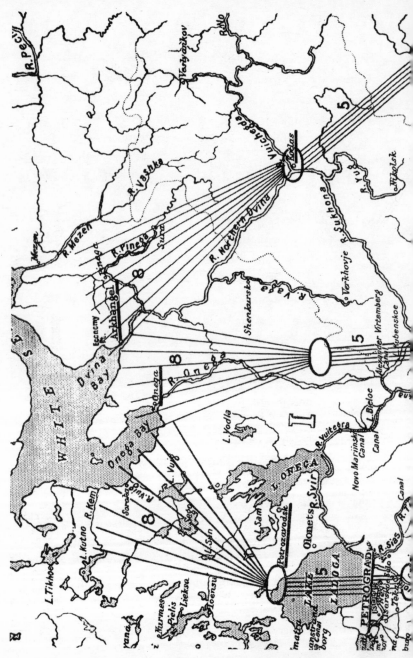

Courier routes used by George Hill and Sidney Reilly
to pass intelligence to the Allied Intervention Force.

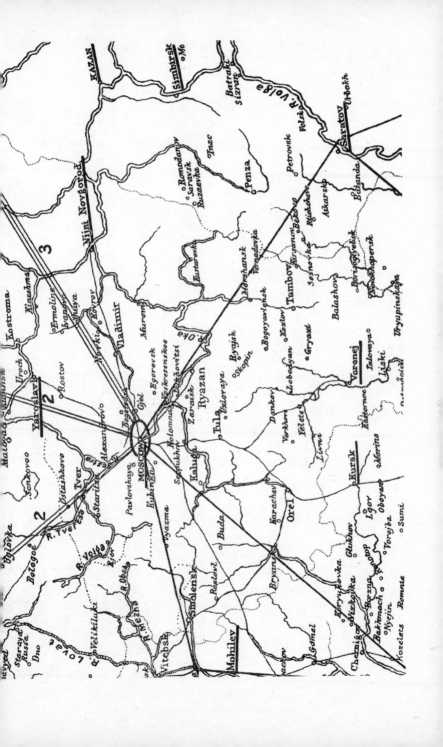

Chapter I

To the word 'espionage', through use and misuse, is attached a stigma likewise associated with the word 'spy', and all that spying stands for – a stigma undeserved yet easy to understand, for it is rooted in the fear of prying eyes from outside, of the stranger within the gates, of the traitor within the camp.

Spying is one of the oldest occupations in the world and, in course of time and by reason of the antipathy noted above, it has become so obscured by the accretion of legend and prejudice that I feel it necessary to define anew the meaning of the words 'spy', 'traitor', 'agent provocateur' and 'patriot' before I embark upon this story of mine, which has to do almost entirely with spying.

Espionage is the collection of evidence which enables one to appreciate the strength or intentions of an enemy, rival or opponent. It is a science blended of many parts. Spies exist all over the world. The greengrocer's assistant who watches the prices in the rival shop-window, the couturière who 'lifts' a model from a rival designer, the theatrical thug who steals a colleague's ideas and embodies them in a production a week before the other opens his show, all these people are spies or employ spies, just as much as do rival states and nations.

Peace pacts or no peace pacts, the Intelligence departments of most nations are still prying into their neighbours' secrets. The rumour of a new gun, an aeroplane engine, a new poison gas or even a gear for releasing or locking an aeroplane will awaken into activity spies, traitors and patriots, and will be protected by patriots, counter-espionage agents, secret police and the CID of New Scotland Yard and its equivalents.

Let me define those words I have already mentioned:

SPY

The meaning of the word 'spy' in its applied sense is very precisely defined. This is as it should be, for, by the Hague Convention, in time of war a spy if caught is liable to the death penalty. We cannot do better than quote Convention Four, Article Twenty, which informs us that a spy is a person who, acting clandestinely or on false pretences, obtains or endeavours to obtain information in the zone of operations of a belligerent with the intention of communicating it to a hostile party. A soldier in uniform is not a spy. A spy must not be shot without previous trial.

In time of peace a spy is one who secretly endeavours to obtain information concerning forces, armaments, fortifications or the defences of a country for the purpose of supplying it to another. A spy in peace time is not liable to the death penalty, but to a term of imprisonment.

In the United Kingdom the Official Secrets Act of 1889 makes it merely a misdemeanour wrongfully to obtain information concerning the Navy, Army, fortifications, naval dockyards, etc. But if such information is communicated or intended for communication to a foreign country the offence becomes a felony. Most of the civilised countries of the world have similar legislation.

A spy carries his life in his hands. His existence is one long hazard, joyous or the contrary. Spies in the British service have commonly taken up their dangerous duty out of sheer love of adventure. British spies have slipped through the Khyber Pass disguised as Afghans, or loitered in Eastern bazaars in the dress of native traders, but it is difficult for a man, however much he has tarried among them, to imitate with faultless exactitude the accent, habits, ways of thought of an alien people, and for that reason the espionage agent finds himself again and again compelled to resort to the employment of nationals. It is because of this part of his work, because of the necessity imposed on him of associating with traitors, that a certain odium has come to be attached to the name of spy.

TRAITOR

A 'traitor' is one who betrays those who trust him; is false to his allegiance to his Sovereign or to the government of his country. His crime is called 'treason'. I am not dealing here with High Treason for which a man like Sir Roger Casement was tried and executed. Whether one regards him as a traitor or a patriot depends on the angle from which the question is approached. An ordinary traitor just sells his country's secrets for his own gain, and very often to save his own skin because of some fault he has committed. Whatever his rank or calling he is a pretty low specimen of humanity.

AGENT PROVOCATEUR

I am glad to say these are not very common in this country, although of late they have been (in my opinion unfortunately) used to get convictions against petty violations of existing licensing laws. The policeman or plain-clothes detective who dons a white tie and vest and takes a pretty companion to a nightclub where, under the guise of an ordinary guest, he manages to persuade the proprietor or waiter to sell him and his guest drink out of hours is just a common agent provocateur.

But the Continental agent provocateur is a very much more dangerous person. He is used by the secret police of most countries to incite students, soldiers, or sailors to illegal activities in order that certain troubles may be artificially fomented, plots brought to light, or in order that people with certain political tendencies may fall into the net of the police. An agent provocateur is a more deadly reptile than an ordinary traitor and the history of the world's revolutions, bound up with secret service and secret societies as it is, unfortunately teems with examples of them.

For instance, Father Gapon, the Orthodox priest who for years was not only a hero to the masses of Russia but was respected throughout the world as the organiser of the Union of Factory Workers in Russia and was also a leader of the work-people in St Petersburg, was found to be an agent provocateur working under the direction of the secret police on that Sunday afternoon in January when a peaceful delegation was shot down outside the Winter Palace. That Sunday afternoon will go down in the history of the world as Bloody Sunday. Unfortunately Gapon's perfidy was discovered too late, but he met a grisly fate one evening in the early spring of 1906 at Terioki, in Finland. Rutenberg, a prominent revolutionary, managed to make him betray himself during a tête-à-tête conversation, when a number of workmen were listening concealed in another room. The proof was overwhelming. Gapon was executed then and there.

Some time afterwards I met one of his executioners. He told me that none of them had ever killed a man before and did not quite know how to set about it. 'Gapon,' he said, 'would not keep his head still when I tried to slip the noose over his head. He kept dodging it about. Finally I grabbed him by the hair and slipped the rope round his neck. Gapon complained that the rope was hurting his neck. I said, "You may as well get used to it now, as it is going to hurt much more before you are dead."' And so they strung him up. After the fall of the Tsarist government, when the archives of the Ochrana were seized by the revolutionaries, the evidence of Gapon's guilt was still nestling in the secret dossiers and was made public.

Counter-espionage agents are those whose duty it is to nullify the efforts of spies. It is the most artful form of espionage, this spying on spies, and those engaged upon the work are often in greater danger even than the spy himself.

PATRIOT

The best type of a spy is a patriot in the highest sense, who for the sake of his country's freedom and rights lives a life of risk and self-sacrifice, knowing that his end, if he is caught, will be far from pleasant.

The spy must of course be familiar with the language, habits, and ways of thought of the people among whom his field of operations lies. He must be gifted with a brain of the utmost agility, able to draw a deduction in a flash and make a momentous decision in an instant, possessed of infinite resource in pulling his neck out of the noose into which he will not infrequently thrust it, equipped with superlative qualities of tact, patience and perseverance. He must have a memory trained to register a photographic impression of a face or a document, and be able to retain with literal accuracy the contents of the latter.

Over and above all this, he must have a genius for organising. What may be called the office work of espionage is apt to be overlooked through the appeal to the popular imagination of the adventurous aspect of spying, but on it the whole success of the undertaking depends. A thousand and one details have to be arranged by the master spy, assigning their several tasks to his assistants, keeping them primed with all vital information that comes to his ears, choosing the many places where they can report to him. Nine out of ten spies who are caught have faulty organisation or communication to blame for their arrest and court martial.

Again, the most accurate and detailed information is valueless if it cannot be conveyed expeditiously to the quarters where it is required. In time of war the espionage agent is often in hostile country, and around him every line of communication is cut. Through the blockade which hems him in his messengers must be continually piercing and in this work many brave men die.

Clever and effective spies seldom get caught, *but the best are not even suspected*.

While I cannot, alas, claim that I was never suspected, I have the satisfaction of knowing that I was never caught.

I have never been caught! I do not say this boastfully, but in gratitude. My days as a spy were a joyful adventure in the pages of my life; had I been caught, the adventure would have come to an abrupt and by no means joyful conclusion.

I little thought as a young man that I should become a spy and be drawn into all the drama and melodrama of such sport during a war. And yet everything that happened to me in my boyhood days was fitting me out for that calling. If I had gone to a special school for years, studied espionage as a profession, I could not have had a better training than life gave me in my early days.

My father was a general merchant with a business that stretched over Russia across Siberia and down into Persia through Turkestan. As a small child I moved with my parents from London to Hamburg, Riga, St Petersburg, Moscow, to the world's fair at Nijni-Novgorod, down the Volga to the Caspian Sea. For days we would stop at my father's depot at Enzalai, and then go by horses to Teheran, back to Krasnovodsk on the Caspian by sea, down the railway that was being built to Merv, by carriage to Samarkand and by camel sledges to Tashkent, back along the line across the Caspian to Baku, along the military roads of the Caucasus to Batum, and via the Black Sea to Constantinople and so back to England.

With my parents I always spoke English. My father was an English pioneer merchant of the best type and our life at home was the life lived by an ordinary English family. English customs and traditions were maintained, nor did my parents ever become good linguists. But I? Well, I had a Russian nurse with whom I spoke Russian; our head man was a Tartar with whom I used to converse freely in Tartar; our coachman was a Persian and I was always in and out of the stables fussing about my pony. There was also a little boy with whom I romped on occasions, an Armenian a year or two older than myself. How I envied him because of the knowledge of life he had!

My parents, of course, had not the least idea as to the things that I heard discussed by various people in various tongues, how I knew the intrigues and love affairs of the people around our warehouses. Had they known I should have been whisked off at a tender age to a preparatory school in England.

As it was they employed excellent German and French governesses, with the result that when still a small boy I had half a dozen languages at the tip of my tongue, had learned to sum up the characteristic qualities and faults of a dozen nationalities, and had acquired an adaptability which has helped me all my life.

As an aftermath to the Russo-Japanese war in 1905 came 'the first revolution' in Russia, marked by widespread disorder and bloodshed. Every stratum of society was affected. There was absolutely no political freedom of any kind, and those who wished for even the mildest and most conservative reforms were branded as dangerous revolutionists. Agitation was so rife throughout Russia that it spread even into the schools. Schoolboys were used for carrying illegal newspapers. They were used for carrying messages and, as a protest to the closing of universities by the authorities, many of the senior schoolboys came out on strike.

It was during this period that I met my first agent provocateur. He was a boy who kept the ball of discussion rolling and then reported the seditious remarks he heard to the police. I leave to the imagination of the reader how mild the sedition must have been in what roughly corresponded to an English fifth form, but we discovered that he was making reports to the police, and the following day he was nearly slain. At this school we wore a type of patent-leather belt with a very fine and rather heavy brass buckle. A dozen of us slipped off our belts and used the brass ends on the unfortunate youth, who never appeared at our school again. The school authorities and the police investigated the case, but never found out the cause of the thrashing.

Coming events, they say, cast their shadows before and, while never being a revolutionary myself, I was constantly mixed up with revolutionaries and counter-revolutionaries, a circumstance which gave me my first knowledge of espionage and counter-espionage work. While still at school I had a policeman friend. He was not really a policeman, but had been an officer in a crack regiment and had to leave it for financial reasons. He joined the gendarmerie which did a great deal of the political spy work in Russia.

He was a splendid-looking man and, for a gendarme, very popular. I first met him during a sailors' Christmas-tree party which the English colony in Riga gave every year to British sailors in the port. Those parties were always jolly occasions which started with a dinner and ended with a sing-song, the sailors as a rule supplying three-quarters of the programme. 'Soldiers of the King', 'Daisy Bell', 'Hearts of Oak', 'Clementine' and 'She was Poor but She was Honest' were the favourites. The evenings always finished up with 'God Save the King' followed by the Russian National Anthem. Yet such were the conditions in Russia that we were not allowed to hold this party without the presence of an official gendarme. That is how I got to know my friend. Young as I was, I discovered that he had a taste for whisky and so twice a week, about the time that has since become cocktail-time, he would drop in for a whisky-and-soda with my father.

I have since wondered whether possibly his visits had an ulterior purpose and whether he was not watching to see that we were not aiding and abetting some of our revolutionary friends.

One morning, walking down the Kalkstrasse, I saw the broad back of my policeman friend on his regular beat in front of me. He always passed down the Kalkstrasse at that time, and I quickened my step to overtake him. Just before I came up with him two men suddenly stepped out of the doorway ahead of him. My friend's right hand suddenly jerked in his pocket, there were two sharp and piercing cracks, and the two men who had stepped out of the doorway dropped to the pavement. Then there came a shattering explosion and I ran like a hare. I knew that my gendarme had shot them, but whether he had been blown up by the bomb or not I did not know. By the time I had recovered my nerve there were police at each end of the street and I went home and told my tale.

Imagine our surprise when at the usual time that night my gendarme arrived at our house, handed his coat and sword to the maid, and unconcernedly came in for his whisky-and-soda.

We chatted on all manner of subjects, but he made no allusion to his morning adventure, so while he was talking to my father I slipped out of the room into the hall and looked at his coat. There, sure enough, were two singed holes through the lining of the pocket.

Then I went back and tackled him. His organisation had been on the track of the two Nihilists who were known assassins and had come to Riga especially to murder the Governor-General. Had he waited to pull out his revolver instead of shooting from his pocket he would have been killed by the bomb.

Murder, assassination, and hold-ups in the street were the order of the day between 1905 and 1907. There were very large warehouses adjoining our house and one night, returning from the port where we had just seen off to England a ship which had been loading very late, we came across our foreman, Pavel Spiridonov, hanging on a disused lamp-post just outside our gate. It was a bitter night. Snow was on the ground. He had been strung up with barbed wire, and beneath the dangling form of the poor wretch was a little pool of blood. On his chest was pinned a notice with the one word, 'Provocateur'.

That summer my father and I went down the Volga as usual to Persia. On the boat, after we reached Kazan, I had my first encounter with a British secret service agent, Major Y.

At our table opposite us there was a rather tall German merchant. At our first meeting we bowed to him as Continental etiquette demands, and he rose in his place and introduced himself in the German manner.

At the second meeting my father's attention was suddenly attracted, for the German had quite unconsciously given a Masonic sign. My father caught the German's eye and returned the sign. This led to the two men becoming very friendly, and we learned that our German companion was making for Barfurush, where we had a depot.

When we were well out in the Caspian our German friend confided to my father that he was really an Englishman and on special service. He took my father into his confidence because he wanted a place at Barfurush where he could stay and whence he could disappear in another disguise.

This was just before the Anglo-Russian agreement about Persia. Both Great Britain and Russia were sending spies into each other's territory and great hostility existed between the two countries.

Major Y. stayed at our house for several days and then, late one evening, the servants were told that he was going away.

His bags were packed and he drove off towards Teheran. Late
the following night he slipped back into our house after the
servants had gone to bed, and next morning a grave, shaven-
haired Persian left for Merv, from where, I believe, he departed
disguised as an Afghan. During the six days that he was with us
we felt that we were really helping the Empire's cause, and the
excitement of aiding a British spy kept my father and myself
happy for many days to come.

Chapter II

'Maxim Gorki is in town' – excitedly the rumour swept the universities and was echoed among the senior schoolboys! Maxim Gorki, the writer on Russian life, the hero of the day, a man of the people, who knew the under-stratum of life and could write about it in a magic way. Maxim Gorki was in Riga. How I hated the idea of going back to school in England at such a time, for sooner or later, if he really were in Riga, he was bound to turn up at one of our friends' houses.

Months previously, intellectual Russia had raged when it became known that Maxim Gorki had been thrown into the prison of St Peter and Paul. He had for some years been working with the Social Democrats, and he was imprisoned for the idiotic reason that he had been a member of an accredited delegation which had presented a petition for political reform to the Tsar's Ministers. The unfairness of the sentence rankled in the breasts of his admirers.

One or two letters sent by the novelist to his wife had been privately circulated, but everyone in the country was waiting for news of his release and to hear of his experiences.

Our home was open to any English people who happened to be visiting the town, and sooner or later most passers-by found their way to us for tea or some other meal. Among such chance visitors was an English journalist who had been waiting patiently in Riga for some days. No one knew exactly why he was there.

On one occasion he was expected to lunch, but at the last minute he telephoned regretting that he could not come. I took the message. He asked me whether by chance I had a camera, and I replied that my father had one. 'Could he bring it along, do you think, to the Hotel Commercial at once?'

I thought this request rather cool. Possibly I was disappointed at our acquaintance not coming, as I wanted to tell him of the Maxim Gorki rumour.

I said, 'I suppose he can as soon as he has had lunch. By the way, it is rumoured that Maxim Gorki is in town.'

'I know,' said the surprising man, 'I am with him now. Don't tell anyone, but that is why I want the camera.'

I almost jumped out of my skin. 'We'll be along in ten minutes.' Slamming down the receiver, I rushed off to get my father.

We did not wait for lunch, but seized the camera and drove off in a sledge to the Commercial Hotel.

Spring had come early that year. The thaw had already set in. There was a slight mist hanging over the town, and the snow looked dirty and muddy. The iron sledge runners kept grating on the cobble stones which were appearing through the yellow slush. All this I remember keenly to this day, and how my heart was beating with excitement at the idea of meeting Maxim Gorki.

He was staying at the Commercial Hotel, under an assumed name, in room No. 7. We found our journalist friend and the author sipping tea out of glasses. There was a samovar gently boiling on the table, and they were eating strawberry jam out of little glass dishes and occasionally cutting off hunks of black bread.

That was Gorki's lunch. He had come out of prison in St Petersburg the day before. He had spent an hour with his wife and had learned that he would most likely be re-arrested on a further charge which probably would mean his exile to Siberia. To avoid this fate his friends had arranged for him to go to Riga and from there to be smuggled out of Russia into Germany. Our journalist friend was very much in sympathy with the Social Democrats and so had been acquainted with Gorki's movements.

By the time we arrived Gorki had already told his story, had given our friend certain letters and made some sketches of his cell and a plan of the prison yard in which he took his exercise.

These letters, which had been written by Gorki in prison, had, of course, been examined by the prison authorities, and they had also been tested for secret writing with a mixture of cyanide which would develop any invisible ink.

Our journalist friend was afraid to send the originals out of the country, for if they came into the hands of the censor they would certainly be confiscated and destroyed. And that was why he wanted the camera.

Gorki was then about thirty-seven, though he looked very much older. He had a mop of hair which was constantly slipping down over his forehead and he had a trick of throwing his head back to get it out of his eyes. I think he had the saddest eyes of anyone I had ever met. He talked to us for an hour about his prison experiences. He was planning to live abroad and to start an intensive anti-Tsarist campaign. We promised to say nothing to anyone until he had been twenty-four hours across the frontier, and he was leaving that evening secretly for the frontier where friends were waiting to smuggle him across.

Gorki escaped safely and finally settled at Capri. I did not see him again for thirteen years, when we met in Petrograd in very different circumstances.

Well, we photographed the documents, the four of us, there in room No. 7 at the Commercial Hotel. And now the question arose, how were we to get the photographs to England? The censorship was so strict that it was impossible to think of using the post as a means of communication, and our journalist friend had some other people to see before returning to England.

I said at the commencement of this chapter that I was just about to return to school in England. I had come to Riga for my Christmas holidays, but had been taken ill and was returning very late in the term. We decided that the best chance was for me to take these photographs back with me in my silk hat.

As soon as the plates were developed and the photographs ready the lining of my hat was carefully removed, the photographs lightly gummed inside, and the lining very carefully put back and tightly gummed down.

I had always loathed that topper with particular venom, for it was uncomfortable and to my very cosmopolitan mind an idiotic form of headgear. But after I had safely crossed the frontier at Wirballen and was speeding towards England and school my feelings changed towards it, and for many years I kept it by me for sentimental reasons.

I was very young and naturally longed to tell my friends in England of my adventure and how the photographs had reached the *Illustrated London News*, but had already learned that in the game into which I had so casually wandered silence was golden, and even when one was safely through a job one did not talk about it – much!

Chapter III

I was an English business man in Russia, and while I was most interested in the political developments, and sympathised very much with the champions of political reform, I did not meddle in the politics of the country. After all, I was only a visitor, even if a permanent one. Nevertheless it was impossible to avoid being involved from time to time in some sort of political affairs. There were in Russia no politicians or liberals of the English type. A Duma had been constituted more or less on the Western model, but most of the political leaders were idealists and students of philosophy rather than practical statesmen.

One of my great business friends was a Mr B., a wealthy Jewish merchant in St Petersburg, with whom I stayed whenever I visited the capital. He was an elderly man, childless, and very unhappy about it. He and his brother were the last of their line and felt keenly, as all Jews do, the fact that there was no male heir to follow them. The brother had a daughter, Sonia, who was studying at the University of St Petersburg, and who was adored by her father and her uncle. Curiously enough, although I was constantly visiting Mr B., I had never met his niece.

We used to dine about four o'clock in the afternoon. There would be vodka in ice buckets on the table, the finest caviar, smoked sturgeon and garlic sausage, followed by a number of Russian dishes. I think his cook made the finest borscht that

I have ever tasted and it was invariably accompanied by a doughnut-like meat pie.

As a rule, on my arrival at the house, my host would be standing in his study door with a broad smile of welcome on his face, rubbing his hands and saying, 'Come along, come along, I have got all your favourite dishes,' and in we would go, more like two old cronies than an elderly, rather fat Jewish gentleman and a very young Englishman. But one day when I arrived he met me with a white, scared face, and tears streaming down his cheeks.

'They have arrested Sonia,' he said chokingly. 'She is in the Schlusselburg prison.'

It appeared that Sonia, while studying at the university, had joined a Social Revolutionary organisation, and the usual sequence of events – expulsion from the university, police court trial and banishment to Siberia – was impending. To make it worse, although she had joined a pacific branch of the SR organisation, she had somehow or other got mixed up more or less unknowingly with a terrorist section.

I had never before seen a man so broken with sorrow.

After weeks of trying and bribing he and his brother finally managed to get Sonia out on bail, which was fixed at £2,000. That sum gives one some idea of the graveness of the charges which were being brought by the authorities against her. The minimum punishment would be exile to Siberia for five years.

Her uncle and father did not care about the £2,000. All they wanted was to get Sonia out of the country.

I had never met Sonia, but could I in decency refuse to help a friend in such an impasse?

My business took me often from Riga to Stettin, and as a

rule I tried to make the two days' journey in the same ship. I think she was the *Regina*. She belonged to a Swedish company and had a delightful captain, while I was also friendly with the officers and engineers of the ship. She was really a cargo boat, but had accommodation for four or five passengers and a tiny cabin de luxe consisting of a twin-bedded state room with an adjoining bathroom and lavatory, which I always booked.

I made up my mind to make an attempt to smuggle Sonia out on this ship.

Her passport, without which she could not officially leave Russia, had been impounded by the police. Even if she could have secured a false one (and they were quite common in those days) the risk of using it would be great, as her full description would have been circulated to all frontier posts.

It was decided that she should be motored from St Petersburg to Riga where she would stay one night at our house. And then I was to try to smuggle her out of the country on the *Regina*.

My plans were rather simple. I had probably made seven or eight trips that year on the *Regina* and was, of course, very well known to the port authorities whose duty it was to search from top to bottom all outgoing vessels. So thoroughly was this search made that the examiners were equipped with long iron rods to poke into ventilators, lifeboats, lockers and cupboards.

The Russians are a charming people, and one of their great joys is to see people off or to go to boats and stations to meet friends. No matter how often I went abroad there would always be half a dozen people to see me off with baskets of fruit, bunches of flowers, chocolates and all sorts of queer, kindly gifts. It was a custom to arrive at least an hour before a train or boat departed and to make a real party, and I am afraid I very often disappointed my friends because I had what they considered an unhappy habit of reaching a boat or train just a few minutes before it left. But nevertheless they always turned up and used to entertain each other pending my arrival.

When the ship was about to sail all the friends who came to take farewell of passengers were put on shore and the gangway raised before the examination of the ship began.

My plan was that Sonia should be among those who saw me off. I would then conceal her in the bathroom and somehow or other prevent the examining officials from examining the place.

When Sonia turned up she proved to be an adorable person, rather small, with jet-black hair, a wonderful peach-like complexion and blue eyes. This is a combination which one meets occasionally in Russian Jewesses. She had a delightful smile, very beautiful even teeth and delicate hands. As a matter of fact I completely lost my heart to her. I think I had been afraid of meeting a stern, high-brow, somewhat vicious Jewish revolutionary.

Everything went according to plan. There were about ten people making a great noise in my cabin. Somebody had brought a case of champagne. The head steward had said with a grin that I would be charged corkage, and I gave him a bottle, telling him to drink it in his pantry and give a drink to the port officials, and to let me have my party to the very last moment.

I had asked my guests as a great favour to make a point of not waiting to see the boat out (luckily it was raining) but to leave as soon as they were ashore, and this they promised to do.

The ship's siren boomed out the warning for visitors to go on shore. The steward came along with one of the port officials to say that my guests must really leave me now, and after one last quick drink they started to file out. Sonia remained behind. I called out to the last guest that I would be up in a moment, and slipped her into the bathroom. Between the bath and the lavatory seat there was a protruding iron bulkhead, and Sonia stood flat up against the wall behind it. She had gone very pale. I gripped her hand. It was icy cold. I whispered, 'Pull yourself together!' and a plucky smile came into her eyes.

I closed the state room door and went on deck feeling none too good myself, for if I were caught not even my British passport would save me from an unpleasant term of imprisonment and possibly a protracted visit to Siberia.

I waved to my departing friends who, true to their promise, were scrambling into cabs. Then I walked aft and blundered into the examining officers, shook hands with one of them whom I knew slightly and received their thanks for my charming thought in sending them the bottle of champagne.

Then I strolled towards the saloon on which my cabin opened. Through a porthole I could see the examining party approaching. I slipped into my cabin, left the door open, and passed into the bathroom.

I had left the bathroom lavatory door unlatched, and now I arranged my clothes and sat on the lavatory seat. After what seemed an hour but was really not more than two or three minutes there came a slight tap on my cabin door, which, you will remember, I had left open, and the examining officials walked in. They gave one glance round the cabin and, as I anticipated, came over to the bathroom door and opened it. I promptly called out and slammed the door, and then as if in a hurry went to the door with my clothes still undone and stood in the opening. The officials were most apologetic, and I replied with a smile,

'That is all right; I should have locked the door.' Then I turned round deliberately and pulled the plug, after which, doing up my braces with some show, I walked into my cabin and offered them yet one more drink, and we opened the last bottle of champagne, tossed off a glass each, and they went out.

All danger was not yet over, as there was always a chance of another inspection at the mouth of the river at a place called Boldera. So Sonia had to stand in her little corner for another hour.

It was most important that the captain should not suspect that Sonia was a political refugee, for, however good-natured he was, it would be more than his command was worth to take such a risk. Accordingly I had made up a story beforehand to the effect that we were lovers and that she was secretly escaping from her parents to be with me.

Boldera was passed, and, as all the world loves a lover, my captain friend and the mate and the first engineer were now grinning at the two of us in a friendly way and telling us both that we were very wicked people. We had a merry dinner that night.

Sonia had never been on a ship in her life before and so was tremendously excited and interested, and the danger she had passed through seemed to have been entirely forgotten.

But I shall never forget that charming person's embarrassment when it came to turning in for the night. All her worldly knowledge, the determined young revolutionary, disappeared, and she was just a very shy, scared young girl. I sent her to bed first, and when I came into the cabin found her with the sheets drawn up right under her nose, and two rather frightened blue eyes peeping out at me. Brute that I was, I yelled with laughter. I slipped into the bathroom, changed into pyjamas, and turned into the second bed.

The crowning jest came next morning when the captain knocked at our state room and came in. He had come to inquire after our health and saw to his dismay that the two state beds were nicely separated, being screwed to the deck. He apologised to Sonia and said that for the second and last night he would instruct the ship's carpenter temporarily to screw down one of the beds next to the other. He meant it very kindly.

For years I wrote to Sonia, but since the war I have lost touch with her.

One evening a little over a year before the war, I boarded the Nord Express for Russia at the Friedrich-strasse Bahnhof in Berlin, and found that I had a travelling companion in my coupé. We bowed to each other and mentioned our names. I noticed that his was German, but his appearance suggested the Slav more than the Teuton. As a rule it is easy to drop into conversation with strangers on trains, but this man was silent, very reserved and seemingly very nervous.

I passed along to the restaurant car for a drink and when I returned found that our bunks had been made up for the night. My companion was standing in the corridor looking more nervous than ever. Suddenly he asked me my nationality and seemed somewhat relieved when I replied that I was English. Presently the ticket inspectors came along. My companion made a tremendous effort to keep calm, but there could be no doubt that he was labouring under a great strain. At first I thought that maybe he was trying to travel without a ticket, but this was not the reason of his agitation, for he produced one which was duly clipped.

Later I noticed a man pass up and down the corridor two or

three times and invariably glance into our coupé as he passed.
My companion took down his bag and went to wash. The
train was slowing down for a station. The man I had noticed
came along the corridor again. The train stopped. He looked in
and, seeing me alone, his whole manner changed. He looked
up at the rack. My companion's bag had gone. He almost
shouted at me, 'Has the other gentleman left the train?' Before
I could reply that I did not know, my questioner had darted
out on the platform. Almost simultaneously my companion
returned, and the train started on its way north again. After
the next stop the guard and a train inspector came along
and asked to see our tickets. This was quite unusual and by
this time I was pretty certain that my companion was under
observation.

Mine was the lower bunk. I turned out my head light and
before I dropped off to sleep the upper berth light was out as
well. Every time the train stopped I woke up, and each time I
noticed in the looking-glass over the washstand the glow of a
cigarette. I do not think my companion slept a wink that night.

About six o'clock, just before dawn, I left the coupé. A man
was leaning up against the corridor at the far end of the carriage.
He was obviously watching.

My companion seemed to be in better spirits by breakfast
time. We chatted and I casually mentioned what had happened
the previous evening. A look of fear passed swiftly across his face.

'Have you seen the man this morning?' He asked the question casually.

'No,' I said; 'but I have a feeling that one of us is under
observation.'

My companion suddenly seemed to master himself. He

smiled at me. 'No,' he said, 'I don't think that we can possibly be under observation,' and lit yet another cigarette. I commenced reading a new Tauchnitz novel.

Presently he started tearing some papers in minute fragments and, opening the window, scattered them along the line. From his bag he took more papers, which I recognised as tracings of some sort, and rather regretfully these too he destroyed. He did this all without any undue hurry, and unless my suspicions had been aroused I should not have given his action a thought.

Gumbinnen was passed and in a few minutes we were due at Eydtkuhnen, the last station in Prussia and the frontier post for Wirballen in Russia.

The man who had been in the corridor since morning came up to our coupé as we pulled into the station. 'The Herrshaften are wanted in the Commandant's office.' Although my conscience was like driven snow I felt uncomfortable. One always does on these occasions. I at once asked why, and was told I would be informed in due course. As we got out of the carriage a detective and two railway police closed in upon us and we and our bags were marched off to the Commandant's office.

A typical Prussian bully (I believe this particular breed is now almost extinct) demanded my passport. I handed it over. 'This is obviously forged,' he said rudely, and I assured him it was perfectly genuine.

He said the same about my companion's German passport, who merely said that he had had it for many years.

'Possibly,' replied the Prussian; 'but we know it is forged.'

Then he started questioning me. I had no difficulty in reply-ing, but because of his rudeness and a sympathy I had for my companion I held my tongue as to the papers I had seen the latter destroy and throw out of the window.

'You will be searched,' said the Prussian.

I protested, but without avail, and an expert at the game ran his hands over my clothes. I do not know of a more humiliating experience than being searched. You are absolutely helpless and you invariably remember the little private things you have forgotten to destroy which are sitting in your pocket-book, or tucked away in an inside pocket, and now prying eyes are running over one's innermost secrets.

I heard the warning bell sound for the departure of the train to Russia. I said it was imperative for me to catch it. The Commandant just looked at me.

'Am I under arrest?' I demanded.

He shook his head. 'Only detained for examination. We will search your bag. Hand over your keys.'

So they opened up my Gladstone bag. It was a beautiful leather contraption in a canvas cover. Why Gladstone bags have gone out of use I, as a traveller, cannot imagine, for they were the handiest form of bag for carrying property, and in my opinion very much more effective than the modern suit-cases. My companion was treated in a similar way to myself, but he did not protest very much. From the questions I was asked I could see that I was suspected of being his accomplice.

The Commandant examined us for about an hour. I demanded to see the British Consul and was told that the nearest one was at Danzig. We were told that we should be interrogated again in another hour's time, and meanwhile, if we desired it, at our own expense we could have some food.

For a moment my companion and I were left alone, and in

Russian he thanked me for not having said anything about him to the Commandant, and added with a twinkle in his eyes, 'I am glad I destroyed those papers.'

Later we were led back for further examination. A detective stepped forward and examined my bag thoroughly. The contents had already been spread out on the floor, but now he ran his hand along the seams of the bag and tapped its bottom, and felt the lining. Then he made a small incision and ran a long steel-like prong between its leather sides. He did this very skilfully and with practically no damage to the bag.

Alas, by the look on my companion's face I saw that all was up with him. As soon as the detective commenced to operate on his bag he felt papers. The bag was ripped open, literally taken to pieces and a number of documents found. My companion was formally arrested then and there on a charge of espionage and sent back to the fortress of Thorn for trial.

By this time apparently the Commandant was convinced of my innocence and within an hour he received telegrams both from Berlin and St Petersburg proving my bona fides.

With many apologies I was put up as a guest of the German government at the local hotel.

The next day I boarded the Nord Express. Before leaving I bought a copy of a Koenigsberg newspaper and found a brief note to the effect that two suspect spies had been arrested on the previous day and taken from the Nord Express.

But the paper was wrong.

Only one spy had been arrested.

Chapter IV

At the outbreak of war I was in Northern British Columbia, fishing on the Skeena River, some twenty miles from Prince Rupert and, like most men, I hurried to join up. Within a week I was in training at the Willows Camp, Victoria. There was a marvellous collection of men at this camp, and it was they who in less than a year made such regiments as the 16th Canadian Scottish and the 30th Battalion famous on the British fronts.

We were equipped at Esquimalt, but there was still a great shortage of uniforms. I am short and very broad, and accordingly the quartermaster gave me a uniform designed for a man about six feet in height, in which misfit, to my shame, I had to march back to the Willows Camp. As soon as parade was over I rushed off to a local tailor and had it remade. In fact most of us obtained our own uniforms – which was certainly against regulations – and spent our money on all sorts of useless equipment. In this connection I met my first wartime spy.

An American drummer, as commercial travellers are called in the United States, was peddling a new kind of canteen. He came in and out of camp frequently and somehow or other the men came to suspect him. At last the suspicion reached the ears of the camp Provost Marshal, who had the drummer watched, and it was found, sure enough, that he was a German-American working for the German secret service organisation in Seattle.

But, owing to a stroke of good fortune, I had been selected to make up a draft for Princess Patricia's Canadian Light Infantry, and was on my way to France before the fate of the American drummer was settled.

Owing to my languages, I found myself a full-blown interpreter as soon as we arrived in France. Arranging for billets, dealing with irate villagers, purchasing food from avaricious shopkeepers was not very amusing, but I was thoroughly interested in the examination of prisoners and their documents, the taking down of their statements, and from little pieces of information building up, as one does a jigsaw puzzle, a complete picture.

The Canadians were in the line during the battle of Neuve Chapelle, and it was at Laventie, near Estaires, that I saw my first spy caught red-handed during the war.

He was an ordinary French peasant, a traitor who had been bought by the enemy and was used as a post office, i.e. he was not actively employed on getting information, but received messages which he attached to carrier pigeons and dispatched across the German lines when the coast was clear.

He had been under suspicion for some days, for he was constantly being found in places where he had no business to be, but he always had some sort of an excuse ready – he was either looking for stray cattle, collecting wood, or searching for something.

The civilian population in the zone of operations caused enormous difficulties to the military authorities, but quite naturally they would not leave their farmhouses unless they were forced. It was a strange sight indeed to see a peasant stoically ploughing his field while shells whizzed over his head and exploded around him.

We actually were billeted in the farm of this particular spy. One evening when he came back to his farm he was stopped and a pigeon was found tucked away in his coat. He was put under arrest, and, of course, knew he was doomed. The Canadians handed him over to the French authorities who I presume dealt with him in due course.

There was a terrible scene just before he was marched off. His wife and sister must have been well aware of his treachery, and their wailings continued long after the man had been taken away.

Early in April we moved up to the Ypres front and I was put entirely on Intelligence work. About the middle of the month our division took up a position round St Julien. We were expecting some sort of an attack at any time, and it was most important for us to know whether the enemy were getting any reinforcements. As my knowledge of German was exceptional, night after night I slipped out between the lines to listen to the German troops in their trenches. One could tell by the accent whether the soldiers were Bavarians or Saxons, and if we knew that a section of line was held by Bavarians, and suddenly either the Bavarians disappeared and were replaced by Saxons, or Bavarians and Saxons were there together, by putting two and two together after a certain time one could reasonably infer whether reinforcements had arrived and whether the German line on this section was being strengthened for the purposes of attack.

It was a nerve-racking business, wandering through no man's land, and horrible, because for months there had been intermittent fighting all round the sodden, reeking, clay fields over which I crawled. One night as I crept through the pitch dark my right hand touched something, and, with a sickening squish, sank through. It was the body of a poor fellow who had been lying there for weeks.

On another night, when I was close to the German trenches, I was challenged and the challenge was followed by a hand grenade. The result was a shattered knee-cap. But my luck was in and I was found by one of our own patrols and hauled back to our lines. When I came to I was lying on a stretcher, and as I looked down towards my feet a sudden horror seized me. When I had crawled out into no man's land I had been wearing a Gordon tartan kilt, for by now I was attached to the Canadian Scottish Brigade. But flung across me hanging over the stretcher was a kilt of the Seaforth tartan. Of course the kilts had been mixed up at one of the advance dressing-stations, but the fact that I was wearing the wrong tartan worried my semi-delirious brain far more than my wound.

A few weeks later I received my commission and after a pleasant convalescence was assigned a post on the Intelligence Staff at the War Office. Then, as I got stronger and was able to walk about again, I was sent to the East coast on counter-espionage work. During this time nothing very sensational occurred in connection with my work, but I was learning the ropes and the experience gained during those six or seven weeks made me thoroughly conversant with the work of counter-espionage service.

A telegram summoned me back to the War Office, where I was ordered to report at a certain room.

'Mr Hill,' said a civilian, who had the bushiest eyebrows of any man I had ever met, 'do you speak Russian?'

'Yes, sir,' I said, and a warm glow crept up my spine. I was very anxious to go to Russia, and to my mind the question could only mean that I was to be ordered to that front.

But the authorities had other ideas, for Dr Ross,[†] who was the civilian gentleman, said: 'Then you will please learn Bulgarian in a month,' and my hopes fell to the ground.

For the next four weeks I was working hard at the War Office with a Bulgarian teacher, and at the same time went through a special course in Intelligence work. It was a most thorough course. Experts from Scotland Yard lectured me on shadowing and recognising the signs of being shadowed. I was taught the methods of using invisible inks. I learned a system of codes and was primed with all the dodges which are useful to spies.

It happened at that time that a British spy had escaped from the German-occupied parts of Belgium. For days before his escape he had lain in a loft watching German reinforcements entraining at a certain junction. Hour after hour he wrote in invisible ink on greaseproof paper the number of wagons, and the type of troops entrained, and counted the guns which were loaded. And at last when he had all the information he wanted, he wrapped his greaseproof paper round some particularly fat ham sandwiches, which he put into the saddlebag of his push-bike, and pedalled off for the Dutch frontier.

At the frontier a long queue of people was waiting to have documents examined, and he whiled away the time by munching his sandwiches as he slowly moved up to the control post. When he reached the examining officials he politely wrapped up those sandwiches which he had not had time to consume and quite openly put them into his saddlebag. The officer

---

†   Now Sir Edward Denison Ross, Director of the School of Oriental Studies.

examined his papers, found them in order, looked through his saddlebag to see that he was not carrying any correspondence, and passed him through into Holland. Within thirty-six hours he was in London, and we were developing the writing on the greaseproof paper.

How I admired that agent and his pluck! I am glad to say he came through the war quite safely, and only a few weeks ago I met him at the Conservative Club.

At the end of a month my Bulgarian was almost word perfect, and I made preparations for Salonica. We had recently stopped a neutral vessel carrying Bulgarians from the United States, and we had reason to suppose that one of them was engaged on a mission of some importance. The Bulgarians were at Alexandra Palace, which had been converted into a civilian internment camp.

It was decided that I should spend a day and a night at the Palace as a prisoner of war, and accordingly (dressed in mufti, and with a second-hand bag which I bought in the Charing Cross Road, and some odds and ends such as a third-class passenger might possess) I set off for the Alexandra Palace in a motor-car, escorted by two military policemen who thought I was a genuine Bulgarian.

The prisoners at the Alexandra Palace were a mixed lot – Germans, Austrians, Bulgars and Turks – but in a way they were well off, as many of them had either friends or wives and relations, who, owing to their British status, were not under arrest, and were able to visit them.

I found my little party of newly-taken Bulgarian prisoners and told them that I had met with a similar misfortune on my way to Copenhagen. My story was that I was a Bulgarian born in America, and that I had decided to go back to do my duty in Bulgaria. It was the man in whom I was particularly interested who gave me hints as to the examination to which I would be subjected, and what I should and should not say and do. He had been through the experience a few days before.

At the end of thirty-six hours I had his story. He had been going to set up a new espionage bureau in Scandinavia which was intended to be a clearing-house for the information collected by his organisation in America about the purchasing of munitions and armaments by the Allies. At the end of that period I was marched off for interrogation, and of course, never went back to the Alexandra Palace. Within a few hours I was on my way to the Near East.

Chapter V

From the harbour Salonica looked like a dream city. It is situated on rising ground, and in those days, before the fire, its buildings were of every shape and colour, and minarets stood out on the horizon like sugar towers on a wedding-cake.

The blue waters of the Aegean seemed to throw a peculiar light over the city, and one was ever conscious of the white top of Mount Olympus emerging from the clouds and keeping watch on the Thessalonica of old.

In fact, from the side of a ship the whole scene strongly resembled the first act of a West End musical comedy, with a Gordon Harker setting.

Ashore, that impression became almost a reality. First one noted the uniforms of the British, French, Italian, Serbian, Russian and Greek officers and men, all – with the exception of the British – wearing their decorations. Mixed in with this throng who had occupied Salonica were Greek *Evzons* in their white, baggy breeches, fantastic red leather slippers and gorgeous blue jackets. Armed Albanians and Montenegrins gave a special colour to the crowds in the streets with clothes which were a mixture of wonderful reds and yellows. Add to all this the peasants in their native costumes, the shepherds in their sheepskin coats and fur caps, which they wore no matter how hot the weather, and you begin to have some idea of the appearance of any Salonica square at the time of my arrival there.

Half the population of the city were Jews – the Sephardi Jews who had fled from Spain and Portugal in the fifteenth century to escape the persecution of Ferdinand and Isabella. By their clothes they might have stepped out of that bygone century, and the women were particularly beautifully dressed.

The rest of the population was made up of Greeks, Turks, Serbs, Albanians and Bulgars, and when found in any quantity they were truly an unwise and ungodly rabble.

Many of them had undertaken missions on behalf of the enemy and a number of them fell into the hands of the military police and were brought to trial and eventually hanged. These trials were conducted with the utmost fairness, which the Levantine population never really appreciated nor understood, accustomed as they were to more rough-and-ready methods.

Flokas Café, the White Tower, and the Odeon were the main rendezvous of the Allied officers, and in consequence the happy hunting ground of every class and kind of male and female spy.

Within a few days I was only too happy to escape from the town and to find myself posted to the XIIth Corps, whose headquarters were situated a few miles away from the town, on the Lembet Road.

At this time Salonica was in a state of siege and a series of fortifications, most suitably known as the 'bird cage', had been constructed from the Gulf of Thinos to the mouth of the Vardar.

I was busy collecting every kind of information I could get from beyond the enemy's lines, and training agents who would make suitable spies. It was not easy work. As often as not the best potential spies were totally illiterate and it was necessary to teach them even how they were to assimilate and remember the information which they gathered.

Some of them took to this work like ducks to water, and on returning from a visit to the Bulgarian lines they would recite without a stop for over an hour all that they had seen.

Information would be given in some such form as this: 'At such and such a village the 22nd Regiment is stationed, and they say that there is very little food to be had in the district and in consequence there is a certain amount of dissatisfaction. There is also a great deal of sickness, and a new hospital has been set up outside the village.

'Two kilometres down the road the bridge over the XYZ River is being strengthened so that it will bear the weight of heavy guns. Eight kilometres from here a new flying-ground is being made. It is most curious, but over the houses they have spread nets and sprinkled leaves.'

From such a report, if it were confirmed from other sources, it would be deduced that at this particular village more troops had been concentrated than could possibly be supplied with food from local sources, that it was likely that the enemy intended to use this as a centre, that it was their intention to bring down heavy guns, that the Intelligence Corps of the enemy were anxious that our aeroplanes should not spot the new aerodrome they were preparing.

Occasionally I managed to get literate agents. These, of course, were more useful because they could get their information back to me very much more quickly.

An illiterate agent had to go into the enemy's country and come back again, but the educated man would slip through the lines with four or six carrier pigeons, write down all the information he collected, slip it into the little metal tube attached to the pigeon's leg, and within a matter of hours the pigeon would alight at the headquarter's loft and be pounced upon by the pigeon-keeper, its message extracted and sent to me. The pigeon would be given a good feed and rest and a few days later be sent out with another agent.

But it was not only natives on whom we relied for espionage. There were quite a number of army officers who were brilliant at this form of work.

One of them was Captain J., a most brilliant creature who revelled in every form of disguise, and who would put his heart and soul into whatever character he assumed. We all knew that he excelled at this form of work, but he took great care that none of us ever saw him in character.

He would disappear for days and then come back with the most accurate information, but as no one ever saw him go or return, some of us would chaff him by saying that we had discovered he never went himself, but employed his own agents to do this work while he stayed with some fair charmer in Salonica.

After one of these periodic raggings he said: 'I bet the mess that I can pass by you between a given time at a certain spot and not one of you will recognise me.' The bet was immediately taken, the loser to stand a first-class dinner with champagne and cigars at the White Tower. Captain J. undertook to pass a certain spot on the Seres Road between eight and nine on a given evening just before sundown.

On the evening that Captain J. was to pass, half a dozen of us took up our position on the Seres Road, which was the main road leading out to the British section of the front. Along it passed army lorries, Red Cross vans, troops on the march, mule trains, dispatch riders on motor-cycles, and staff cars. Sandwiched in between this military traffic was the movement of the civil population. For the most part the Macedonian peasantry walked from place to place, but occasionally one would find a hefty, prosperous peasant riding a mule while his wife walked on foot just behind him, in her left hand carrying heavy packages and in her right a stick with which she would belabour the mule which her lord and master bestrode. And then donkey caravans passed by, belonging to the more prosperous Macedonian merchants or shopkeepers. Tiny, mangy donkeys with great oil-jars slung on each side of their flanks carrying sunflower or olive oil, or with a carpet saddle stuffed each side with vegetables. Some would carry petrol tins hermetically sealed, and others petrol tins full of water with their tops already ripped off.

We scrutinised everybody who passed, looking for Captain J. Once or twice we suspected some foreign officer and even a Greek gendarme, but in each case we were wrong.

Presently another of these caravans came down the road. The owners of these donkeys were known for their cruelty, and as this particular caravan drew alongside of us we saw the owner urging the poor little beasts along by means of a longish board tipped with a rusty nail. The flanks of two of the donkeys were running with blood. As he passed us the driver gave one of the animals a vicious prod, and one of us indignantly snatched his implement from his hand and gave him a particularly hard kick on the seat of his trousers.

Presently the sun set and we were all quite sure that for some reason or other Captain J. had failed to come down the road, and that we would enjoy a very good dinner at his expense.

Late in the evening J. came in, to be greeted with much joy and the news that he owed us a dinner. He assured us that we were wrong and that he had passed us. We called on him to prove it.

'I can prove it all right,' he told us, 'for I can hardly sit down owing to that kick you gave me as I prodded Neddy when passing you.' Captain J. was the driver of that donkey caravan.

Unfortunately he lost his life a year later in going up on one of his usual trips during a heavy Bulgarian bombardment, when he was trying to penetrate the lines.

Chapter VI

From January to March 1916, there was practically no fighting on the Salonica front. The Allied troops were preparing to move out in front of the 'bird cage', and to occupy the Struma valley, which at that time was being patrolled by the South Midland Mounted Brigade, who formed our advance guard.

Under King Constantine, the Greeks were still maintaining a benevolent neutrality. The Struma valley was nominally Greek territory, and throughout this region five Greek divisions were distributed with the purely theoretical purpose of guarding the Greek–Bulgarian frontier. A quite Gilbertian situation.

Nominally attached to the mounted brigade, but otherwise quite independent, Lieutenant L. and myself roamed over the Struma valley on our own account. We each had a groom and a batman, and one pack mule which carried our fodder, supplies, and kit. We never slept two nights in the same camp and were always on the move, always watching the Greeks and the local villagers, and keeping ourselves informed as to what was happening just over the frontier in Bulgaria.

The season of wild flowers, almond and fruit-blossom which in March and April made this valley a setting for a midsummer night's dream, passed away beneath the scorching rays of a sub-tropical sun by the middle of May. It became more and more difficult to do our usual patrols, and we began sending messages back to headquarters every third day in place of every day as before.

On 23 May the Commander of the 10th Greek Army, General Biras, intended to hold manoeuvres at Seres, and he kindly invited Lieutenant L. and myself to attend.

I obtained permission from headquarters, my chief remarking that, as he presumed we would meet Turkish, Bulgarian and German officers as guests of the Greek Army Commander at these manoeuvres, he wanted us to behave ourselves with the utmost correctness, and suggested that if it were possible we should attend the manoeuvres unarmed, with the exception of swords. On 22 May we left Orljack for Seres in the cool of the evening, a distance of about twenty kilometres, and passed over the Struma River by Kopriva Bridge.

About three o'clock in the morning we made camp some four kilometres from Seres and took a few hours' sleep, after which our chargers were groomed, our head-ropes blancoed, and our equipment specially polished. We decided to leave in camp our batmen, and handed over to them our rifles, revolvers and ammunition, and with field-glasses slung across our shoulders, and no war-like equipment but the swords attached to our saddles, we rode off into Seres.

Seres is an Oriental village with large tobacco warehouses, being one of the centres in which Turkish tobacco is grown and cultivated. The village was the scene of a battle between the Serbs and Bulgarians in 1913 and part of it was still in ruins.

We rode up to headquarters, where a Greek orderly officer was appointed to be our host during the period of the manoeuvres. We lunched with the Commander-in-Chief and his staff, who were very pleasant to us during the meal. I do not suppose that he knew that I had been personally keeping his dossier for the last three or four months, and through various sources knew a good deal about his correspondence and private opinions. He explained with many apologies that he would be unable to entertain us at dinner that evening, and we were invited to dine with the chief of the Artillery staff.

My delight was great when I found that the wife of this officer was a Russian lady who had lived in St Petersburg and had met her husband while he was on a visit to Russia. This gave me a highly appreciated ally in the camp, and while the lady never betrayed a single thing in connection with her husband's work or the army, it was quite simple for me, in the course of conversation, to draw my own conclusions as to what was happening.

At five o'clock the following morning the manoeuvres started. Sure enough, round the Commander-in-Chief of the 10th Greek Army there were ranged two German officers, four or five Bulgarians, and two Turkish officers with their respective orderlies, and to my great joy I noted that every one of them was armed to the teeth. However, I said nothing at the time. We rode up to the General and saluted him, and then saluted the foreign officers present, who most punctiliously returned our salute.

The manoeuvres were rather a simple affair, and were a blind for the events which were happening behind the scenes. There was an inspection of infantry, cavalry and artillery which ended up in a march past, and then a midday meal was arranged some miles from Seres under trees.

I took this opportunity of approaching the senior aide-de-camp with a very polite but very firm protest against the breach of etiquette of which the other neutral officers were guilty, in bearing arms. The aide, very embarrassed, promised that he would mention the fact to the General.

The following morning there was to be a special review of the artillery, and when we reached the rendezvous I was delighted to see that none of the foreign officers was carrying arms. But if looks could have killed I should have been a dead man from the stares I got from the two German officers.

The manoeuvres were due to finish that evening, and never once did we speak to our enemies, nor did our enemies speak to us. I must add that the Greek staff was very tactful, at every meal placing a couple of Greek officers between the officers of the hostile armies.

That evening, after the manoeuvres had ended and we had taken our leave of the Greek C.-in-C., I went to pay my respects to my hostess of the previous evening, the Russian lady. I found her in tears and very agitated. Her husband had just been ordered to Demihissar, a town at the foot of the Rupel Pass, and the key to the Struma plain. Her husband was anti-German. He knew that orders had been issued from Athens that the Bulgarians were to be allowed to come through the pass to invade Greek territory. This act meant that Greece would, in any case, be involved sooner or later, whether she came in on the side of the Central Powers or on the side of the Allies.

I comforted the poor lady as best I could and then hurried off to find Lieutenant L., and without any delay we made for our camp outside Seres.

We sent one of our batmen back at once with coded messages to Orljack, where our yeomanry outpost had charge of the telegraph line to headquarters. And then, after a very short rest, we started out in the direction of the Rupel Pass. Ahead of us were trekking two Greek mountain battery brigades whom we had been watching that morning. At any moment their guns might be turned against us on the Struma.

About one o'clock in the morning we halted for sleep. All of us were pretty well exhausted, and I set the alarm in my wrist-watch for three o'clock and slept with my head upon it.

Just after dawn we made a small camp-fire and cooked a billy-can of tea, which was very welcome with the addition of a tot of rum. Then we proceeded in the direction of Demihissar. Our progress was naturally slow, as we had to go through the process of 'drawing' every village that we came to. This manoeu-vre consists in trotting up to the village at a good pace, then suddenly halting one's horse, turning round and galloping off in the direction from which one has just come. If there are hostile forces in the village or an ambush has been prepared, it is ten to one that fire will be opened at once.

About six o'clock we knew that we were not on a wild-goose chase and that the Greeks were letting the Bulgar-German Army through the Rupel Pass, for we met the first refugees from the surrounding villages fleeing before the invading army.

Refugees in time of war seem to behave in the same way the world over. They load themselves up with the most useless things and hang on to these burdens at the risk of their lives. I remember an old man pushing a heavy wheelbarrow into which he had put an ordinary deal kitchen table. He was doing this under a scorching sun along a very rough unmetalled country track. By his side walked a young woman with a baby in a shawl slung on her back. In her right hand she carried two live chickens by their feet with their heads down, and in her left she held a small tin plate with two eggs and an apple upon it.

Why the wheelbarrow and the table – what were they hoping to do with them, and the pathetic tin plate with its two eggs and one apple?

This was but one of a hundred pictures. Heavy objects seemed to have a particular fascination for the refugees.

For the most part these people passed us without any sign of recognition and it seemed to be a matter of complete indifference to them as to what army we belonged to. I cross-examined a number of them to try and get information, but they had not much to tell. When the Bulgarians invaded the Struma valley in 1913 there had been great excesses. The villagers had not forgotten and were flying before the new invasion.

As the day wore on it got hotter and hotter. A Varda wind was blowing, and a Varda wind means hot, dry air that has caught up every particle of loose dust and sand, which penetrates through one's clothes into one's skin. And every kind of beetle, bug, mosquito, and sand-fly pestered both horse and rider alike. This, I think, was our greatest torture.

Finally we came in sight of Demihissar. About a kilometre from the town I met the first Greek soldier we had seen that day. He happened to be a man who had lived in Chicago and spoke English fluently. From him I learned that Demihissar was still in the hands of the Greeks, but that an advance guard of Bulgarians had been allowed to come through the pass into Greek territory, and had occupied the villages to the west of the pass in order to form a flanking party for the main body of the invading army which was coming through that evening.

From a map it will be seen that the Rupel Pass is the

only gap along the Bela Shitza range of mountains, and that without what seemed treachery on the part of the Greeks, the German-Bulgarian Army could not possibly have got into the Struma valley.

Beyond Demihissar we could see Fort Rupel, the key position to the pass, but the Greek flag was no longer flying there.

After a short rest and a consultation, Lieutenant L. and myself decided that we would push on into Demihissar with one man, so we left our two orderlies with messages and instructions to proceed back to Orljack unless we returned by sundown.

We were taking no risks and rode into the town with our revolvers actually drawn. A Greek sentry stopped us and said that we could not go into the town. We demanded to see the Commandant and after some delay were allowed to proceed to his office.

He was extremely rude, and said that he expected the town to be occupied by the Bulgarian Army at any moment, and that unless we got out immediately he would make it his business to arrest us and hand us over to the Germans.

I asked him with a smile about Greek neutrality, and he replied that that was a thing of the past and he thanked God that Greece had gone into the war on the winning side, and that we English would find ourselves very shortly driven back to our ships, which would be undoubtedly sunk in the Gulf of Salonica by the German submarines waiting there specially for our coming.

Altogether a charming person to meet at the end of a tiring ride.

We picked up our two orderlies and decided that we would make for a ridge in the mountain wall which runs out to the

east of Demihissar whence we could get a commanding view of
the pass and the Struma valley.

As soon as we reached this ridge and managed to find a
bit of shade for ourselves and our horses we had the first meal
of the day, and then Lieutenant L. and I took it in turns to
watch the pass while the other slept.

Chapter VII

About six o'clock Lieutenant L. awakened me with the news that he had observed a large body of troops marching through the pass.

We trained our glasses on the road and made out that they were Greek troops retiring from the Rupel forts. They marched by Demihissar and camped in a valley below the ridge we occupied.

They were shortly followed by three or four battalions of Bulgarian troops and a regiment of cavalry, and then the road was occupied by cars and dispatch riders, which we rightly took to be the headquarters of an army arriving. Through our glasses we saw the cars pull up outside Demihissar and the Greek staff come forward to welcome the invaders. A battalion of Bulgarian troops took over Demihissar and set out pickets around the town.

We knew that we were running a very grave risk of being cut off from our line of communication, and that if we were not very careful we should certainly be taken prisoners. However, the information which we were getting was of such importance that we felt ourselves justified in staying as long as we could.

The Bulgarian Army filed through the Rupel Pass rather like a great snake. Battalion after battalion followed each other, deploying left and right as they reached the valley and spreading out along the banks of the Struma. Bivouac fires were built, and we saw the marvellous sight of an army in the field, very, very different from seeing one entrenched.

Meantime there was a stir among the Greek troops. Some sort of parade was evidently being organised. One battalion seemed to refuse to parade and the officers of other battalions went over to it. Then there seemed to be a conference of officers. Finally the reluctant battalion apparently agreed to parade, and within a few minutes a Greek general was addressing the assembled troops.

All this was rather like watching a silent film. We could see beautifully through our glasses, but imagination had to suggest to us the way in which the drama was unfolding.

As soon as the Greek general had finished his address and the troops returned to their bivouacs, I left Lieutenant L. to watch the pass and slipped away to find out what the trouble had been.

The first group of soldiers I met were gathering scrub for firewood, and seemed quite friendly, but I could not make myself understood, until one of them – when I had produced a little money – promised to fetch someone who could speak English. Presently he came back with a man who had lived in Canada, where he had been in one of the construction gangs which ran the final railway line of the Grand Trunk's trans-continental line into Prince Rupert, BC.

This made a link between us, and I quickly learned the situation from him. It appeared that a good part of the Greek Army, although anti-Ally, very much resented the fact that the Bulgarians should be allowed to come into the Struma valley, and were horrified that the Greek command had evacuated the Rupel forts to them. Some of them felt so strongly on the subject that they wanted to fight the Bulgarians then and there and drive them out and across the frontier while yet there was time. The general who had addressed the troops had explained that they were acting on orders from Athens, and that the Greek Army would withdraw to Seres. But there was a great deal of dissatisfaction in the Greek camp.

I told my Greek informant that I was going back to Salonica, this being in the direction exactly opposite to that in which our camp lay. Night was now rapidly approaching, and giving the Greek a fifty-drachma note I slipped off in the direction which I had indicated. As soon as I was sure that I was not being followed I made a detour and returned to Lieutenant L.

From our ridge we had a marvellous view of the Bulgarian Army and of the Greek detachment, for now the positions were picked out by thousands of little camp-fires which gave a most picturesque effect to the scene.

I told Lieutenant L. of the feeling which existed in the Greek camp, and we wondered whether we might turn it to some good account.

We remembered the action of Stalky in Kipling's *Stalky and Co.* when he was besieged in a fort on the North-West frontier between the Malots and Khye Kheen tribes, and played the one side against the other. We felt there was a great similarity in our own position.

Our plan was to creep out on to the Greek flank which was nearest to the Bulgarian troops, and under cover of darkness to open rapid fire on the Greek camp in the pious hope that the Greeks, justifiably angered by what they would take to be Bulgarian treachery, would attack the Bulgarian camp and start a nice little row between the two parties.

But while the plan was feasible enough, we did not know whether such tactics would be justified, for perhaps this penetration of the Bulgarians into the Struma valley was all part of a plan of the Allies who were working out their own tactics. We also knew that it was important for us to get back as soon as possible with our information. So, after a very long discussion, we decided that we had no business to attempt to stage our plot.

We had unfortunately been guilty of one great oversight. We had seen the Bulgarian cavalry come through the Rupel Pass, but we had not noted where they had bivouacked, and it suddenly struck us that they would probably have put out a protective screen, and that there was every chance of our running slap into a Bulgarian patrol. That made us decide not to return by the route we had come, for obviously if the Bulgarian and German cavalry were out along the road to Seres they would be keeping watch on the Kopriva Bridge. We therefore decided to pass the Greek camp, follow the line of the Struma River, ford it as soon as possible, strike out towards Poroi and recross the river in order to get back to Orljack.

At that time we were still using the Austrian staff map of the Struma valley which, though the best available, was very far from accurate, some villages being as much as five or six miles out.

By six o'clock we had cleared the Bulgarian flank, but all danger of running into hostile cavalry was not over and we still had to take the precaution of drawing every village as we had done on the previous day.

About midday we entered a village which we subsequently discovered to be pro-Bulgar. We had as usual drawn it and no one had fired at us, and so we felt fairly safe in approaching it. We bought some eggs and bread, and went on our way. On the outskirts of the village we met some angry villagers who hurled stones at us and somebody fired a couple of shots.

As we were not there for guerrilla warfare, and did not know what forces were against us, we galloped off. Unfortunately one of the stones flung hit me on the head and knocked off my slouch hat, and I could not risk stopping to pick it up. The stone had drawn blood and made me feel very sick, and as the day wore on the burning rays of the sun penetrated the handkerchief I had tied round my head and made me feel very ill. Lieutenant L. and two of the men had been suffering with an attack of dysentery before we had even left Seres. I was developing in addition to my other aches and pains an attack of malaria.

The horses were absolutely dead beat, and by the evening my mare developed colic.

The next five hours' ride was a complete nightmare, and at the end of this day I nearly committed murder.

The sun had already set when we got to the village of Cavdalar. We had not the least chance of getting back to Orljack that night unless we could find a guide, for we had found the Austrian staff map totally unreliable for the part of the country we were crossing.

I staggered into the village inn, a dark little mud hut with a couple of tables and a small bar lit by a smoky kerosene lamp. There were half a dozen louts in the bar, and the air was heavy with the sour odour characteristic of unwashed peasantry. I made myself understood, and said that I wanted a guide to take us to Orljack. One of the number, a particularly sneaking-looking Greek, said that he would act as a guide providing I stood his friends, who were *comitadjes*, a drink all round. The *comitadjes* are brigand peasants who roam all through

Macedonia and have the unpleasant habit of shooting first and asking questions afterwards.

I was weak enough to stand a round of drinks.

My Greek guide asked for another round, and I suppose it was because I was so tired that I complied with his request, and then he demanded yet another round, which I bought.

'Come on, now we go,' I said. He leered at me and then spat contemptuously on the floor and intimated that he would be damned if he was going to guide any Englishman to Orljack.

I completely lost my temper. I drew my revolver and rammed it into the middle of his back and then kicked him with all my might towards the door and continued to kick him down the path.

It was a crazy thing to do, for ordinarily I could have expected half a dozen bullets in my back from the *comitadjes*.

But I just did not care, and can never understand how it was that in my fury I did not actually kill that Greek. I can only account for it by the fact that I was getting a savage satisfaction by brutally kicking him.

Lieutenant L. said he had never seen anything quite so unpleasant and yet so funny as my anger.

I made the Greek walk by my stirrup and kept the barrel of my revolver scratching the back of his neck for the first hour.

Then Lieutenant L. took charge of the guide, and about midnight we slipped into Orljack and started passing our dispatches down to the signal section for telegraphing to headquarters.

When the last word was written we just pitched forward and slept until late next morning.

Chapter VIII

Ours was a sad little camp next morning when we tried to parade. Lieutenant L's dysentery was very much worse and he could hardly stand. Two of our men were equally weak.

The sun beating through my handkerchief had given me a mild attack of sunstroke, besides which, I was alternately shivering with cold and unable to keep my teeth from chattering, and running a high temperature, the usual distressing symptoms of malaria.

The Brigade Veterinary Officer had condemned my charger to be shot. And so by eventide four out of six of us were being jogged down in an ambulance to Salonica and our little outfit, which had been organised as an independent observation unit on the enemy's movements in the Struma valley, was broken up.

Those weeks had been one of the happiest times I lived through during the war. The hardships, the torture of the flies, the pitiless blazing sun, the long hours in the saddle and the dizziness caused by my eyes trying to penetrate through the mirage, have not been forgotten but toned down in my memory. The things that stand out are the quiet cool nights spent under a starlit heaven, the black walls of the mountains that surrounded the valley with their snow-clad tops lit by a silver moon, the excitement of gathering information under the very nose of the enemy; the good-fellowship that prevailed in our small outfit. The joy of eating a lamb roasted over a char-coal fire, and the occasional praise received from headquarters. These are the things that make me look back on that summer with regret. It was a time which can never come again.

I was in hospital for a fortnight and on being discharged was attached to the Intelligence Headquarters at Salonica. This meant office work, and while it was interesting to start with, I soon got tired of the monotony of the work and longed for something more active.

I felt that with my experience of Intelligence work I could be of greater use if I learned to fly, and luckily was able to bring my chief round to the same view; and in due course I became a fully-fledged pilot in the RFC.

One of my reasons for joining the RFC was to be able to drop our spies into enemy territory.

Nico Kotzov was one of my first passengers. He was a Serbian patriot who had been in the enemy's country nine or ten times and always brought back very accurate and valuable information. He was a big-boned, tall man with a long grey beard, and had a very grand manner. He wore native dress, a sheep-skin cap and a heavy brown homespun cape, and always carried a shepherd's staff.

We wanted information from an inaccessible part of the country, and as this information was urgently needed it was decided to drop him by aeroplane. I took him up for a couple of trial flights, and although he did not enjoy the experience very much he was quite determined to go. He knew the country where we were going to land, and I explained to him that I wanted the landing-ground to be as much like our aerodrome as possible.

During the trial flights I asked him to point out to me, when we were flying low, grounds that he thought were suitable, and while occasionally his judgment was very much at fault, on the whole I thought that he had grasped the general requirements necessary for a landing-ground.

With luck, providing you are not attacked by enemy fighting planes, there is no difficulty in flying over strange country, but the art of dropping a spy consists in doing so unobserved. It is necessary to land your man and get away unseen, so the operation is conducted as a rule just before sunrise, after sunset, or on a very brilliant moonlit night.

The Hague regulations respecting the customs of war were drawn up before man learned to fly, and in consequence there was no rule under the general spies clauses of these regulations regarding an airman who dropped spies in enemy's territory. But the Germans and Bulgarians had intimated that they would treat the actual pilots of aeroplanes landing spies as spies and shoot them.

This added to the risk of dropping a spy over the line, for if one made a bad landing and crashed one was for it.

General aviation had not then been developed to the perfection it has reached today, and there were no aeroplanes fitted with air brakes to make a low-speed landing possible.

Early one morning I collected Nico from the hut he had slept in and took him across to the hangars where my machine had already been wheeled out and was waiting.

Despite a large mug of hot coffee I felt very cold and shivery.

Once again I pulled out the map and worked out the course with Nico, who told me where I would find a suitable landing-field; we were to arrive a little before daybreak, when there would be just sufficient light to land.

As we climbed into the machine the sergeant in charge of the pigeons brought along a little cage with six of our best carrier pigeons in it, and at the last minute a felt cover was slipped over them to keep them warm at the altitude we should reach during our journey.

I ran the engine up. Everything was all right.

I signalled to the sergeant to pull away the chocks and we taxied out into the dark aerodrome. I opened the engine full out and we were away.

I had to do a stiff climb in the air in order to be able to cross a mountain range, and the higher I got the less I liked the job before me. The flight was uneventful. I picked up the various objectives that were serving me – together with a compass – as a guide, and got over the country that we were to land upon in the scheduled time.

It was getting light and I throttled back my engine, so that it was just ticking over, in order to land.

We lost height rapidly and I could faintly make out the ground below me, which seemed fairly suitable. As a precautionary measure I made up my mind to circle it just once more. Suddenly I noticed that the whole of the field selected by Nico for our landing was dotted by giant boulders. To land on that field would be suicide. I climbed into the air again, and when I had got sufficiently high, switched off my engine so as to be able to make Nico hear me and told him that his selection was no good as a landing-ground. He said simply that I had told him nothing about boulders, and that he imagined we would hop over them. We were in a BE2E bus and the only way to start the propeller going was to dive vertically. The force of the air drove round the propeller and if all went well one's engine started again. So I dived. The propeller started and we climbed once more into the air.

All hope of landing that morning had to be given up, but as it was rapidly getting light I hoped to be able to pick out a suitable landing-ground for the next day, and through my glasses located a dry river bed which promised to be the best place for landing, and back we went to the aerodrome.

Nico was most crestfallen at his mistake, and thought that I had been so angry with him that I had dived purposely to punish him, and it took a couple of hours of hard talk and a thorough exposition of aero engines before I could convince him that I simply had to dive to start my engine going.

Next morning we made the trip again and I safely landed my passenger. Within ten days he had dispatched all six pigeons and on the return home of the last one I took over a further cage of pigeons and dropped them from a parachute over the spot where I had landed Nico. These also returned home safely. In all I dropped Nico three times over the line.

But not all my passengers were as good as Nico.

On one occasion it was essential to drop a spy over the lines before we had even had time to give him a trial flight. The passenger was a Greek. He was looking forward to his flight and was a boastful creature.

It was a dirty morning with bad visibility and gusts of strong ground wind swept the aerodrome. My attention was fully occupied in taking off and gaining altitude. I had to climb through four layers of cloud, and in those days once one got into a cloud one was completely blinded. Now there are special instruments to make cloud-flying simple. We had been in the air half an hour before I had a moment to turn round to see how my passenger was getting on.

He was petrified with terror. His eyes were starting out of his head, and he was being violently sick. I smiled and tried to cheer him, but it was no good. I did not think it was possible for any man to be as sick so long and so regularly. I picked out the landing-ground, planed down and made a beautiful landing, but on turning round found that my passenger had gone into a dead faint and was huddled up in the cockpit. It was no good landing him in that condition and so back I went to the aerodrome. My passenger was still unconscious, and nothing ever induced him after he had recovered to go into the air again.

One of my other passengers was a man called Petrov who loved flying, and even when not being dropped over the lines would come down to the aerodrome to cadge a joy ride.

One evening, just about sundown, he climbed into his seat behind me and was given a basket with four pigeons and off we went.

He was a joyous passenger and would sing Serbian songs at the top of his voice, and even the roar of the engine could not drown the bass sounds coming from his lungs.

Those flights over the Balkans were wonderful. The mountains beneath looked like the great waves one sees in the Atlantic.

The sun had just slipped behind a mountain, and the valley in which we were to land was plunged in shadow. I spiralled down in order to lose height rapidly and circled round our landing-ground. Everything seemed clear and there was not a soul about – the conditions appeared ideal.

How often ideal conditions are a snare and a delusion! On

landing we struck a furrow which jarred the bus badly, and worse still, stopped the propeller.

The only way in those days to land a spy and to take off successfully after having done so was to throttle back one's engine so that the propeller just kept turning round. As soon as the spy had landed one revved up the engine and took off again. When I first did this work it had always been a nightmare to me that my propeller might stop, for even under good conditions propeller swinging was a tricky operation and required a great deal of knack.

When learning to fly one was instructed in the art of propeller swinging, and before qualifying one was given practical tests. I was never very good at this business, principally because of my build.

I am not tall and have very short arms, I have always been rather round, and it was all I could do to reach the propeller, let alone swing it and swing myself clear in so doing. Failure to swing clear means nine times out of ten that the propeller will hit the swinger, and many a man has been knocked out at this job.

And here we were in the enemy's country with a propeller that had stopped. Petrov hopped out of the bus, and at once volunteered to swing the propeller, and I showed him how to do it.

The process in theory is quite a simple one. The pilot calls out to the swinger 'switch off', and the swinger then turns the propeller in order to suck sufficient petrol vapour into the cylinders. When this has been done the pilot switches on the ignition and the swinger calls out 'contact', which is the signal for the propeller to be given a sharp, quick swing and for the person doing it to step aside.

Should the engine for some reason or other not start, the man swinging the propeller calls out 'switch off', and the process is started all over again.

For ten minutes our voices could be heard calling, 'Switch off – contact – switch off.'

But nothing happened, the engine simply would not fire.

Petrov was running with perspiration due to his exertion. I was bathed in the sweat of fear.

We rested for a moment, then I climbed out of my seat and went over the petrol leads and magneto points. Everything seemed in order. Then to our horror in the rapidly deepening twilight we saw a cavalry patrol approaching.

Petrov said that he would have one more swing, but before doing so we decided to release the carrier pigeons.

We had instructions in the event of likely capture immediately to get rid of the pigeons, so that the enemy could not use them to send information calculated to mislead our Intelligence department. Off flew the four pigeons. And then like a demon possessed, Petrov started swinging the propeller. Still nothing happened.

The cavalry patrol had spotted us. I think at first they thought it was one of their own machines. Then they must have got suspicious, for they started trotting over towards us. Suddenly the engine fired. Petrov raced round to the fuselage and leaped into his seat. The cavalry patrol broke into a gallop and called upon us to stop. I opened up the throttle and we were away, but before we had left the ground the patrol had opened fire. Their shooting was good, for we found when we got back to our aerodrome half a dozen bullets' holes in the fuselage.

Rapid as was the communication by the means of aeroplane,

pigeons and spies, there was a system used by the monks of Mount Athos which seemed to be quicker for the transmission of startling news than any system devised by the Intelligence sections. Occasionally it was unbelievable how rapidly important news reached them, and I spent some time at the monastery at St Panteleimon, the retreat of the Russian monks, and from its friendly close tried to study the inmates at the Chiliandri monastery which was inhabited by Serbian and Bulgarian monks, among whom, owing to the war, there was considerable political friction.

But I never learned how the speedy regular communication was kept up between Athos and the enemy's country.

Athos has a unique group of twenty monastic communities clustered round the village of Kayes; except for the two monasteries mentioned, they were made up of Greek monks. All the monks belong to the order of St Basil, and the brethren on the whole are friendly to male visitors, but no woman is allowed to land on the isthmus. The entire population is male. So strict are the monks that they will not even tolerate a cow or a female goat upon their domain; such things as milk, butter and eggs are brought to them from outside.

The monasteries are all fortified in an old-fashioned ramshackle way, and as a rule consist of large quadrangles enclosing churches, houses, stores, and they look wonderful from the sea. Within these quadrangles there are precious Byzantine art treasures and some of the world's rarest manuscripts. But nothing in them compares with the beauty of Mount Athos itself. The peak rises like a pyramid with a steep summit of white marble to a height of over six thousand feet above the sea. At sunset it can be seen from the plain of Troy on the east and the slopes of Mount Olympus on the west.

But even this beautiful, peaceful, ascetic retreat was affected by the repercussions of war. Many an Intelligence officer spent a long weekend there, outwardly resting, sight-seeing, but in reality watching men and events.

Writing of Athos reminds me of yet another religious retreat I used to visit at Salonica. It was the house of the Sisters of Charity of St Vincent de Paul, where Sister Augustine had been working for over fifty years.

Sister Augustine was an English lady who had lived through wars and revolutions, and under the rule of both Turks and Greeks. Nothing in the world could surprise or shock her; she was loved by rich and poor alike. She was known as 'The Wise Woman of Salonica'. She was undoubtedly one of the best-informed persons in the Near East, and a marvellous linguist. She was over eighty when I knew her, but she was never too tired or too busy to advise and help me when I wanted local knowledge.

Meanwhile what was left of the Serbian Army had been shipped from Corfu, reorganised in Salonica and was now fighting with the Allies on the Macedonian front. Within a few weeks Monastir had been recaptured, and once again the Serbians were on home soil and with a dogged persistence set about clearing the Bulgars out of Serbia. I was temporarily working with the Serbian counter-espionage staff.

Monastir had only been captured two or three days when two Bulgarian spies were caught. There was a drum-head court martial. The evidence was overwhelming against the two spies, who had been directing the fire of Bulgarian batteries on certain of the crossroads which intersect Monastir. The Bulgarians had left a field telephone hidden in a cellar, and while one of the spies observed the traffic on the roads the other waited for signals from his colleague and then would tell the Bulgarian batteries when and where to open fire. Some deadly work on the crossroads had been done before these spies were caught.

They were both sentenced to death.

Although I should have very much preferred to miss the ordeal, it was necessary for me to be present at the execution.

In front of a whitewashed wall two stakes had been hastily driven into the ground. A battalion had been formed into three parts of a square in front of the stakes.

The late mayor of the town and about four hundred citizens had been ordered to attend and were paraded in front of the troops.

The two spies were marched into the square by the field gendarmes. A firing-party of twenty men was drawn up in front of the stakes. The promulgation of the sentence was read over to the two prisoners and they were asked if they had anything to say, and both of them just shook their heads. Then a Serbian officer read out the names of, and the charges against, the two spies to the civil population.

The firing-party was called to attention. The two spies were marched up to the posts and tied up to them. Two white handkerchiefs were produced. One prisoner allowed his eyes to be bound, the other man refused the bandage.

There was a horrible stillness in the air, and one could hear the deep breathing of all those who were standing around. I saw two or three people cross themselves. The officer in charge of the firing-party gave the order to present arms. This order struck the still air like the crack of a whip.

'Long live Bulgaria!' said the spy who had refused to have his eyes bound, in almost a conversational tone.

The officer in charge of the firing-party held up a handkerchief and then dropped it, and before it had reached the ground twenty rifles had belched out flashes of flame which were followed, after what seemed a long time, by the crack of rifles.

The two spies crumpled up and sank down as far as the cords would let them go, and blood poured down over them and their clothing. The wall behind, white a moment before, was scarred by bullet marks and bespattered with blood, just as if a paint-brush had been dipped into a pot of red paint and flicked on the wall.

The firing-party was marched off. A Red Cross van drove up to the posts to take away the bodies. I hurried off to find a spot where I could be sick without disgracing myself.

The execution had brought my theoretical education of spying and its conclusions to an end, and in the abstract there was not a thing that I did not know about the business.

The taking of human life can never be right, but in time of war I have no hesitation from my own personal experience as a spy in advocating that the death sentence should be carried out on those who are caught spying.

Chapter IX

I first met Venizelos in Salonica. He had spent the winter and spring in endeavouring to compel King Constantine to change his policy of benevolent neutrality for full participation in the war with the Allies. But he had not succeeded. It is not my purpose here to go into the rights and wrongs of the policies supported by Venizelos on the one side and King Constantine on the other.

Despite everything that had been happening in Athens I was pro-Constantine and anti-Venizelos, and therefore my early meetings with the Cretan were somewhat of an ordeal.

Eleutherios Venizelos had been an obscure lawyer in Greece. He was of dark complexion, his hair already turning grey, and his face was somewhat disfigured by a number of rather notice-able warts. He drove about Salonica in a limousine, and wore an outrageous silk hat and a very queer frock-coat. But for all his eccentricity he had very intelligent eyes, a persuasive sympa-thetic voice, and a mind as sharp as a needle.

Early in October 1916, he broke off negotiations with his Sovereign, founded at Salonica a provisional government which a few weeks later was recognised by England and France, and issued a proclamation calling to the colours all the Greeks outside the domain of the Royalist forces. These Greek divisions were meanwhile being formed and equipped by the Allies.

As a reprisal to his activities the Royalists persuaded the Archbishop of Athens to pronounce a solemn anathema against him, and he was excommunicated with all the pomp and ceremony of the Greek Orthodox Church.

I do not think this ever worried Venizelos. His reply was to form the *Corps de la Sûreté* for the protection of himself and the provisional government. This corps in time became extremely powerful, and after King Constantine's abdication played a part very similar to that of the old Russian Ochrana and the Bolshevik Cheka.

Politicians seem to have a habit of forming these institutions in good faith, but sooner or later the arm which they create for their protection is the means of their own overthrow. I think that Venizelos owed his downfall to the tyrannical activities of the *Corps de la Sûreté* during his absence at the Paris Peace Conference.

Fate decreed that we should stay at the same hotel in Paris during the Peace Conference; we had adjoining rooms, and it was then that I really came to appreciate his brilliance and grasp of international affairs. One day I asked him what his feelings were when he heard that he had been excommunicated. Venizelos smiled. 'Within a year,' he said, 'at the same cathedral a Te Deum was sung as a thanksgiving for our formal entry into the war on the side of the Allies.'

In time I was ordered to Egypt and embarked in a wartime sloop which was ultimately bound for Alexandria, but on the way called at various islands in the Aegean, and also dropped anchor at Piraeus, where Compton Mackenzie, the Military Control Officer, was running a brilliant secret Intelligence department against the Germans. By correspondence I had known of his activities for a long time, and I admired the masterly way in which he organised his section. But it was not for his military achievements that I thrilled to meet him, but as the author of *Sinister Street*.

At Alexandria I waited for fresh orders and whiled away the time by roller-skating in the afternoon at the local rink. On my second afternoon a trim figure came on the floor, who skated with wonderful grace and charm. As she came round I recognised her as one Minnie Klein, a German lady who belonged to the oldest profession in the world, and was one of Germany's more important spies in the Levant.

We had with great difficulty expelled her from Salonica. I say difficulty for, despite her German nationality, she had an irreproachable Greek passport, and we had only succeeded in getting her banished as far as Athens. She had been clever enough never to get technically caught, but she was rightly suspected, and had a marvellous way of getting information out of officers, old and young alike.

I did not know how she had got into Egypt, but I knew she had no business there. I took care to keep out of her way for fear she should recognise me and take fright, but I never let her out of my sight while I sent a messenger to the Provost Marshal, who sent an officer with a polite invitation for Minnie Klein to visit his office.

Minnie was most indignant. Her defence was almost convincing. But alas, though she had changed her name and her passport, she had failed to change her face. Fate was against her, for there was a photographic record in the possession of the counter-espionage section at Salonica. When this arrived at Alexandria and her identity was definitely established she was shipped off to Malta and interned for the duration of the war.

Cairo and Alexandria were hotbeds of intrigue and international espionage. I was associated with a man called Theorides who was a spy in the service of the Greek government. He controlled a band of cut-throats who hovered round the bazaars and were used for all sorts of illegal work. It was Theorides who first told me of the marvellous work that was being done by an Englishman who was disguised and lived as an Arab, Colonel Lawrence of Arabia.

I met Lawrence once while in Cairo. He was a quiet, reserved man, and it was only from his colleagues on the staff and from my ruffian friend Theorides that I learned of his work. Subsequently, when in Russia a year later, I tried to employ some of the tactics against the Germans that Colonel Lawrence had used against the Turks.

Another man with whom I spent many hours in Egypt was Linkevitch, a Russian revolutionary who had been exiled from Russia and picked up his living in devious ways. He was a queer fanatic but was very well informed and knew everything that was happening in Cairo. He also had certain secret sources of information, and he told me of the abdication of the Tsar of Russia and the establishment of a revolutionary government in Petrograd within a few hours of its happening. This was two days before any official telegrams had reached the staff or the press in Egypt. But I never discovered how he obtained his information.

Chapter X

While on leave in July 1917, I was suddenly ordered to join the RFC Mission in Russia, and it was with a joyful heart that I left King's Cross by the midnight train for Aberdeen to find out the real situation in a new strange Russia. Early next morning the train crossed the Forth Bridge. Below us the Grand Fleet was spread out, while in the air above hung observation balloons from which a ceaseless look-out was kept in case a German submarine somehow or other should manage to slip into the Forth. The bridge was strongly guarded, and I wondered how much a German spy would give for the privilege of spending an hour upon it.

A terrific storm was raging over the North Sea, and Aberdeen was being shaken by the gale when I arrived. Obviously we were doomed to a dirty crossing. Really bad weather makes submarine work difficult and I was glad to find the risk of being torpedoed reduced to a minimum. Of course, there was always a risk from floating mines – horrible things to meet in a rough sea – but since the *Hampshire* disaster of over a year before, when Lord Kitchener and all but half a dozen of the ship's personnel perished on the way to Russia, very special precautions were taken.

I think I crossed in the *Jupiter*, but I am not sure. In any case, she was a yacht-like ferry-boat with a very low line, and was reputed to be very fast. She looked to me to be far too small to face the storm which was raging outside the harbour.

There was a queer collection of passengers on board, among them a number of Russian and Jewish politicians who had been living in exile in the United States, and were now, owing to the fall of Tsardom, going back to Russia. With the exception of the ship's company everyone was in mufti. There were also several British and Allied officers on board, but as we were going through neutral countries to Russia we could not wear uniform.

My military uniform, sword, revolver and kit were nailed up in crates and labelled for Haparanda-Torneo, the Swedish-Russian frontier posts. To send one's military kit in this manner did not constitute a violation of the neutrality of the Scandinavian countries.

We steamed slowly out towards the breakwater straight into the teeth of the gale, and then dashed across the North Sea to Bergen. It was one of the very worst of the many bad sea crossings I have experienced. A pretty girl with whom I had become acquainted in the train on the way to Aberdeen was now a poor little wreck hanging on to one of the settees and moaning to the stewardesses, 'Oh, please; oh, please, let me be dropped overboard.' What a relief it was to steam into Bergen and to be in the shelter of the fiord! I took the night train to Christiania and was lucky enough to secure one of the few sleeping-berths. From Christiania I hurried on to Stockholm, where I was to stay a week.

The economic situation in Sweden was very strained. As good merchants the Swedes had sold, during the second year of the war, most of their food supplies to Germany at a very good price, but now, although money was plentiful and the merchants' coffers were full, they found that they could not buy food for themselves owing to the Allied blockade. If Sweden chose to sell her food supplies to Germany it was her affair, but the Allies could not afford to let her replenish her stocks from abroad at their expense. In consequence of the blockade Englishmen were not very popular in Stockholm.

The Swedes were not instinctively pro-British like the Norwegians. Before the war they had the closest economic relations with Germany. For centuries Sweden had been anti-Russian and the bad feeling which existed between the two countries was not improved by the intrigues of German diplomats and agents.

Germany had one of her principal secret service organisations in Stockholm and the town was full of spies watching the railway stations, the hotels, the restaurants and the night clubs. Of course the Allies also had their secret service sections watching the Germans; using Stockholm as a base from which to survey the German coast and to test that the efficacy of the blockade was as watertight as possible. The principal agents of all these secret service organisations had to carry out their work without violating Swedish neutrality or sensibility, and were forever trying to placate the Swedish authorities.

Neutrals coming out of Germany could reveal the conditions of the day before in that country. Hamburg, Cologne and Berlin newspapers arrived in the city in less than twenty-four hours after they were printed and were scanned by the various Intelligence organisations. More than once the German secret service had made use of this fact and printed a special edition of one of the principal newspapers, by which they passed out information calculated to mislead and misinform the Allied staffs. I stayed at the Grand, one of the most luxurious hotels in Europe, and its winter gardens were thronged with people throughout the twenty-four hours. No one ever seemed to go to bed in those days.

As soon as I had registered at the hotel and produced my passport to establish my identity I was watched by German agents. The first time I left my room someone managed to slip in and examine my luggage and papers. Of course the hotel authorities were not aware of these irregular proceedings, which otherwise they would have stopped at once. But the smaller secret service agents have to take these risks and to develop the skill of a professional burglar in getting in and out of rooms without detection.

I had been warned that my things would be examined, and had taken precautions to leave nothing which could be of the slightest importance. The consciousness of being watched breeds a very uncomfortable feeling, and is a nerve-racking experience. After a very short time one knows the watchers and gets to hate them. Time and again you feel that you have shaken them off and then suddenly when you least expect it one of them will turn up again. Important public men who are watched by detectives for their own safety and protection grow to loathe their protectors, and often cheerfully take the risk of assassination for the relief of being for a few hours unwatched.

One afternoon, when I came into the lounge I spotted the brigand who had been watching me. He was talking to a man with his back turned to me who, when he turned round, I recognised as Hans Hartvig, a Russian subject of German origin whom I had known years before as a boy at school.

The lounge was full of people, but I managed to get a small

table and ordered my afternoon coffee. A minute or two later one of the senior waiters, whom I knew to be a German agent, very politely asked me if I would allow another gentleman to share my table. I gave my willing consent, and chuckled to see Hans Hartvig led up to me.

Would he recognise me, I wondered. But he did not. He had taken a new name. It was not Hans Hartvig, nor in fact was it Teutonic at all. He had also learned to speak perfect English and had come to my table deliberately to get into conversation with me. Of course he claimed to be a Swede and very pro-British.

He was very clever at his work, but it was a case of Greek meeting Greek with the advantages slightly in my favour, as I had recognised him and was on my guard. For two or three days he took every opportunity of talking to me, and we even lunched together.

I had been to the British Consulate and had also paid my respects to the British Legation. Owing to some trouble on the Russian frontier during the Kornilov affair it was necessary for me to go to the Russian Consulate and to the house of the Russian military attaché before I left for Petrograd. To all these places I had been shadowed by my pet aversion, the brigand. Hans Hartvig also decided that I was worth cultivating, and invited me to dine with him one evening: 'Just a little dinner party for four of us. It will give me great pleasure if you will make the fourth,' he said. The morrow was to be my last evening in Stockholm before I went north, and I gladly accepted. Of course Hans did not know that I was leaving. The following evening, as arranged, I asked for his table and found that it was secluded in one of the alcoves of the huge restaurant. As he rose to meet me he was full of regrets that the other lady had been prevented at the last moment from joining us that evening, and he, too, would have to leave quite early, but would I be so kind after he had left as to entertain the lady he was about to introduce?

The idea, of course, was to leave me alone with a lady in the hope that she would be able to abstract from me information which Hans did not feel he could manage to get himself. This is one of the oldest secret service dodges employed. He introduced me to Miss Irma Johansen, a very beautiful woman exquisitely dressed.

But the fact is that, though Hans believed Miss Johansen to be one of his very best agents, he was sadly mistaken. In reality she was one of our star agents of the British Intelligence section, and was working in our counter-espionage organisation.

Hans had ordered an elaborate dinner. We had lobster, spring chicken, and pineapple melba with which we drank a most excellent icy cold vintage Liebfraumilch. When the mocha coffee had been served Hans begged to be excused. He certainly had been a charming host and had thought of everything. He had given orders to the maître d'hôtel that we were to be served with liqueurs, fruit and a bottle of Mumm in order to keep us happy for the evening, and he begged me to order at his expense anything else we wanted, then off he went.

Irma Johansen knew who I was, and I knew who Irma was, and we had a very merry evening at Hans's expense. Irma told me how Hans had primed her and the questions she was to ask me. We made up the replies that I was supposed to have made to these questions, and I suppose that Hans got Irma's report next morning about the time that I was speeding north for Lapland.

Russia was cut off from the rest of Europe except for this route through the very northern Scandinavian and Swedish Lapland. The passport formalities on the Swedish side were very strict. In the customs shed I found my military luggage which had been sent on in advance, and had some difficulty in getting it, for every kind of formality and difficulty seemed to be put in my way. From the customs shed I could see the River Tornea, and on the other bank was Finland, then part of the Russian Empire.

Finally, all the passengers were ready and we proceeded into Russia. The luggage was loaded up into trucks and, escorted by Swedish gendarmes, we were solemnly marched over the wooden bridge, half of which belonged to Sweden and half to Russia, both countries having their frontier guards at their respective ends.

Tornea is a more miserable and squalid village than Haparanda, and whereas the station at Haparanda was neat and scrupulously clean as all Swedish stations are, the big waiting-room at Tornea was dirty and terribly dilapidated. The revolution had already put its stamp on the northern frontier town. There was no discipline among the soldiers, the gendarmes had been done away with and everything was lackadaisical.

No one knew when the train for Petrograd would leave. They hoped to collect sufficient railway carriages to make up one that evening, but it was rumoured that there was some difficulty with the engine, there being only one in a fit condition to take a train south.

There was, however, a delightful British RNVR [Royal Naval Volunteer Reserve] passport control officer at Tornea who looked after British interests and British travellers coming in and going out of Russia, and he took me along to his room and made me comfortable until such time as a train had been made up. I had my case opened and changed into uniform in his room.

After two or three false alarms the made-up train ambled into the station, pulled by a disreputable-looking engine burning wood and shooting sparks with great energy from its cone-shaped funnel.

No one knew when we would arrive in Petrograd, but I did not care, now that I was back in Russia.

Chapter XI

Three days later, at eventide, we pulled out of Terioki – the last town in the province of Finland – and made for Beloostrov, where the Russians had built a frontier station within their own kingdom. Despite all that M. Sazonov, the famous Russian statesman and Minister of Foreign Affairs, may have held, Russia was always Russia and Finland always Finland, and the two had never been really one. Little did I think as we came into Beloostrov that in less than a year I would be crossing the frontier again into Russia, not by means of a train and the railway bridge, but by wading in ice-cold water and swimming across the stream which forms the barrier.

About one o'clock in the morning we arrived at the Finland station in Petrograd. With his usual kindness General Poole had sent down Sir Victor Warrender, who was on his staff, to meet me and to tell me that rooms had been reserved for me at the Hotel de France. Nothing could have pleased me more, for in the old days I had always stayed at the France, and knew its proprietor very well.

To me, as I drove through the silent streets, St Petersburg – that city of distances – did not seem to have changed very much since I had seen it last. The still waters of the Neva flowed past the famous grey-and-pink granite embankments as silently as ever. The spire of the Peter and Paul fortress gleamed in the moonlight as of yore, while the coachman pulled off his hat and crossed himself at every shrine we passed. Had the revolution really come, I asked myself? Had Petrograd really changed in anything but name? The night was kind, and hid much from my eyes. It was not until next day that I began to realise how very much not only St Petersburg but the people of Russia had changed, under the stress of war and the destructive forces of revolution.

There was not much prospect of flying activities on the Russian front. Hostilities had practically ceased after Kerensky's ill-fated offensive in July. The British RFC unit had withdrawn to Moscow pending the arrival of new machines and within a couple of days I set off to join it. Outwardly Moscow seemed to have been less affected by the war than Petrograd. It was hundreds of miles away from the front, and while there were certain restrictions, and bread and other staple foods could only be obtained on ration cards, there was a noticeable absence of that tension which prevailed in other European towns.

It did not take me long to look up my old friends and to begin to enjoy the city life. At the opera Chaliapin, Sobenov and Nezdanova appeared on the same evening, while on the ballet nights Karsavina, Mordkin, Hessler and others of the famous Moscow school of ballet made one feel that one was living in a beautiful world of colour and movement, and not in the gory war-stained reality of Europe. The social world was considerably enlivened by the presence of some of the younger Grand Dukes. Relieved of their appointments through no fault of their own, they had to find some outlet for their energies, and with some of them I spent wild nights at the Gypsies.

After a short time however, I was ordered to attend a special conference at Mohileff. It was in this town that the C.-in-C. and the Russian General Staff had their quarters, and accordingly it was known at the time as Stavka, which is the name applied always to the seat of the Headquarters Staff of the Russian Army.

I found Mohileff to be a provincial town on the Dnieper, a mean and dirty little place, inhabited mostly by Jews and Catholics who were forever at loggerheads with each other, and, since the arrival of the Commander-in-Chief, a very hotbed of intrigue.

The situation on the front was critical. The Russian Army as a fighting machine was slowly but surely crumbling to pieces. Much of this was due to the natural war weariness which was affecting most of Europe at that time and to the terrific sacrifices which had been demanded of the Russian armies in the first three years of hostilities. Some of it was due to the general backwardness and the economic situation of the country. The revolution had had a disastrous effect on the morale of the army, which had been further smashed by the well-meant but fatal No. I order issued by the provisional government, an order which virtually abolished any discipline in the army. But that military operations were conducted in a manner fantastic and frivolous was chiefly due to Kerensky, with his naive belief that the armies' spirit could be resuscitated by melodramatic speeches from the War Minister and his idealist associates.

I met Kerensky and Savinkov on the same day at Stavka, two big men to meet together – Kerensky, then virtually Dictator of Russia; Savinkov, the great Nihilist who was Kerensky's Minister of War.

Savinkov I will describe later in my narrative, for I

subsequently had many dealings with him. Kerensky I met only once again before he was overthrown by the Bolsheviks. He was about thirty-six or seven at the time, a short slim man, with dark hair and a very pale face. He was wearing khaki uniform, and a military cap which he carried very much at the back of his head. He had a nervous manner and in conversation with him I gained the impression that everything he said was simple pose, that he was everlastingly playing for effect. I must confess that I took an instant aversion to him. To say that he was a nonentity would be absurd. But his great forte was stump-oratory, and he had the power of winning over in an amazingly short space of time mobs of hostile and infuriated soldiery. It is an unkind thing to say, but I always feel that Kerensky 'meant well'. Unfortunately for him, although he had the power of raising a fierce enthusiasm for any cause in his listeners, as soon as his presence was removed the enthusiasm evaporated with startling rapidity.

On the occasion of this visit of his to Stavka he was engaged in some bickering quarrel with General Dukhonin, the Commander-in-Chief, a fact which he did not disguise from the Inter-Allied representatives at Stavka.

The Inter-Allied officers all messed together at the Bristol Hotel. It was a queer assembly of representatives – British, French, Americans, Serbians, Japanese, Belgians, Italians, Rumanians. At the head of each delegation was a general who had a staff of three or four officers of his own nationality attached to him. General Bazoroff, with a staff of Russian offic-ers, acted as host. Each of these Missions was there to represent the views of its own particular country, and there was naturally a good deal of difference of opinion among various representa-tives, who in their turn were split up into divers factions.

These delegates acted as liaison, and also as official observers of the Russian armies' activities, and quite naturally the German secret service had an organisation at Mohileff to watch the Allied representatives.

I had my first encounter with the German secret service organisation at Madame B's house. She was in the Russian counter-espionage service, and made it her business to collect any pro-German Russians at her house. At this stage of the war there were quite a number of genuine Russian patriots who were pro-German, and to this number were added many more Russians who were frankly traitors. On one of my visits to Madame B's house I purposely gave tongue and was extremely indiscreet in what I said about the pro-German factor in Russia. A day or two afterwards Madame B. warned me that my remarks had been noted and that I had better be on my guard. I was therefore not surprised when I had only gone a little way from her house to find that I was followed. Unfortunately my way took me into an ill-lit street and here it was that my followers started to put on speed, and I suddenly realised that two thugs were after me. Just as they were about to close with me I swung round and flourished my walking stick. As I expected, one of my assailants seized hold of it. It was a swordstick, which had been specially designed by Messrs Wilkinson, the sword makers of Pall Mall, and the moment my attacker had the scabbard in his fist I drew back the rapier-like blade with a jerk and with a forward lunge ran it through the gentleman's side. He gave a scream and collapsed on the pavement. His comrade, seeing that I had put up a fight and was not unarmed, took to his heels while I withdrew, and fumbled for my revolver. Meanwhile the man I had run through staggered off, leaving my scabbard on the pavement, and I went back and recovered it. That sword-stick thereafter had a value in my eyes. By the irony of fate I lost it some years later at a lecture in which Sir Paul Dukes described his own experiences in Russia.

Arrived at the Bristol, I went straight up to my room, examining the blade on the stairs, anxious to know what it looked like after its adventure. I had never run a man through before. It was not a gory sight. There was only a slight film of blood halfway up the blade and a dark stain at the tip, but I was so occupied in the inspection of these phenomena that I did not notice a man in the uniform of a British officer waiting at the top of the stairs until I had blundered into him.

The stranger was a powerfully built, square man with a rugged countenance, blue eyes and a great mane of iron-grey hair, and he seemed highly amused at the examination I was making of my blade. It was my first meeting with Colonel Joe (better known in some parts of the world as 'Klondyke') Boyle.

Colonel Boyle was an Irish-Canadian who as a boy had run away to sea and worked his way up until he had taken a mate's certificate. He had been a fireman in the Chicago fire brigade. He had been amateur heavy-weight boxing champion of the United States, and had fought many a battle at the National Sporting Club in London. He had been manager of the great Frank Slavin, heavy-weight champion of the world.

In 1898 he took part in the Klondyke gold rush and staked out valuable claims for himself, ending by founding a Canadian gold-mining company. By the outbreak of the war he was a millionaire, and at his own expense equipped a machine-gun detachment on certain theories he had of how such a unit should be organised and equipped. This detachment he sent direct to

England, where it was disbanded by the authorities as being unsuitable and its personnel drafted into the Canadian overseas contingent. By the irony of fate and as a result of bitter and practical experience a British machine-gun corps was formed three years later on lines almost identical with those worked out by Colonel Boyle.

Colonel Boyle had been sent to Russia and Rumania to assist in the coordination of transport and to organise the auxiliary Decauville Railways, which were being constructed from the main lines to form a network of communication along the Russian and Rumanian fronts.

He was a born fighter, a great talker and blessed with an exceptional amount of common sense. He was independent to a revolutionary extent. Etiquette and procedure meant nothing to him, especially if a job had to be done. He was in Russia to get on with the war, to harry the Germans and to help the Allies, and in doing so he cared not over whom he rode roughshod.

Such was Colonel Boyle, a man whose equal I have encountered neither before nor since, and to have enjoyed his friendship and to have worked under and with him will always remain one of the proudest memories of my life.

Chapter XII

My last interview with Kerensky at Stavka – prior to his return to Petrograd – left a very bad impression on me. The situation on the front was going from bad to worse. From every sector there was mass desertion. The soldiers' committees were expelling, persecuting and murdering all officers who tried to keep some semblance of law and order. Kerensky – the last hope – was a vacillating and bombastic weakling, who played ducks and drakes with his own party, with his supporters, and with his country.

On 6 November 1917, when the situation was already beyond repair, he declared, in the name of the provisional government, the outlawry of the Military Revolutionary Committee of the Soviets which was controlled by the Bolsheviks and Mensheviks.

Lenin had organised at Petrograd a Red Guard composed of soldiers, sailors and workmen, with its headquarters at the Smolny Institute. The Military Revolutionary Committee's reply to Kerensky was to give battle. Street fighting started in the afternoon and by the following morning Petrograd was in the hands of the Bolsheviks and Kerensky in ignominious flight. The following day the Soviet government was formed by decree. A few days later, after stubborn and sanguinary street fighting, Moscow was captured from the Whites and a Soviet regime established in that town. Meanwhile the agents of the Bolsheviks were working everywhere through the country, agitating for the establishment of a Soviet regime. In this task they were helped by agitators in the pay of the German secret service, for Germany wished to smash the Russian Army, disintegrate the country, and have in power a party whom they believed would eat out of the hands of the Wilhelmstrasse and meekly carry out the orders of the German High Command.

Following the flight of Kerensky, General Dukhonin, as Commander-in-Chief of the Russian forces, assumed the obligations of the provisional government. Dukhonin was a pawn of fate, thoroughly unfitted for the post he occupied. He had been used as a stop-gap by Kerensky and, although an excellent executive soldier, was unfit for administrative work and was no statesman. He always impressed me as being a very simple Russian soul on two occasions I stood just behind him during mass at the Mohileff Cathedral, and the sincerity with which he carried out his devotions and his general humbleness convinced me that he was far too much of a fatalist to be a good fighter. He was surrounded by intrigue, which was not lacking even among the senior commanders of his personal staff. The whole of the general staff showed a lack of initiative and cooperation. Everyone was waiting for someone else to do something. Only the Soldiers', Sailors' and Peasants' Councils were active and their activity, directed by the German secret service, was the activity of destruction.

The military duty which had brought me to Stavka vanished with Kerensky's government. I tried to form the junior officers into some sort of an organisation but without success. Then I decided to begin propaganda among the regimental Soldiers' Councils, and here I was rather more successful. I found that

Colonel Boyle was doing the same thing. He did not speak a word of Russian and had to employ an interpreter, but little things of that kind were not allowed to stand in the way of Klondyke Boyle. He was living in a very ornate, up-to-date saloon railway carriage which he had fitted out delightfully, and in which I spent many happy hours. Boyle and I had many interests in common. He knew the Pacific Coast from A to Z, and he was very proud of the fact that his collar and shoulder badges were made of Yukon gold. My residence in British Columbia and my own knowledge of the Yukon made a tie between us, and we were united in our view that the situation in Russia might still be turned to the advantage of the Allies.

The Allied Military Mission were doing their best to expose the Austro-German machinations by propaganda among the rank and file of the Russian Army. The German agents spotted this at once and started an agitation among the members of the Soldiers', Sailors' and Peasants' Council at Stavka, to have the Allied Missions thrown out and, if necessary, murdered.

One afternoon I learned that the Council was in special session debating our fate. A few minutes later I happened to meet Boyle in the street and told him what was toward.

'I wish I had my interpreter with me,' was Boyle's comment; 'I would go and address the Council.'

'I will interpret for you,' said I.

'Done!' said Boyle.

We arrived at a packed hall. On learning our purpose in coming the President of the meeting was most unwilling that we should speak, but we pressed him so hard that finally he agreed to put the matter to the vote of the meeting. Boyle and I were standing just inside the wings of the tiny stage when the motion was put. It was received with a howl – of ferocious intensity – the angry howl of an infuriated pack.

And in the middle of all that turmoil of wrath and hatred, and without waiting for anyone's leave, Boyle stepped on to the stage. I followed. He gazed for a moment at the audience, and then spoke. His voice was clear and musical, his sentences short and crisp. It was a terrible moment. At first the crowd was taken by surprise. Then there was a move to rush the stage. But it was too late. Boyle had got hold of his audience, while I translated sentence for sentence, though I do not mind confessing that I did not find it at all easy to keep my voice level, and my manner calm and undisturbed.

Boyle knew crowd psychology. He gripped the attention of his hearers. He began with stories about Canada. Then he switched into Russian history. The speech did not last more than fifteen minutes, and concluded with a stirring perora-tion in which he reminded his listeners that Russians never surrendered. They might retreat into Russia, as they did during Napoleon's invasion, but it was only to return to the attack with renewed ardour. 'You are men,' he concluded, 'not sheep. I order you to act as men.'

Thunders of applause followed. A soldier jumped up on the stage and shouted 'Long live the Allies. Down with the Germans!' The ovation continued for some minutes. Finally Boyle and I were escorted by the mob to the hotel and an enthusiastic demonstration in favour of the Allied Military Mission was held which was addressed by each of the Allied Generals in turn.

After this Boyle and I decided to join forces. We both believed that cooperation with the Bolsheviks was the best means of serving the Allied cause against the Germans in Russia. Neither Boyle nor I at any time subscribed either to Bolshevik policy or doctrines, but we felt that these were things apart and would be dealt with in due course by the Russian people. Our job was to harry the Germans and Austrians and in pursuit of this end we decided to go to Petrograd and see what we could do at Bolshevik headquarters. A further reason for going was that, owing to the civil war which had been raging, the important railway junction known as Moscow Knot was hopelessly choked. Supplies going to the south-western front had been stopped, and Boyle, who had been in charge of this area, had received a telegram from the General Officer in command of the south-western army, saying that the mass desertion of his front was due to the absence of supplies. We hoped that we might be able to untie the Knot. However, we did not get to Petrograd without an attempt at revenge on the part of the German agents.

We travelled from Stavka with a huge crowd of soldiers hanging on to the open platform at the end of our carriage. The train, like all Russian trains, was packed and passengers had to travel as best they could. At Orsha, an hour out from Stavka, our carriage had to be switched from the Moscow train, to which it was attached, to the waiting Petrograd express.

It was shunted, and then deliberately smashed into lined buffers at high speed. The car was wrecked. Boyle and I were unhurt, but some of the soldiers on the outer platform were killed. For a moment the air was rent by terrible screams. Then there was a stupefied silence. Boyle and I scrambled out on to the line. After the crash the car had rebounded, and one poor soldier was pinned beneath a wheel of the carriage. I think he was already dead, but all our efforts to get him out were unavailing. Meantime the engine-driver had fled. However, we found another and ordered him to back the wreck so that we might be able to get the body clear. But while we were working hard to free the poor wretch, the shuntsman suddenly blew his whistle and the whole car was run over the pinned body. Then Boyle rose in anger, and with a smashing blow hit the shuntsman square in the mouth. I fancy that after coming to that fellow found he would never be able to use a whistle again with any comfort.

No more was to be done. We had seen the last of our saloon car. We transferred our belongings from the wreckage to an ordinary sleeper, and in due course arrived in Petrograd.

Chapter XIII

Our first task after arrival was to get possession of a new saloon carriage since, owing to the terrible congestion, travelling in ordinary carriages was almost impossible. No matter where the train was going it was not only full to suffocation inside, but also crowded outside, with men and women. People would huddle together on the roofs of the carriages and quite cheerfully travel in this way for a journey lasting three or four days.

I went down to the yards to look over available special carriages and chose one numbered 451. If not as modern or ornate as that which had been wrecked it was more solidly built, and equipped with bullet-proof walls. It had been the private car of the Empress Marie Feodorovna, and consisted of an observation dining-saloon, a combined state bedroom and sitting-room, five coupés with the usual double sleeping-berth in each, a small pantry with a stove and a plant for heating the carriage, and finally a lavatory. Moreover it was equipped with a self-generating electric-light plant. Though I expended the utmost care on the selection of this carriage I did not think at the time that I was going to live in it and make it my home for nearly seven months. Number 451 was in the care of a fierce, rather elderly, very competent conductor named Ivan, of whom more anon.

It took us a day to provision the car and install ourselves in it, after which we had it transferred to a reserve platform on the Nicolai station with the intention of using it in preference to an hotel.

The following morning we buckled on our swords and drove off to the Smolny Institute.

The Smolny Institute had been a boarding-school for the daughters of the nobility – the female Eton of Russia. Lenin considered that both for strategic reasons and because of its large size it would be the most suitable site for his headquarters, and therefore, early one morning, one of his detachments had swept down on the place and kindly but firmly ejected from its precincts all the trembling young ladies, their governesses, teachers and the principal.

It was a low, grey, colonnaded building with a dome in the centre, and was surrounded by a fairly high brick wall, which was topped by a fence of iron railings. Its courtyard was full of men: members of the Red Guard, unmilitary-looking soldiers, civilian workmen, and a fair sprinkling of sailors. The sailors in their black leather jerkins and sailor caps caught the eye at once. They were the best-armed men in the crowd and moved as a trained body among that disorderly jumble. The workmen and soldiers were armed according to no order. Some had rifles, others just bayonets and pockets bulging with hand-grenades, and the prevailing fashion seemed to be a machine-gun belt full of cartridges wound round the body. Where this indisciplined horde crowded thickest stood a couple of armoured cars. Boyle and I fought our way through to the entrance of the building, where we found ourselves faced by the muzzles of a couple of field guns. The place was well fortified though had those guns ever been fired, the recoil would have carried them through the wall and brought the whole entrance down on top of them.

The entrance hall was fuller, if anything, than the courtyard. Nobody seemed to be doing anything in particular, and we wandered around, poking our heads into various corridors until at last we reached one where a sentry was on duty. We were brusquely informed that we were not allowed in there. Clearly this was the entrance to the inner sanctum of the Bolshevik leaders.

'I want to see Comrade Joffe, the President of the Petrograd Military Revolutionary Committee,' said I to the sentry.

'Well, you will find him somewhere down this corridor,' answered the sentry carelessly, and let us through.

Again we wandered along the passage, looking into various rooms, all of which were almost bare of furniture but quite full of people. I called out for Comrade Joffe, and at each door was referred to another room. However, at last we traced him. We were among the very first of the Allied officers to penetrate Smolny, though I think that both the French and American representatives had forestalled us by a few hours. Joffe came forward in quite a friendly manner and apologised because there were no chairs for us to sit on.

The room was full of hangers-on. From the moment of seizing power the Bolsheviks had declared that an end had come to all secret diplomacy, that the proletariat were in duty bound to assist in the affairs of state, and that they were cordially invited to attend all government offices and see that matters were being conducted to their satisfaction. Hence in the early days of Smolny anyone was admitted. But this Utopian state of affairs lasted only a few weeks, and within a month it was more difficult to see Messrs Lenin, Trotsky, or their confreres than it is to see any cabinet minister in England.

We explained to Joffe the work we had been doing with the provisional government, and told him that we were willing to go on with it provided that we had the support of the Bolshevik authorities. In particular, we pointed out to him how the south-western army was starving owing to the congestion of the railway Knot at Moscow, and that it was essential to get food supplies down to it.

To this Joffe replied that it was not only the south-western army that was being faced with starvation, but that Petrograd likewise was threatened, and that the Bolsheviks would be quite ready to give us every facility they possibly could to further our work.

Ruthless, ignorant, pig-headed, seeking to conduct affairs on a strict adherence to a few second-hand phrases, the Bolsheviks yet had a rough-and-ready system of working by rule of thumb, which is at the root of any success which they have attained.

Joffe hurried off and fetched Podvoisky who had just been appointed Minister of War by Lenin. Podvoisky was a most undetermined sort of man, being unique in that respect among all the Bolsheviks I have ever met. I think that Joffe must have sensed that the interview was not going any too well, for he bustled off again and this time brought in Karahan, a good-looking Armenian who was very well turned out and had a rather distinguished manner.

I think it was Radek, with his very bitter tongue, who once in my hearing described Karahan as 'a donkey of classical beauty'. But Karahan was no fool (he is still a People's Commissar for Foreign Affairs). He saw at once the importance of our demands and went off to fetch Lenin.

Lenin ambled in, Karahan in his wake. The outward appearance of the Dictator was that of a strong and simple man of less than middle height with a Slavonic cast of countenance, piercing eyes, and a powerful forehead. He shook hands with us. His manner was not friendly, nor could it be said to be hostile; it was completely detached. He listened to what Joffe and Karahan had to say about us, and when they had finished, nodded his head two or three times and said, 'Of course, they must be given full facilities for the work they are doing.' Now that the Commissars had got him there, they plied him with questions concerning other matters which they had in hand, and I noticed at once how ready he was with well-reasoned advice, which he gave with disarming simplicity. In a few minutes he had polished off their questions and then bowing to us strolled away with his hands behind his back.

Meanwhile I explained to Joffe that we should require passes from him authorising us to do the work which had been agreed upon, and he promised that we should have them without delay provided that he could find a typewriter. At once half a dozen of the hangers-on and a couple of so-called secretaries were sent scouring the building for a typewriter, and after about twenty minutes a dilapidated machine was brought in. Then he found that there was no table on which to put it. Joffe always stood at the window-sill when he wanted to write.

Off went another messenger and returned with a school desk. Then another hitch occurred. Nobody there knew how to type. Finally one of Joffe's three or four secretaries volunteered to make an attempt.

Stationery had already been produced with the Smolny heading and the crossed sickle and hammer – the sign of the Peasants' and Workmen's Republic – embossed in the left-hand corner.

I dictated the very fullest of powers for Boyle and myself, which Joffe scribbled down on paper, agreed to without alteration and passed over to the lady who had volunteered to do the typing. It was a lengthy business as she only used one finger, and was not very adept at manipulating a rubber. Finally the document was ready. On reading it through I noticed that the typist on her own initiative had changed 'Colonel Boyle and Captain Hill' into 'Comrades Boyle and Hill'. I was inclined to let this pass, but Boyle stood upon his dignity, insisted on our proper titles, and at the direction of Joffe the document was retyped, and once again in agony we watched that solitary finger wander over the thirty-six letters of the Russian alphabet.

Finally Joffe's signature was appended to the document, the necessary seals affixed and counter-signed by a secretary and we took our leave.

I have always had a friendly feeling towards Joffe, and was sorry to hear some years ago that he had taken his own life. A queer fate has overtaken many of those Bolsheviks whom I met when they were in power in 1917–18. Volodarsky, Vorovsky, Uritsky died by assassination. Dzerjhinsky and Sverdlov died suddenly and under suspicious circumstances. Lenin survived two attempts of assassination and died as the result of a painful illness. Trotsky is in exile in Turkey. Rakovsky and Kamenev are likewise in exile. Only Stalin has kept on the crest of the wave. Truly those who live by the sword…

Chapter XIV

There could be no doubt that the population of Petrograd was on the verge of starvation. We had undertaken to help to get provisions to the town, and so we ordered our special car to be attached to the midnight Moscow express, there to untangle the trouble. Trains were still designated as express, fast, and slow, but the difference was purely nominal. They all travelled at the same rate. The railways had become disorganised, and an ordinary twelve-hour journey might take anything from eighteen to forty-eight hours.

We arrived in Moscow the following afternoon. It was a dismal winter day. The station and the square outside were deserted but for armed guards. Dotted here and there all over the snow-covered square were dead horses, their bellies so swollen that they looked like inflated balloons. These were the outward signs of the street fighting that had taken place when Moscow had changed from White to Red during the previous week.

After some delay we secured a sledge drawn by a poor half-dead grey nag with ribs almost bursting through its hide, and set off to the Central Railway Board, which was housed in a great building in the middle of Moscow. We jogged along for some time, Boyle expressing doubts whether the poor beast would get us to our destination. It did not, but it was not the fault of the nag. A fierce fight started in one of the side streets, the first warning of which was the rattle of rifle and revolver firing, then came the pat-pat-patter of machine guns, and our horse pitched forward with a bullet through his head. We paid the driver the full fare we had bargained for and, leaving him weeping over his horse, proceeded to our destination on foot.

Before the Bolshevik revolution Boyle had been unofficially controlling the south-western railways, and was very well known to the executive boards of the Russian State Railways, by whom he was liked and trusted. The technical boards were staffed for the most part by anti-Bolsheviks and, as a counter-attack on nationalisation, confiscation, and ill-treatment of the bourgeois classes by the Bolsheviks, they had commenced a system of sabotage on the railways. This, of course, was tanta-mount to cutting off the nose to spite the face, and our purpose was to persuade the railway board – at our direction – to put a stop to the sabotage, and assist us in untying the Moscow railway Knot. They did not require much persuading to use their authority as far as it extended, but they pointed out that they could do nothing with the personnel or with labourers in the railway yards as these were controlled by their unions who, in turn, were directed by the Soviets and the Bolsheviks. We undertook to bring the Bolsheviks into line, and went off at once to Bolshevik headquarters.

The streets were for the most part deserted, the houses pockmarked with machine-gun and rifle bullets, and in the neighbourhood of the Kremlin buildings were smashed up by shell fire. In the centre of the town there was hardly a whole shop window and the broken glass had been replaced by rough wooden screens. An air of gloom and depression hung over the town like a pall. The Bolsheviks had their headquarters in a building of which the imposing exterior only accentuated the filth and squalor within. As at Smolny, the building was packed with unwashed soldiers, workmen, hooligans of the city, and convicts who had been indiscriminately released from the prisons by the Bolsheviks. Through the mob we fought our way to the commander of Moscow, a soldier named Muralov. Pending his arrival we were entertained by his adjutant, an overdressed dandy who had decorated himself with a couple of Mauser revolvers, three or four hand-grenades of the German pattern, on longish sticks, two whistles, and a policeman's truncheon, and drenched himself with at least a bottle of cheap scent. The effluvia wafted from his person did not improve the general stench of the ante-room, the air of which was thick with the odour of unclean humanity and cheap tobacco smoke. In a business-like way and none too gently the adjutant cleared off three or four dirty-looking individuals from a gorgeous Louis XV couch. But out of reverence for their entomological companions we declined the invitation to be seated.

Muralov was a pleasant surprise. He was a tall, dark-bearded Russian with a frank face and intelligent eyes, a hand on him like a leg of mutton and a very deep voice. We took a liking to each other at once. We showed him Joffe's document and, stating our business, explained the arrangement we had made with the Central Railway Control Board and asked for his cooperation, which he readily gave us. What was more, he gave us complete liberty of action within that area of hundreds of junction lines, loading platforms and shunting sidings which formed the Moscow railway Knot.

It was in his room that we drew up drastic plans for the following day and explained the proposed arrangements over the telephone to the Central Railway Board, who agreed to carry out our plan. We returned to our carriage feeling that we had done a good day's work.

The following morning at the principal depot, the railway staff were ready to do their part, but the engine-drivers, the lorry drivers and the working gangs had not turned up. As all these people came under the orders of the Bolsheviks we went off and complained to Muralov. Muralov summoned the men's leaders, to the number of about twenty-five, and asked why his orders had not been carried out. There was no explanation.

'If your gangs are not in place and ready to commence work to-morrow morning at seven o'clock,' said Muralov, 'I shall shoot six of you, and it will be decided by lot which of you are to be executed.'

The Bolsheviks had been in power less than a month, but Russia already knew that they had an unpleasant way of carrying out their threats to the letter. Accordingly I was not surprised that the gangs were in place at seven o'clock on the following morning. We cleared that congested knot in two days. Whole trains were pitched over embankments, empty trucks run out along the lines and pitched into fields. Our methods were very much criticised by the technical staff; but I think that we were justified, for within three days the lines were cleared, the confusion remedied, and trains able to proceed with much-needed food supplies to Petrograd, and rations and fodder in the opposite direction to Kieff and the south-western army. It was owing to this timely arrival of supplies that the general in command of the south-western army was able to keep three hundred thousand men in their trenches and engage the attention of an equal number of Germans.

Chapter XV

About this time the Bolshevik papers gave details of an armistice which Lenin and Trotsky had proposed to the German High Command with a view to negotiating an immediate peace. General Dukhonin, at Stavka, had refused to transmit these requests to the Germans. Dukhonin was dismissed by the Bolsheviks and the chief command of the Russian armies given to a subaltern officer, Ensign Krylenko. Dukhonin refused to leave his post. It was rumoured that Krylenko was moving against Stavka. Boyle and I decided that there would probably be work for us at Stavka, and we had our special car transferred from the Petrograd to the Briansk station along the Knot which we had opened.

On our way to the station we encountered the gigantic funeral procession of some four hundred of the Red Guard who had been killed in the recent street fighting. In Russia it is the custom to carry the coffin opened to the place of interment. Many of the bodies had remained in the frost for days, and owing to the immense number for burial and the hurried preparations for the interment, some of the corpses had been placed in the coffins more or less in the positions in which they had frozen. The dead were interred by the Kremlin Wall in the great Red Square, where Lenin's mausoleum now stands, with their graves on either flank.

The weather was so cold that the windows of our carriage were covered with frost, and as we pulled out of Briansk station the setting sun lit up the frost crystals on the windows into a myriad jewels of flaming opal while the whole western horizon blazed like a fiery furnace.

At Orsha, where only a little while previously our saloon carriage had been deliberately wrecked, we ran into a detachment of Comrade Krylenko's force, consisting of Red Guards and sailors from Kronstadt. Everything was in a state of chaos. There must have been two or three hundred camp-fires alight in the station yard. For fuel they had used the spare, valuable and irreplaceable oak sleepers. The station-master was cowed by terror, and dared not protest, for his assistant had been executed as a counter-revolutionary for objecting to the use to which the sleepers had been put.

We had our carriage coupled to the train which was conveying a small detachment going to reinforce Krylenko at Stavka, and were informed that Dukhonin was a prisoner, having been treacherously surrendered by some of his own guard. At last our train drew up at Stavka station opposite a stationary one some five platforms away. The entire space between the two trains was a howling mob of armed men, who kept baying like hungry wolves, 'We want Dukhonin.' Suddenly a little figure with a bearded face came out on the platform of a first-class carriage opposite our own and tried to address the mob. It was Krylenko. The mob would not listen to him, but howled him down; his courage failed him and he slunk back into the carriage, while the fury of the crowd surged up higher than ever.

Then someone else appeared on the carriage platform and held out in his hands two large, heavily tasselled silver epaulettes.

There was a moment's silence. 'These are Dukhonin's,' called out the man and flung them to the crowd. They were seized and torn into a million shreds. It was like watching a pack of wild wolves. Then the baying recommenced. 'We want Dukhonin ... *We want Dukhonin* ... WE WANT DUKHONIN.' The man who had held the epaulettes vanished into the carriage, and a moment later reappeared pushing someone in front of him. I recognised Dukhonin.

For a moment he stood on the step, clutching the rail and looking down at the inhuman frenzy of the crowd. Only for a moment. His foot might have slipped or he might have been pushed from behind. I do not know. But suddenly he lurched forward, was caught by a thousand hands and hurled into the centre of the crowd. There was a scuffle. It ended. There was a pause. A circle was being formed in the middle of the crowd and then, as a man is tossed in a blanket, Dukhonin was thrown into the air. Round the circle came a crackle of musketry, and as his body fell it was caught on the waiting bayonets. For a moment longer the corpse was worried on the ground. A hush fell on the crowd. Even those hundreds of yards away knew what had happened. Someone laughed, and a voice said, 'Well, he's dead!' The sadistic lust of the mob was satisfied and it started to disperse. A few curious persons pressed forward to look at the poor mangled body as it lay oozing in its pool of blood. Then the station rapidly emptied until between our carriage and that of Krylenko there was only the mutilated body of the Commander-in-Chief. A station sweeper came forward, in a mechanical way crossed himself, and dragged the remains unassisted down the line and over a platform into a goods shed. Someone descended from Krylenko's carriage and a few minutes later I noticed that an armed guard had been placed at the door of the shed in which the body lay.

Thus was butchered Dukhonin, Commander-in-Chief of five million fighting men. *Requiescat in pace.*

We had witnessed the whole horrible affair, and had been able to do nothing. Of what had happened in Stavka itself and of the fate of the Allied Mission we knew nothing. We decided to go and investigate. The station yard was empty, and we rightly assumed that most of the crowd had gone off to loot the town. We commandeered a dilapidated Renault car which was standing there unattended and drove to the Bristol.

On our way we compared impressions of the crowd. We agreed that there had been a number of men who were neither soldiers, sailors nor workmen, but were of quite a different stamp and who had acted almost like stewards. One or two we had previously noted working in the soldiers' committees, and were pretty confident that they were part of the German secret service organisation. Many years afterwards, through the memoirs of various German, Austrian and Hungarian generals and officials, our suspicion received confirmation.

At the Bristol Hotel we discovered that, luckily for them, the Allied Missions had left Stavka by a special train for Kieff half an hour before Krylenko's horde had occupied the station.

There was no more to do. We returned to the station only to find that our carriage had been shunted out to the depot with orders that it was not to be moved, and that there would be no trains leaving Stavka that day.

'Who gave this order?'

'Krylenko.'

'And there are to be no more trains today?'

'So Krylenko says.'

'Then you will please put us on a special.'

'I can't do that.'

'Then who can?'

'Krylenko.'

'Where is Krylenko?'

Our informant pointed out a heavily guarded railway carriage, and Boyle and I marched over to it and demanded to see Krylenko.

After some delay he came out of his car and descended on to the platform. He was a shorter figure than I had first of all thought him to be, a most unpleasant creature, deadly pale, with a queer head, and small shifty pig eyes. He was surrounded by his staff, personal guards and some of the actual murderers.

We produced our Joffe document and demanded that a special train should be put at our disposal to take us to Petrograd. Krylenko fawned on us and promised to put an engine at our disposal immediately. In a sheepish way he made an allusion to the regrettable incident which had just taken place and explained that it was no fault of his. When I translated this to Boyle it was too much for him.

'Tell him', he said in a loud voice, 'that anyone who allows his prisoner to be taken from him and lynched in his sight is no man. What you have done is no business of mine, but I am told that you are keeping the body. If there is a shred of decency left in you you will hand it over to the General's widow. Will you undertake to do this?' Krylenko turned scarlet, and said that the body would be given up immediately. Then he turned his back on us and swung himself up into his carriage.

Two hours later we had our special engine, and were en route for Petrograd.

Chapter XVI

Our first visit on arrival in Petrograd was to Joffe, whom we found much impressed by what we had achieved in Moscow. We did not disguise from him our disgust at the murder of Dukhonin, nor did we mince our words in assigning the responsibility for the outrage. At first Joffe tried to make excuses, but eventually finding it of no avail he rather cleverly changed the subject and told us of the progress which the Soviet government had made since we were last in Petrograd.

They had established a full government. Comrade Nevski had been appointed Minister of Railways. A War Affairs Collegium had also been formed and he was certain that we could be of assistance both to Nevski and the War Collegium.

So we got into touch with Nevski and the War Collegium, to whom we were able to be of considerable use, at the same time contriving that the armies in the field continued to receive their supplies.

But the Bolsheviks feared the army and were in terror that it might be organised for use against them.

They had signed a ten days' truce with Germany. It began on 5 December 1917, and under its general terms the Central Powers agreed not to transfer German or Austrian troops from the eastern to the western front, though in fact the Germans did move several divisions from the Russian front to France before the end of the year. Meantime Krylenko had returned from Stavka and was conferring with Lenin.

His return entirely changed the feeling among the members of the War Affairs Collegium, and on his advice the demobilisation of the army was determined on. Boyle and I were present at most of these sessions and fought them tooth and nail. We proved to them conclusively that the demobilisation of the army at this moment would culminate in an economic disaster of unparalleled magnitude. It would choke up the railways, it would add to the confusion existing in the area between the front line and the towns of Central Russia, and it would mean starvation in Moscow and Petrograd. But it was all to no purpose. They were determined to have their own way, and on 7 December a general demobilisation order was circulated by wireless to all units on the front.

Subsequent events showed that Boyle and I were right, though we had not foreseen anything like the actual extent of the effects of the demobilisation order which was the main origin of the successive famines which for the next three years swept through Russia.

The Railway Minister and War Collegium having rejected our advice we changed our *point d'appui*, and were preparing to visit Rumania and the south-western front to see what could be done there, when the Rumanian Ambassador, M. Diamandi, asked us to call on him.

We found him in despair, not only because of the situation in Russia and the immediate prospect of war between Rumania and the Soviets, but also because of the state of affairs in Rumania itself.

'I tell you, Colonel, the position is desperate – desperate. In

Rumania there is no money. You know that when Bucharest fell we sent our gold reserve, the crown jewels, the Foreign Office archives and our reserve of paper currency for safe keeping to the Kremlin. It is still in Moscow, and now that the Bolsheviks have seized and nationalised everything and are forcing this war upon us we will lose the very last of our resources. We have not even a printing press in Jassy capable of printing paper money. *Mon Dieu*, it is appalling.'

The Colonel grunted enigmatically.

'If only a part of that treasure could be returned to Jassy, what a relief to my poor country,' continued the minister.

Boyle looked at me, and I looked at Boyle. The same idea had occurred to both of us. 'Well, why not?' we said.

The minister leaped to his feet. 'If you gentlemen succeed you will be our saviours. If you say it can be done I know it will be done.'

We explained that we did not share his confidence in the certainty of our success, but that we were prepared to do our best if he would undertake the responsibility of giving authority for the treasure to be handed over to us for transport to Jassy.

M. Diamandi was nominally in complete charge of this treasure, and he hastened to give instructions to the Rumanian authorities in Moscow that the valuables in question were to be handed over to us, if we on our part were able to persuade the Soviet authorities to allow them to go out of their charge.

M. Diamandi had not exaggerated the position of Rumania. It was, as he said, appalling. For the first few weeks after her entry into the war on the side of the Allies she seemed to be carrying all before her. And then General Mackensen with new German, Austrian, and Bulgarian armies turned on her and

inflicted defeat upon defeat. Fighting doggedly the Rumanian
Army retreated. Bucharest was surrendered, and gradually the
gallant little army was forced back until it held only the north-
eastern provinces of the country and was almost in Russian
territory. Jassy, a small provincial town, had been made the new
capital. The Rumanian Army was reinforced by Russian divisions who had lost all discipline since the revolution and were
contaminating what was left of the Rumanian Army.

The previous year, when the Rumanians felt that they had
reached the low-water mark of their misery, they did have
the feeling that if the worst came to the worst the court and the
government could withdraw into Russia. Now this great Ally
of theirs had suddenly become an enemy. The Bolsheviks were
determined to crush them. They were between the devil and the
deep sea. Their line of retreat was cut off. They were surrounded
by enemies, and their life blood was stored in the Kremlin
at Moscow.

That evening we left for Moscow. I felt that it was time that
I propitiated the hostility of Ivan, our conductor, for although
we had now made three trips in number 451, the tall, elderly
man of the white beard and venerable physiognomy remained
surly and aloof. I knew that beneath that forbidding manner he
must have a good character, for the Provodnik, as conductors
are called in Russia, of the Empress's carriage would have been
specially selected. I wandered along to his pantry, where I was
received very ungraciously. The conductor was a Royalist, who
loathed the Bolsheviks and looked down upon anyone who was
not of the Blood Royal. Nor had he a very high opinion of
the new foreign tenants of his beloved 451. I tried to get into
conversation with him, and he answered me in monosyllables.

'No, yes, no. No, I don't drink. I am of the sect of Old Believers. We don't touch alcohol.' I knew that he was wondering all the time what my little game was, but I refused to take a rebuff. Presently he asked me if he could take two pieces of sugar a day from our stores. Sugar was terribly scarce and expensive in those war days and beyond Ivan's means. Gladly I gave my permission. I had penetrated his armour – I had found his weak spot – he had a sweet tooth. Forthwith I returned to my coupé, and took out of my kit a large slab of chocolate which I carried along to the pantry.

I had always found the value of including in my kit a certain amount of good plain chocolate, half a dozen pairs of ladies' silk stockings and two or three boxes of the more expensive kind of Parisian toilet soap. My experience was that, presented at the psychological moment, they would unlock doors which neither wine nor gold would open.

Ivan's eyes gleamed. 'For me?' he said.

'If you will accept it.'

From that moment Ivan was my friend. He was always crotchety, but his manner hid a fiercely loyal heart of gold.

In Moscow the Rumanian authorities looked askance at M. Diamandi's order that the Rumanian treasure was to be handed over to us, and put every difficulty in our way.

'Where's the stuff?' we asked.

'The crown jewels are in the Kremlin vaults, the royal jewels in the state bank vaults, and so is the paper currency.'

'What is the value of the paper currency?'

'One hundred million lei' (£4,000,000 at par), said the nervous official; 'and, anyway, the Bolshevik canaille will never let any of it go.'

'That is our business. You get through to M. Diamandi in Petrograd by telephone, or you will be sorry.'

Off we went to interview Muralov, the Bolshevik commander of Moscow.

Muralov was genuinely delighted to see us and welcomed us very heartily, for had we not alone and unaided averted the threatened famine by opening the Moscow Knot, and were we not even now keeping the transport system of Russia in operation? Not only was he grateful, but he trusted us.

'Well, we have helped you,' said we, 'and now, for a change, with your assistance we are going to help Rumania.' We told him the truth without any beating about the bush. We wanted to remove the Rumanian jewels, the paper money, the Foreign Office archives and some Red Cross stores from Moscow to Jassy. Muralov's reply was the Russian equivalent of, 'Well, I'll be damned!'

A lengthy discussion ensued, and finally Muralov said that the authority did not rest with him, but that he would give us his decision on the morrow. When we called the next day, with a twinkle in his eye he gave us written permission to take everything we asked, with the exception of certain treasures stored in the Kremlin vaults.

I do not think that Muralov had acted on his own. I imagine that he had instructions from the People's Commissars at Petrograd, to make Boyle and myself happy by this concession. Not that they supposed, for one moment, that they would be involved in any loss, or that we would get to the frontier with skins and treasure intact. But if a couple of mad Englishmen were bent on the experiment, it was their own business.

Half a loaf is better than no bread, and we returned to the

Rumanian officials in a state of considerable elation. They simply could not believe their eyes when they read Muralov's permits.

It would of course be impossible to obtain an escort which would be adequate to guard that vast treasure. Between Moscow and Jassy we must pass through a country overrun by civil war, and our journey would probably take us through five or six fighting fronts. A glance at the map will show that actually we passed through seven separate battle areas.

Through these fighting areas a certain number of trains continued to make their way, but without any regularity. Once or twice a week a post train, which stopped at every station and took anything up to ten days to do the journey, would leave Moscow for Odessa or Jassy. On one of these post trains we decided to hitch our saloon and as many trucks as would be necessary. Our one hope of success was to convey that vast treasure as casually and informally as possible.

We explained to the Rumanian officials that the archives would be packed at once in two railway trucks, the Red Cross stores in two other trucks, and that these four wagons would be hitched to our special carriage, in which we would also take the 100,000,000 lei and the jewels.

'How are the jewels packed?' we asked.

'In steel cases.'

'Very well,' we said; 'the steel cases will be brought to the Rumanian Red Cross warehouse which is under your charge, and the contents there be repacked into ordinary wicker baskets.'

'Does untold wealth travel about in wicker baskets?' squeaked the Rumanian.

'It does not!'

'Well?'

'Well! That is why we are going to carry it that way.'

The Rumanian lost his nerve.

'I must get instructions from the government at Jassy.'

'Go ahead,' said I – I did not speak Rumanian, so our conversation was conducted in German. 'But remember, the treasure has been handed to us by the Bolsheviks and we shall do as we like.'

A few hours later he informed us that the Rumanian government had instructed him to hand everything over to us, but that they had suggested we should take with us two Rumanian Treasury officials, who were then in Moscow.

'Very well,' I said; 'but tell them that they won't be comfortable.'

Later this timid official also asked us if we would take back to Rumania eighteen Rumanian soldiers who had been acting as guards to the Rumanian Red Cross depot. As there would be sufficient room for them if huddled close together in one of the wagons containing the Red Cross stores we naturally agreed.

Reluctantly the Rumanians repacked the contents of the steel cases into ordinary wicker baskets.

The trucks containing the Red Cross stores and the Foreign Office archives were coupled to our carriage, which was to be attached to a post train. Everything was ready.

Chapter XVII

The following day I started out with sledges to collect the wicker baskets, and was to arrive back at the station twenty minutes before the train was due to depart, which would just give us time to take the treasure aboard. Boyle and his interpreter, Sandy, a charming Russian officer who spoke perfect English, remained at the station.

It was a golden afternoon, and everything worked smoothly. The sledges were loaded and I was ready to move off. 'Go,' said I to the leading driver, and as I spoke, behold, eighteen Rumanian soldiers with fixed bayonets distributed themselves round the sledges, and two beaming gentlemen, one tall and thin, the other short and fat, emerged from the building and joined us.

'This is ludicrous,' I protested. 'Why have an armed guard? The Soviets are on the eve of war with Rumania. The light green uniform of your soldiers is likely to act on the mob like a red rag to a bull.'

'But monsieur has so kindly promised to take these men on their leave,' blandly remarked the tall man; 'they must naturally march to the station. Go ahead? Come after? *Mais mon, monsieur le capitaine*, it is impossible.'

It was now clear to me that the Rumanian had lied when he asked us to take some soldiers back to Rumania – as they were no longer required. It was nothing of the kind. It was an armed guard for the treasure.

I pictured Boyle's face if, owing to this argument, we arrived late and missed the train; I pictured our march through the mob-infested streets with our fabulous wealth and that guard simply asking for trouble. But there was nothing for it. I shrugged my shoulders, wrote a protest in my Field Book, made the senior Rumanian sign it, and off moved my cavalcade ten minutes behind scheduled time.

That walk stands out as the longest, most slippery and most anxious of my life. Three times we were stopped by Bolshevik patrols:

'Comrades, what carry you there?'

'Stores,' I answered to the challenge, and the reply got us safely to the station.

Boyle, tremendously anxious, was at the entrance. I will never forget his face, nor the strength of the language which he used. It was not a habit of his.

'What the — are you doing with that — guard?'

Explanations were useless. I showed him my Field Book which the Rumanian had signed.

'You did quite right, Podge.' He always called me Podge when he was excited. 'I'll take charge of the baskets. Make those men put their rifles on the sledge and send them back where they came from. The soldiers can travel unarmed.' Then looking at the Treasury officials with dislike, he added: 'And for God's sake get rid of those two fools.'

Politely I told the fat and the thin Rumanian to get into the station. Then we started to transfer the wicker baskets one by one into number 451.

'Mind my carpets,' growled Ivan.

'Your carpets be damned!' said I. 'Get these baskets into the coupés as quickly as possible.'

The jewellery and the paper money completely filled three or four coupés from floor to ceiling, which meant that I had to turn out of mine and sleep in the dining saloon, and this fact did not add to my good humour.

The Rumanian Treasury officials, whom from the moment I first saw them I had named A. and O., proved a tremendous nuisance and wanted to count each basket as it came in, and separate the jewels from the paper money. It must be remembered that we were moving this vast treasure without any guard, since our surest way of doing so safely was by not attracting attention. Finally, in despair I locked A. and O. up, much to their annoyance, in the coupé which we had put at their disposal.

Then when everything was safely aboard an argument commenced outside the carriage.

'Our goods wagons,' said Ivan, appearing from his pantry, 'are being uncoupled.' He spoke with relief, for he disapproved of trucks, especially of these into which the whole leave party had been dumped. 'What would the excellent one' – he always gave me that title – 'like me to do?'

'Send for the station-master.'

Arguing with an official is always a difficult matter, and especially if the official happens to be a Russian station-master. I argued and expostulated on the platform, for naturally I did not want him in our carriage, and the usual crowd collected round us.

'Post trains never carry trucks,' he said in a surly fashion.

'This one does,' said I, and at that moment a new Bolshevik Station Commissar, an unkempt Jewish ruffian, appeared.

'What's all this about?' he demanded. The matter was explained to him. He scratched his head for a moment. 'The wagons are to be attached. Get the train off.'

Amazed at this unexpected decision so quickly made, our interpreter caught my eye and negligently followed the Commissar and the station-master as they walked down the platform. The departure bells rang, the train jerked forward, our journey had begun.

Sandy swung aboard as we cleared the platform.

'We are to be allowed to go fifty miles down the line,' he said. 'The Commissar is telegraphing instructions for the wagons to be detached there. He says: "The fools of bourgeois will be asleep by then."'

We looked meditatively at the roof of the saloon in which we were standing.

'Hill,' said Boyle, 'you and I are going to have a nasty time up there,' and he smiled happily.

Chapter XVIII

Our train crawled along slowly. It was heavy and long, the engine was old and dilapidated and was burning damp wood. We estimated that it would take us about three hours to reach the spot where the wily Commissar proposed to unhitch our wagons.

In the middle of that cold and dark night, when we judged the time to be ripe, Boyle and I stepped out on the running board and then scrambled to the carriage top, and lying flat on our stomachs awaited events.

At last we pulled up at a tiny wayside station, where we were halted for some minutes. Just as the train was starting a ruffianly figure, unshaven, unkempt and filthy, stole along and uncoupled the wagons. We dropped quietly to the ground and crept up one on each side; then in the darkness of the night the Colonel's fist crashed out and the man went down like a log. Hastily we recoupled the trucks and the train moved forward, dragging our four wagons along with it.

Throughout the night we watched lest a further attempt at uncoupling should be made. But whether it was that the people at the station which we had left imagined that the trucks were still standing in the darkness there, or that it was too much trouble to telephone the next station, no other attempt was made to molest us that night.

The train went ambling on through the snow-covered coun-tryside at about ten miles an hour. This speed does not indicate our real rate of progress however, for we sometimes spent hours at small stations waiting for engines, waiting for fuel, waiting for engine-drivers. Whenever we did stop at a station it was the signal for a free fight. The carriages were packed with travellers as tight as they could be and humanity swarmed on the top of every car except our own, from which we ejected all invad-ers, sometimes not without force. This work had to be done by Boyle and myself. The two Rumanians were useless, and we could not call on Sandy to help us as, the murder of Russian officers being a national pastime, we did not dare to let anyone catch sight of him. For ten days Boyle and I never removed our clothes. We took turns for sleeping, but we were both always up at every station or stop.

At Briansk we ran into a battle which was being fought between the troops of the Soviet Republic and those of the Ukrainian Rada.

The Soviet troops were trying to capture Briansk station, which was being defended by the Ukrainians with machine guns, reinforced by a couple of armoured cars. Both sides fired indis-criminately at the train. There were no killed, but about forty people were wounded. For the first time our train moved like an express, and we shot past that station and did not pull up until we had passed it by three or four miles. Two of our windows had been smashed and the side of the car marked by bullets, but thanks to the steel walls we had been comparatively safe.

That night, when I was on duty, I observed a glare in the sky and judged that there was trouble ahead. The country into which we had now passed was in the hands of the Soviets. As we approached nearer to the glare I found that it was caused by a vodka factory which had been accidentally set on fire by looters during a debauch. Our train lurched to a halt, and instantly a swarm of people emerged from the carriages and made for the factory.

It was a weird sight, the blazing factory, the snow-covered fields and the hundreds of people rushing across from our train to get a little vodka for themselves. The crowd burst open the warehouse, and men came staggering out from its doors carrying six or seven bottles of vodka. Many of them could not wait until they got back to the train, but knocked off the head of a bottle and drank as they came. When after an hour we moved forward we had hundreds of drunken men aboard.

The following morning, when we pulled into one of the larger stations, a grey, old wooden ramshackle building, the train was surrounded by a detachment of Bolshevik troops, while a Commissar at the head of a search party and an armed guard began a systematic search of the train. Stepping on to the platform I walked up to the end of the train at which he had begun and noted that he was doing his work very thoroughly, and that he was an aggressive type of bully. I went back to report to the Colonel and we ordered Sandy and A. and O. to go to their bunks and to remain there without talking or even daring to cough. I took the further precaution of locking their coupé doors with my pass-key.

By the time the Commissar, at the head of his party, had arrived at our carriage, I had decided that a good bluff represented our only hope of safety, and I gave the Commissar the best salute I could muster, and gravely shook hands with him.

'You cannot bring your party into our carriage. We are a

Foreign Mission and are not subject to search. By doing so you would violate the exterritoriality convention which exists between our country and the Soviet Republic.' A bit of me inside chuckled, for I knew that our government was most unlikely to recognise the Soviet government for many years to come, and for us to claim exterritoriality in our position was really the height of impudence.

The Commissar hesitated for a moment. Then his jaw set. He felt very strongly that it was his duty to search our carriage.

'My friend,' I said, 'you will be doing a great wrong if you do come in, and our country will never forgive the insult.'

'What is your country?' he asked.

To say that we were English would not help us, for at that time our country was neither popular nor very much respected in Russia, so I replied, 'We are the Canadian Mission.'

'Canadian – Canadian. Is that the American Republic?' asked the simple Commissar.

'Yes, rather!' I replied. 'Now look here, come in and see Colonel Boyle, the head of the Mission. I know that he will be very glad to make your acquaintance, but you must leave your detachment here on the platform and I will send them some Canadian cigarettes.' The Commissar stepped in, while I distributed packets of Gold Flake among the soldiers, who apparently found 'Canadian' cigarettes very much to their taste.

I introduced the Commissar to Boyle, produced brandy, bread, ham, sausage and butter and we had, much to Ivan's anger, an informal meal. I was afraid that Ivan might let his feelings get the better of him, and went along and explained that what we were doing was absolutely necessary. He shook his head and said in a low tone, 'If only the Commissar would touch the Colonel I would be glad, for the Colonel would kill him with a blow, and that would be good, except if the pig bled on my carpets.' The Colonel and I had let Ivan into the secret of what we were carrying, for we knew that was the safest way of securing his help and cooperation; indeed, once he realised that we were carrying royal treasure back to the King and Queen of Rumania he ranked us with peers of the realm at least. Ivan knew the pedigrees of the royal families of Europe backwards – their names, their marriages and their relationships. He knew infinitely more about the royal house of Windsor than I did, and spoke of King George, the Royal Family and their relations as if they were personally known to him.

Our conduct, supplemented by the effects of brandy, food and cigarettes, finally allayed the Commissar's suspicions and he rose to depart and took leave of Boyle with much clicking of heels. But when we had passed into the corridor of the carriage he turned to me and said, 'And you have this beautiful carriage all to yourselves? May I just look in at this coupé?' putting his hand on the door of one which contained the baskets of treasure.

'Of course,' said I. He opened the door.

'What is this?'

'Baskets,' I replied.

'Baskets?' said he, with suspicion in his voice.

'Yes,' I said; 'with decorations.'

'Decorations?' he queried.

'From the President of the American Republic for Russian and Rumanian soldiers.' I made my voice as impressive as possible.

The Commissar positively beamed at me, and naively asked

whether I thought that I could get him an American decoration as he would very much like to have one. I said that I
could not possibly promise, but that I would telegraph to the
President from Kieff. He shook me warmly by the hand. 'Please,
please do.'

At last he was out of our carriage, and a few minutes later
the train moved on.

It had been a very narrow escape. Once the true character of
our cargo was known it was a hundred to one that we should
be held up and robbed of it. Even in a law-abiding country that
treasure would have been a fine prize and an irresistible tempta-
tion for a gang of enterprising thieves.

Early next morning, when we were about 120 miles from
Kieff, our train stopped in the middle of a forest. There was
nothing unusual in this, for it had the habit of stopping at
all sorts of queer places, but when at the end of an hour we
showed no signs of moving I went along to investigate. The
snow around the railway track was five and six feet deep, and it
was no easy task to get through to the engine, where I learned
from the driver that the engine had broken down, but that he
was confident that in two or three hours he would be able to
make the necessary repairs.

I think I should explain here that there was no traffic on the
lines, as communications had almost entirely broken down by
this time. Thus we ran little risk of trains running into us, but
at the same time we could not hope that a train might come
along from Kieff to take messages to the nearest station or assist
us in repairing our damaged engine. We had to do the best we
could ourselves.

I was anxious. The black clouds were threatening snow. I

had no desire to be snowed up. Indeed, it was by the merest chance that two days before we had come through this part of the country a snow plough engine had cleared the tracks for a Bolshevik troop train.

A few hours later I returned to the engine. The repairs were going along famously, and a little later the engine-driver was satisfied that we could go on. But now the stoker had his little difficulty. He had kept steam up as long as he could, but had run completely out of fuel and the steam pressure was rapidly falling in the boilers.

'What can we do?' I asked.

'Nothing,' replied the engine-driver and stoker together.

Somewhere and somehow we must find fuel. Was there anything in the neighbourhood which could be used as such? Boyle and I climbed on to the cab of the engine and surveyed the country around us. About three-quarters of a mile away we saw that there had been a clearing made in the forest, and we told the engine-driver to do his best to get us as far as that. He did his best, but when the train came to a stop again it was still some hundreds of yards short of it. Boyle and I went along and reconnoitred. Luck was with us, for the crust of snow was hard enough to bear our weight, and at the very edge of the forest in the clearing we found that there were some stacks of sawn and split logs. Back we went to the train and called a meeting of passengers, to whom we explained that as the steam-heating could not be kept up they would all be frozen during the night and that somehow or other the timber would have to be fetched. The passengers saw the point at once, and we organised a living chain party which started to pass logs back to the engine tender. Some of the men were almost up to their armpits in the soft snow as they passed logs for all they were worth. I suppose the chain consisted of some four hundred men and it was rather an inspiring sight. Soon the tender was piled high with wooden logs. Snow was used to replenish the water supplies, and sufficient pressure raised in the boilers to enable us to resume our journey to Kieff.

Three hours later, firing told us that we had reached the Ukrainian outpost, we pulled up with a jar. The stoker had been hit, and the engine-driver badly frightened. A Ukrainian detachment in picturesque scarlet caps with magnificent golden tassels came to investigate our train. They had thought we were a Bolshevik military detachment, and were considerably relieved to find that it was just an ordinary passenger train which also contained a Foreign Mission. But when I reprimanded the commander of the detachment for firing at a train without finding out whether it was friend or enemy, he merely shrugged his shoulders and said he was sorry but gave us to understand that he was taking no chances.

When we arrived the following night at Kieff it had taken us just over five days to do the trip from Moscow which ordinarily should have taken twenty-eight hours.

Chapter XIX

Kieff is a picturesque town with hundreds of churches, and was the ancient capital of the Russian Empire. It is situated between the rich metal and coal mining area of the Donetz Basin and the fertile black-earthed region of the Steppes.

The Ukrainians – who used to be known as Little Russians – are wide-headed, tall, long-limbed and broad-shouldered. They are dark-haired, and have dark eyes, bright complexions and straight noses. The women are small, more often than not beautiful, and nearly always vivacious, and I hoped that we would be able to rest for two or three days at Kieff.

All thoughts of this vanished after I had had a talk with the station-master, who said: 'I hear you are carrying a great treasure with you. Why are you doing so without an armed guard?'

I assured him that we were doing nothing of the kind, and at the same time learned that there would be a train leaving for the Bessarabian frontier that night.

I discussed the station-master's words with Boyle, and we decided that it was essential to leave that evening, and gave the necessary instructions to have our carriage and wagons attached to the out-going train.

At the end of November the Rada (parliament) proclaimed Ukrainia to be a Republic and entered into separate peace negotiations with the Central Powers at Brest Litovsk. This

Ukrainian government was composed chiefly of youthful idealists, and it was a simple matter even then to predict that its life
would be of a very short duration.

The streets of Kieff presented a most animated spectacle. The
military tailors of the town must have made a fortune, for all
the officers were in a hurry to exchange their Russian uniforms
for the new Ukrainian ones, though out of economy the old
grey military great-coats were retained. They had also revived
the cockades and fantastically shaped, brightly-coloured head-
dress of the ancient fifteenth- and sixteenth-century national
costume of the Ukrainians. Everywhere were tall men who
looked splendid, wearing red, green and blue velvet or plush
head-gear lavishly decorated with gold and silver braid, and set
off with tassels or other decorations.

I spent some time driving round the town, and then wallowed
for a couple of hours in a hot bath at the Continental Hotel.
While at the hotel I met an old friend who was in the Chevalier
Guard, and who spoke English perfectly. He had distinguished
himself by conspicuous bravery on various occasions in the
early days of the war, and now wished to go to Bessarabia. I
saw the value of having one more reliable man with us in case
of danger, which became more likely as our journey advanced,
and so offered to take him with us. Colonel Boyle approved of
this and Captain Y. arranged to join us.

In the afternoon Boyle went off to interview the railway
authorities at the headquarters of the South-Western Railway,
after which he intended to have a bath before rejoining us. He
went alone, for the people at the railway headquarters and the
hall porter at the Continental Hotel spoke English, and he
would not need an interpreter. Accordingly Sandy remained

with me to guard the train, while A. and O. went to see their Consul.

About seven o'clock our carriage and wagons were attached to the train which was due to leave for Bessarabia at eight o'clock.

At half-past seven the first bell announced the impending departure of the train. There was no sign of Boyle. The minutes went by as I waited there. The second bell clanged out. Ten minutes to go. Still no sign of Boyle. I began to be anxious. What could have happened to the Colonel? It could only be something really serious which would detain him at a time like this. I took a turn down the platform. It was eight o'clock. The third and final bell clanged out and Boyle had not arrived. More than anxious over his absence I asked the station-master to delay the departure of the train for fifteen minutes. It was rather reluctantly that he agreed to do so, for although there were only two or three trains per day leaving Kieff in any direction he was trying to re-establish law, order, and punctuality in the Ukrainian Republic.

The fifteen minutes sped by and still there was no sign of Boyle. I would have had our carriage and wagons disconnected, but as it was very doubtful when another train would be leaving for the Bessarabian frontier, I determined to hang on as long as I possibly could. I engaged the good station-master in conversation, presented him with a cigar, and insisted on him smoking it there and then, but nothing I could do would make him take his eyes off the clock. At half-past eight he arose and said firmly: 'The train is now going,' and I went back disconsolately to see that our carriages were disconnected and to tell Sandy what had happened.

But Sandy had observed something in my absence. 'The Colonel may still arrive at any moment,' said he. 'Tell them that our carriage is going, but there is no safety communication cord attached to our wagon. If the station-master is working strictly to regulations he will have to have the wagon in front of us and our wagon linked to the engine by cord.'

Russian trains were connected to the engine by means of a rope which was looped along the outside of the carriages on keys and hung down almost level with the tops of the carriage windows. The rule was that it should be an unknotted cord leading from the engine to the last carriage.

Sandy's idea was splendid. It meant that it would be necessary to relink the whole train: the cord obviously was not long enough to reach as far as the last two wagons and the rule was that it must not have a knot in it.

The station-master was a stickler for regulations, and when I pointed out the difficulty of the communication cord he gave the order that the train was to be restrung. It took over half an hour in the doing. I knew that the station-master would send the train off the moment the work was finished, and stood by with Sandy and Captain Y. to unhook our carriages from the train.

But it was not necessary. At the very last moment Boyle turned up clutching a very large parcel. He explained that his business had taken him much longer than he expected, but that he should have got back in time had he not been caught in a street raid and knocked nearly senseless by the explosion of a large bomb, the percussion of which had thrown him into a provision shop. The people in the shop had been very kind to him, had brought him round with brandy and insisted on his lying down, and when he tried to get up they had forcibly prevented him from doing so. They could not speak a word of

English, and he could not make them understand that it was important for him to get down to the station. He had to think of some other way. From the temporary couch where he lay he could see a magnificent turkey already cooked. It was only a few days to Christmas. Boyle raised himself on his elbow and by signs intimated his desire to buy the bird. The good Samaritans I suppose took this as a sign of his complete recovery, wrapped up the bird for him and let him go.

After supper, when we were well under way once more, I persuaded Captain Y. to bring out his balalaika. He had a beautiful voice and sang gipsy songs exquisitely. We finished the evening with choruses, and Ivan brought in long glasses of hot tea and lemon, not without a good allowance of rum. It was a perfectly delightful entertainment, and the train for a change was doing the regular ten miles an hour. We passed through the territory of the Ukrainian Republic without hindrance, and even crossed the frontier which led into Soviet territory without being stopped, for the guards on both sides were fast asleep. And so at last we reached Jamerinka some forty miles away from the Bessarabian frontier.

All the troubles we had so far encountered had been fortui- tous. Now that we had reached the last stage of our journey we might expect to encounter organised opposition and a serious attempt to take the treasure from us.

Sandy and Captain Y. had got out a large-scale map and were ticking off the miles and working out the hour at which we should arrive at Jassy, where they planned a reunion lunch at the house of Captain Y's friends.

'Don't you be so sure that we shall ever get to Jassy,' said the Colonel. 'Our real troubles are ahead of us.' And so it proved to be.

At Jamerinka we were not visited by a Commissar, an event so unusual as to fill me with deep suspicion. We were being left alone. To a man who knew Russia that was not a good sign. Our train moved on and reached Vapnyarka. At Vapnyarka a nervous station-master entered our carriage.

'Orders have been given that no train is to leave for Bessarabia, and that your carriages are to be shunted to a siding,' and without more ado he proceeded to carry out the orders in question.

After a short time the passengers came to the conclusion that the Bolsheviks had meant what they said and that there would be no train for Bessarabia, and accordingly took themselves off to the village either to put up there or to hire horses and sledges which would take them on their way.

Meanwhile I went to the station-master's office, where I adopted a high-handed manner and demanded an engine. And at that very moment a Bolshevik general turned up accompanied by his staff.

'You are under arrest,' he said.

'You must be mistaken,' I replied. 'We have a mandate from Joffe,' and produced the document.

He merely glanced at it and returned it with a contemptuous raise of the shoulders.

'We have no desire to examine your carriage or your trucks,' he told me. 'But you will not be allowed to continue your journey. Your Mission is covered by two batteries of guns eight hundred yards away, and if you attempt to move they will open fire.'

'When will we be allowed to go?' I demanded.

'I don't know, perhaps never,' replied the rabid general. 'We know you are stealing something from Russia to give to Rumania.'

'Come and have some tea,' said I, but he refused and repeated that he would carry out his orders if we tried to move.

I went back to our coupé. We decided that for the moment we could do nothing, and that we must play for time. So Captain Y., Sandy, and I passed the time with picquet and drank hot tea.

The minutes seemed to creep by like hours. We were on the verge of something portentous. My mind went to zero hour at Ypres or on the Somme. Captain Y. must have been thinking along the same lines for he said, 'I feel just as I always feel on the eve of battle.' A. and O. as usual were troublesome. They fidgeted nervously and asked inane questions as to what we were going to do.

Then we heard the noise of an engine exhaust. Somewhere in the station yard there was an engine with steam up, and out I went to investigate. It appeared that under the old regime a shunting engine had been kept on duty at this station throughout the twenty-four hours, and as no one had ever countermanded the order, despite the fact that there was really nothing to shunt, there the engine had always remained with steam up. I made friends with the driver and fireman, gave them cigarettes, and took some food along to them from our carriage. They proved friendly, and utterly tired of the conditions under which they were living, and they had many tales to tell of their hardships. Boyle and I decided that some time that night we would commandeer the shunting engine and make an attempt at escape.

Our first step was to send Sandy along to the station-master's office to create a row and to demand further interviews with the authorities. He was also told to find out where the station telephone and telegraph lines were connected on the station. While he was doing this Captain Y. and I went off to reconnoitre the

position of the batteries, and found them with their guns trained
on the station sure enough. Some of the gun crews were standing
by, while the remainder were huddled round a miserable camp-
fire. When we reached the station again we found that a small
detachment of infantry had arrived to watch us, who for their
comfort had commandeered the tiny waiting-room and left just
one sentry outside the door to watch our carriage.

We had supper, which was not a very cheerful meal. Boyle
then conceived the idea of a concert to show that we did not
care, and at the same time to dispel any notion that we were
conspiring to escape.

The concert was a great success and the soldiers, muffled
up in their great sheepskin coats, gathered round our carriage
to listen. I told Ivan to put on our largest samovar, a great
copper tea urn. When it was ready I made a strong brew of tea,
poured it into the largest copper cooking pot which the pantry
possessed, and added sugar and the contents of a whole bottle
of rum and about half a bottle of brandy.

When all was ready I took it out to the soldiers, and in a
friendly manner suggested that they should drink it with our
good wishes in the station room. Gladly, they carried off the
pot, and even the sentry followed them into the waiting-room
to make sure that he had his share.

What a beastly night it was! Clear enough, but a howling
wind swept that ill-lit station. Just a few flickering oil lamps
guttered here and there. Once the soldiers had gone in to have
the drink I had brewed for them there was not a sign of life on
the station.

A piece of semi-detached iron roofing was flapping monoto-
nously in the darkness. Somewhere a dog howled.

Chapter XX

Against that eerie background we were working out our plan of campaign. At midnight we were to turn out all the lights in the carriage, at one o'clock action was to commence. Sandy was to cut the telephone and telegraph wires which we had marked, and then with his revolver to cover the door of the waiting-room in which the guard was gathered. If anyone were to come out and give the alarm he was to shoot and keep the door covered at all costs. For this purpose we gave him two extra automatics and an ample supply of ammunition.

Captain Y. was to stand by the carriage and act as a support to Sandy if anything happened to him.

Boyle and I were to capture the shunting engine, force the crew to back it on to our carriage and compel them to take us over the frontier.

In the meantime Sandy and I went out to collect two or three strands of long rope which Boyle wanted for some purpose of his own.

By one o'clock a gale was raging. The howling wind caught up the snow on the ground and drove particles of frozen ice into our faces and eyes. We waited until Sandy had cut the wires and taken up his post opposite the waiting-room door, then with drawn revolvers Boyle and I boarded the engine from opposite sides simultaneously. The stoker was raking the fire and so had his back to us. The driver was dozing, his head resting between a pressure-gauge and a box. He awoke with a start. The stoker spun round. They found themselves looking into the muzzles of our revolvers. We told them what was required of them. We promised to pay them a substantial sum of money and obtain permission for them to live in Rumania. And at last they agreed to run the engine for us.

The fireman went off to set the points, and Boyle went with him revolver in hand. I remained with the engine-driver and told him that at the slightest sign of treachery I would fill him with lead.

The points were set. Very slowly and silently we ran down the line, but to me it seemed as if we were making a terrible clatter. The howling wind was, however, our ally. The engine-driver backed gently – very gently – on to faithful 451. The coupling took three or four minutes, as the irons and the brake attachments had become frozen, and we had to pour boiling water over them in order to loosen them without making any noise. At last we were hitched on.

A low whistle from Boyle and Sandy ran up.

'All correct, sir.'

'Thank you,' said Boyle. 'Get aboard.'

I remained on the engine. I had been carefully watching the driver during the manoeuvre and knew that if it came to a pinch I would be able to take control. We were off. Would the batteries fire?

Over on the left I could see the glow of the camp-fires round the batteries; but not a shot was fired.

As we cleared the station I saw the waiting-room door open and two or three men come out and run along the platform. It was bitterly cold, but it was excitement and not the frost which caused my teeth to chatter. Boyle had ordered that we should stop when we had covered ten miles, and we pulled up at a spot even more desolate and windswept than the station itself.

'I am not going to take a chance,' said Boyle. 'We must destroy the telegraph wires. That is why I wanted the rope.'

In the wind we found it no easy task to throw the rope over the telegraph wires which were suspended some thirty feet high on their wooden posts. Finally however, by tying weights to the ends of the rope we managed to get three or four strands over, only to find that all our combined efforts could not snap the wires. Then the stoker came to the rescue with the suggestion that we should tie the rope to the engine tender. The wires parted with a clang and we were on our way again.

But we had taken too long, and the people at the station had managed to get a message through. Twenty minutes later we saw ahead of us red lights being frantically waved in the darkness, and as we slowed down we made out that the gates at the level crossing had been closed to bar our way.

'Go through them,' I said to the engine-driver.

'I dare not, sir; it is too risky!'

I gently prodded his ribs with my revolver. 'Go on,' I said.

'Even if you shoot me I won't do it. I am responsible for the lives in the train as well as myself.'

I knew that he was right and I knew that I was right. I turned towards him and brought my knee sharply into the pit of his stomach. He rolled on the floor of the engine in agony.

I grabbed hold of the lever, pushed it forward and opened the throttle to its full. Wind, particles of snow and flying cinders stung my eyes and made them water. Gaining speed with every second we charged straight at the gates, and smashed into them with a crash. There was a horrible jerk, while I wondered whether we were going to keep the line, and then the good old shunting engine carried everything before it in its stride. On through the night we rushed.

Presently the engine-driver recovered.

'You are driving too fast,' he said; 'we are nearing a dangerous curve. Let me take charge,' and my short career as an engine-driver was over.

'We must be near the Rumanian outposts now,' muttered the engine-driver, and almost as the words left his lips there was a terrific grinding, the engine rocked and swayed and after a moment came to a standstill against a mound which the Rumanian outpost had piled over the line as protection. Ahead of us the outpost opened fire. I crouched down in the engine cab until the fire ceased and yelled, 'We are friends,' and explained to a Rumanian officer that we were an Allied Mission.

Our nine days' journey was over. The treasure was safe. On Christmas Eve we arrived at Jassy. From the frontier A. and O. had telegraphed the news to the Treasury that they and the treasure were in our care. As we pulled into the station two hundred and fifty railway gendarmes closed round the small train of four wagons and our special saloon. A detachment of cavalry surrounded the gendarmes in order to safeguard in Rumanian territory the national treasure which without escort had been brought all the way from Moscow through a lawless countryside overrun by civil war. A. and O. were very happy. They felt that at last their priceless charge was being treated with the respect due to it. Boyle looked at me sardonically and smiled.

The Rumanian Minister of Foreign Affairs and the Railway Minister were on the station to welcome us. Half an hour later we were receiving the congratulations and thanks of the Prime Minister, M. Bratiano.

That evening we returned to 451 and made a good supper of the cold turkey Boyle had brought from Kieff. Then at last, after ten days, we were able to undress for bed and to fall immediately into an untroubled sleep.

In recognition of this service HM the King of Rumania conferred on Colonel Boyle the Grand Cross of the Crown of Rumania, and on me the Order of the Star of Rumania. For a subsequent service Boyle received the Grand Cross of the Star of Rumania while I received the Order of the Crown of Rumania. It was not until a year after the conclusion of hostilities that I actually received these decorations, when on a visit to Bucharest I was publicly invested with the Crown. But HM Queen Marie, with a kindness which I immensely appreciated, summoned me to the Kotrechinie Palace and in the course of a personal and informal audience decorated me with the Order of the Star.

Chapter XXI

The situation in Jassy was terrible. A small provincial town had been turned overnight into a capital and had to house not only the court, the government and the thousands of refugees, but also the Rumanian general staff and the administrative branches of the army together with the Foreign Missions and Embassies. The result was chaotic. In 451 we lived in comparative comfort, but we felt it necessary to take our midday meal at the General Staff mess in order to keep in touch with the heads of the various branches.

I cannot describe the misery of these midday meals. Jassy was on starvation diet and the menu never varied. It consisted of soup with shreds of horseflesh and cabbage, followed by boiled, baked or fried maize with one small piece of black bread and was washed down by a pale pink, vinegar-like wine, while coffee made from dried acorns, bitter and beastly, ended this apology for a meal.

In the town people died every day of starvation, and the mortality among children was terrible. Nor were the beasts of the field spared. There was no fodder for the horses, mules and oxen. It was revolting to see their bones almost breaking through their hides. One morning I witnessed a driver trying to get one of two buffaloes yoked to a cart to rise from the ground where it had settled from exhaustion. He pulled and tugged, whipped and kicked at the beast who simply refused to stir. Finally he picked up in the road a small handful of wood shavings and after forcing them under the poor beast's tail, set them on fire; in agony the beast rose. Tears were streaming down the driver's face. The cart crawled along for about forty yards, then the buffalo collapsed again. In desperation the driver unspanned the buffalo and left it in the road to die.

The Russian Army in Rumania was giving trouble. Some of the divisions had gone Bolshevik, and there was an agitation on foot to depose the King and Queen of Rumania.

One corps in particular had been attacked by German agents, and systematically starved by the Bolsheviks in charge of its supply column, with the purpose of making the men revolt and start looting the impoverished countryside. At the request of General Prezan, the Rumanian Chief of Staff, and General Tcharbatcheff, the harassed Russian Commander, Boyle and I went off to inspect the corps and see what could be done. We found it in a really bad way. The tales of starvation had not been exaggerated. But we found an easy means of immediately improving conditions. We had half the horses of the corps shot, and the soldiers and civil population received rations of horse-meat. As it was winter the meat that was not immediately used was frozen and kept as reserve rations. The remainder of the horses now had sufficient fodder until such time as we could get at the root of the sabotage in the supply column. We removed the people responsible by the simple expedient of telling their comrades what they had been doing, and the comrades remembering the dreadful days of starvation were ready to lynch the offenders.

The Rumanian Army was surrounded on three sides and

was expecting daily to be stabbed in the back by Russia. One of the coolest and bravest of men was General Bertelot, the head of the French Military Mission of some four hundred picked French officers. Bertelot planned to meet every situation and was determined to fight the Germans as long as it was possible. His scheme of defence was known as 'the triangle of death', for he was prepared to take on the Germans, Austrians, Hungarians, Bulgarians and Bolsheviks simultaneously, and fight until the supplies and ammunition had given out; this plan had the support of the King and Queen of Rumania and the general staff. It was hard to conquer depression, for everyone knew that it was only a question of time before the enemy would overrun the last corner of Rumanian territory and sweep on into the mining areas of the Donetz Basin, where they could get the supplies of coal and petrol they so badly wanted from the Caucasus. But before they did this Bertelot was determined to stand and make the enemy pay dearly for their victory.

The situation was indeed something more than desperate, and at all costs Russia had to be called off. One evening, the Prime Minister, M. Bratiano, called on us in company with M. Také Jonesco. We had accomplished what seemed impossible in bringing the Rumanian treasure safely from Moscow. Would we now attempt a task even more hopeless of achievement, and try to prevent the Bolsheviks from carrying out their threat of declaring war on Rumania? Také Jonesco expressed the opinion that Rumania was going to pay very dearly for her refusal to take part in the Peace negotiations at Brest Litovsk. The Bolsheviks were determined to wipe out the Rumanian Royal Family and establish a Soviet regime. Hence they were doing everything to pick a quarrel. Both Bratiano and Také Jonesco thought that, though they might deal with German enmity or Bolshevik intrigue if they could take them on separately, they had no chance if they were to be subject to the attack of both at once.

M. Bratiano also explained that Rumanian troops were moving into Bessarabia where they would occupy strategic points along the River Dniester, not with the purpose of occupying the country, but solely to protect the Rumanian war supplies and grain. Like all the other larger governments of Russia, Bessarabia had declared herself an autonomous republic. She was ruled by a council named the Sfatul Tzerie, which was being courted by both Rumania and Soviet Russia each for their own ends. While the Rumanian decision to take up strategic points on the Dniester was quite understandable, we knew that it would probably be the final pretext for the Bolshevik declaration of war. Bratiano as well as ourselves realised this danger, but in the position felt that he had chosen the lesser of two evils.

M. Bratiano asked us to explain Rumania's position to Trotsky and laid stress on the following points:

1. That they could not and would not allow Russian troops to leave their positions on the front, march armed through Rumania and pillage the country as they had been doing. All Russian troops would be allowed to leave Rumania as soon as transport was available for systematic evacuation, but they must leave their arms which would be returned as soon as transport could be arranged.

2. The Rumanian troops would be withdrawn from Bessarabia as soon as Rumanian property and stores had been

transported into Rumania. The Rumanian government had no territorial designs on Bessarabia.

3. The Rumanian government had not arrested any of the Soviet delegates and if any arrests had been made it was at the orders of the Russian Commander-in-Chief, General Tcharbatcheff.

4. They could not in future allow agitation by Bolsheviks in the Rumanian Army without taking steps against the agitators.

Boyle and I had begun to feel that it was time for us to return to Petrograd and accordingly we consented to act as legates for the Rumanian government. We travelled by another route as far as Kieff so as to avoid Vapnyarka, where we felt that we might not have a good reception. Before we left I bought a large oxidised silver Ingersol watch and had it engraved, 'In gratitude from the President of Canada', in case we ran into the Commissar who wanted a decoration. A watch I felt, would do as well. It was a very happy inspiration. We did meet him on our return journey. A rumour had reached him that he had let a great treasure slip through his hands, and he was none too friendly. But the gift of the watch changed his attitude completely.

Petrograd looked a little shabbier, a little more dilapidated, a little more squalid than when we were last there. In the streets there was no semblance of law and order. Fighting between the Red Guards and the anti-Bolsheviks was constant, and executions in the streets were quite common.

At this time the Cheka had only just been established, and an important part of its work consisted in the suppression of looting.

At the outbreak of war the Tsar had decreed that Russia should go dry, and while prohibition was not very strictly observed it had been difficult to get vodka and wine. But now the last vestiges of the restraint imposed by the Tsar and enforced by his myrmidons had gone. The great idea of the rabble was to get alcohol, and alcohol was ready to their hand. In all quarters, in the cellars of hotels, in government warehouses, in private residences, there were stores of the precious liquid, and the undisciplined mob had started raiding such places.

It was a terrible sight. Down would go the doors, and barrels of wine would be rolled into the street and opened on the pavement. Bottles would be carried out by the case, the necks knocked off against a wall and the contents drunk there and then. Within a few minutes would collect a great mob of work-men, soldiers, sailors, cab-drivers and men and women of every class. The gutters would run with wine, and the streets be full of reeling drunkards before the military guard could turn out.

On arrival in Petrograd I found it necessary to make the acquaintance of the famous Jacob Peters, who was head of the Cheka in that city. He was a quiet, sad-faced Lett, who had been a revolutionary all his life. He really hated the work he was doing, but felt that it was necessary. He had lived for many years in exile in London, where his English wife was still living with their daughter. He was extremely fond of them both and very distressed that, owing to the complete breakdown of the postal service, it was impossible to get letters to them, and he asked me as a favour to have a letter carried to his wife by an English courier. He wrote the letter before me and handed it to me in an unsealed envelope and I was glad to be able to transmit it for him.

President Wilson's 'Fourteen Point' speech had just been made. An American secret service agent, Mr Sissons, who worked under the cover of the American Press Bureau, had the speech translated into German and Russian in record time, and I think something like a hundred thousand bills were posted up all over Petrograd. It was a very smart piece of propaganda work, as was the way in which Sissons managed to distribute the 'Fourteen Point' speech to the German Army on the Russian front.

Intellectual Russia had not a very high opinion of the 'Fourteen Points'. I was discussing them one day with a well-informed Russian, who summed up the Russian attitude when he shook his head gravely and said, 'The dear Lord God Himself could only think of ten commandments in His interview with Moses, but Wilson – true, it is five thousand years later – has managed to think of fourteen.'

I do not think anyone realised at the time what a part that 'Fourteen Point' speech of President Wilson was going to play. It was certainly not very popular in England or France, but during the next nine months it had tremendous influence in Germany. For, when she discovered that she was being worn down, she commenced to build her hopes on a peace based on the Fourteen Points. Perhaps it would have been better for the world today if the Fourteen Points had been more closely followed and the Treaty of Versailles never signed.

It did not appear that we had come at the most propitious time for delivering M. Bratiano's message to the Soviet Foreign Office. That very day the Bolsheviks had thrown M. Diamandi, the Rumanian Ambassador, into the fortress of St Peter and Paul. This last effort to precipitate a quarrel between the two countries was a gross violation of the principle of diplomatic immunity and contributed a challenge to every ambassador in

Petrograd, each one of whom realised that unless something was done he might very shortly be sharing the fate of M. Diamandi.

The Diplomatic Corps therefore made a united démarche against the incarceration of Diamandi. At the time Trotsky, Minister of Foreign Affairs, was absent at Brest Litovsk for the negotiations, and so it was Lenin and Zalkind who received the deputation at the Smolny Institute.

Within an hour Boyle and I were at the Foreign Office, whither Zalkind had moved from Smolny.

M. Zalkind was Deputy Foreign Commissar, a most unpleasant hunchback with the viciousness of a rat. He loathed England and despised Rumania, and was as rude to us as he could possibly be. Both Boyle and I had the greatest difficulty in refraining from personal violence, and only kept our tempers by a miracle, but naturally the interview came to nothing.

Late that night M. Diamandi was released and diplomatic relations between the Soviet and Rumania were broken off. M. Diamandi received his passport and promise of safe conduct to the Finnish frontier. He was to leave on the following day. Before going to Rumania I had started a little private bureau of information and during the evening one of my agents told me that orders had been given by the Bolshevik secret service for M. Diamandi to be murdered, and that a similar fate was to befall the two deputies of the Constitutional Assembly and late Ministers of the Kerensky governments, Kokoshken and Shingarev. We hurried round to the Rumanian Embassy at once and warned M. Diamandi not to leave his house unnecessarily and when he did start for the frontier to see that he was properly guarded. I am glad to say that he reached Finland in safety and as far as I know is still alive. But K. and S. met the fate which had been designed for them. They had originally been imprisoned in a damp, filthy cell in the St Peter and Paul fortress whence, having contracted pneumonia, on the strong representations of brother Socialists they were moved to the Marinsky Hospital. But this failed to save them. Within a day or two they were brutally assassinated in their sick beds at the hospital. The official Bolshevik papers declared that this killing was the work of agents provocateurs, but all our evidence was to the contrary.

Though we failed to avert war between Soviet Russia and Rumania we entertained hopes that we might be able to stop hostilities. But to do so we must get at the man who was conducting the operations – Christian Rakovsky, who was far away in South Russia.

To have suggested to the Soviet authorities that Boyle and I should act as mediators between Russia and Rumania would, of course, have been tactless in the highest degree. But there are more ways than one of killing a cat, and fortune smiled on us again. Commissar Nevski implored us to go to South Russia to get train-loads of crude oil and petrol into Petrograd. The machine of State was going to wrack and ruin for lack of all the essentials of modern civilisation. Hundreds of railway wagons were ruined because there had been no crude oil to smear round their axles.

Anywhere in a southerly direction suited our purpose and we joyfully accepted the task. We had made up our minds that we would get to Rakovsky somehow or other. It was no light task which we had set ourselves. For weeks now the King's Messengers had been unable to travel between Petrograd and Jassy, and there was a great accumulation of bags containing mail, parcels etc., for the British Embassy in the temporary Rumanian capital. But we were so confident of our ultimate success that we offered to take these bags and Mr Lindley (now Sir Francis Lindley, Ambassador Extraordinary, and Minister Plenipotentiary at Lisbon) who was then chargé d'affaires at Petrograd, was very glad to hand them over to us.

I think that Ivan must have thought that the bags contained further royal treasure, for he did not once mention his carpets when they were taken aboard 451. A Russian friend of ours, whom I will call the Major, joined us on this trip. Our plan was to go first to Kharkov, and from there work our way down to the Black Sea. All went well until we were about a hundred miles from Kharkov when, just outside Orel, there was a head-on collision between our train and another. I was thrown to the floor out of my bunk, but picked myself up, pulled on a pair of gum boots, and slipping a coat over my pyjamas went out to investigate the damage. As a result of the collision our train had caught fire and was burning furiously, while the wind was carrying the flames along the train. However, we organised parties and manhandled the carriages which had not yet caught fire away from the area of the conflagration.

Poor old 451 was badly damaged, our buffers smashed and the lavatory and pantry telescoped into one. In the morning she was towed back to Orel, where we offered the repair shop a huge sum to mend our car in twenty-four hours. Inspired by this inducement, they worked like Trojans and completed the repairs in record time.

To while away the time the Major took us to friends of his who had a delightful house on an estate not far from the town. Our host and hostess were living with their children in fear of their lives, and everything, with the exception of the house itself, had been confiscated and taken away from them. Food was practically unobtainable; but the house had a cellar marvellously stocked with old wine, champagne and Napoleon brandy, which were used more or less in its place.

The family owed their lives and the possession of their house to an elderly, small, grey-haired English governess who had been with them for many years. She had been born in Finsbury Park, and was the eldest of ten daughters of a doctor who practised in North London. When the revolution broke out she marched down to the local Soviet and bullied them into handing the house and her employers over to her care. She had, I was told, a bitter tongue, knew all the scallywags who were in the Soviet, and whenever she was displeased would go down and lash them for all she was worth. She was adored by the family, and to meet her at table one would imagine that she could not say boo to a goose.

As soon as our car was ready we proceeded to Kharkov, which was in the hands of the Bolsheviks. The commander of the garrison had given himself the title of Admiral and had at his disposal a detachment of sailors who terrorised a town considerably larger than Manchester.

The commander himself, as a young man, had nursed a rancorous hatred for his own father and, one day, when a more bitter quarrel than usual had broken out between them, he had killed the old man with a chopper. There was no capital punishment for passionate crimes in Imperial Russia, and the young man, sentenced to imprisonment for life, had been sent to the island of Sakhalin. He had escaped from there at the outbreak of the revolution, and had been very active in the capture of

Petrograd by the Bolsheviks. There could be no doubt that the man was a homicidal maniac and I had one or two very unpleasant interviews with him. 'Off with his head' was his formula for anyone who displeased him or stood in his way, and the pirates round him were not slow to carry out his instructions.

One day I saw two black-coated sailors empty a crowded station platform by a wave of the hand. The Western world has learned to think of the Cossacks as the terror of Russia, but they never inspired one thousandth part of the fear which, in less than three months, the sailors of the Baltic and the Black Sea managed to instil into the hearts of the people.

There was no hope of doing anything in Kharkov with this maniac at the head of affairs, and so off we went to Kupyansa – a day's journey south – to interview the Bolshevik Commander-in-Chief who was conducting a very skilful campaign against the White troops in Southern Russia. It was this White Army which later, under the command of General Denikin, very nearly swept the Soviet power out of Russia.

Commissar Antonov, though only about thirty-five years old, was a veteran revolutionary who had spent many years in prison for political offences.

For his activities in the 1905 revolution he had been condemned to death, but the sentence had been commuted to twenty years' imprisonment, during which he had been confined on the terrible island of Sakhalin. He was a thin, emaciated figure of a man and wore dark blue spectacles which gave him a most sinister appearance. He was a brilliant strategist, a man of action and had the heart of a lion.

The innate honesty and courage of the man are exemplified by the following. Some weeks before we met him he had been captured when the Whites seized the central telegraph and telephone office during one of the risings in Petrograd. The coup had been badly planned. The building had been seized by cadets – boys of fifteen, sixteen and seventeen years old – who, when they saw that the position was hopeless, took Antonov from the cellar in which they had imprisoned him and promised to release him if he would negotiate a truce and secure them a free pardon.

Antonov gave his word and was greeted with thunderous cheers by the Red Guard when they saw him come out of the building unharmed. For the Red Guard who surrounded the building loved Antonov and thirsted to wipe out the Whites who had captured him. At once he was surrounded by delighted crowds, who crowded round, embracing him and shaking him by the hand. 'Now we will go in and wipe out those White dogs.'

Then Antonov made himself heard above the din. He said that a truce was to be made and the defenders allowed to leave the building unmolested.

For a time it was uncertain which way the fortunes of the day would go. The Red Guards were stubborn. They insisted on the massacre they had promised themselves. 'Very well,' said Antonov, walking back to the building. 'I will fire myself on the Red Guard, and you will have to pass over my dead body before you can get at the defenders.'

We explained to Antonov our mission in the matter of oil and supplies and added that nothing could really be done while a maniac was in charge of Kharkov.

Antonov, who had known the man at Sakhalin and, although he admired him as a fighter, realised that he was quite unfitted for his present position, at once had him transferred to a fighting detachment. On our suggestion Antonov then reinstated many of the old traffic experts and within twelve days the supplies going north to Moscow and Petrograd were increased by 47 per cent.

Meantime the Soviet delegates were not prospering at Brest Litovsk and the German Army had commenced a systematic invasion of fresh Russian territory. This gave us our cue. We pointed out to Antonov that the campaign which had been waged by the Soviet troops against Rumania was only putting Germany in a stronger and stronger position. He agreed with us. He was powerless to do anything himself, but suggested that we should repeat what we had told him to the Supreme Council at Sevastopol, which was conducting the operations against Rumania.

At Sevastopol there had just been a terrible massacre of the officers of the Black Sea fleet by their men. The news had spread throughout Russia, and the Soviets had put the whole of the Crimea under martial law. Nevertheless Antonov gave us a permit to travel there.

Two days later we had left the icy Steppes behind us and entered a southern land basking in the sunshine of spring. However, the German secret service had word of our enterprise and was determined to stop us at all costs. We learned of their activities from the honorary British Consul, who was still in residence at Kherson. They had thrown off all disguise and were openly saying that in a few weeks the Crimea would be occupied by the German Army. To this news they now added further information and in honour of ourselves were circulating more disquieting rumours. They said that seventy-nine British warships had forced the Dardanelles and that a flotilla was even now on its way to Sevastopol with the avowed intention of smashing the Russian fleet and punishing the men who had murdered their officers. The advance guard of this punitive expedition was coming by train in the shape of two British officers, who were to have everything ready in Sevastopol for the arrival of the fleet. The Germans had bought a Sevastopol newspaper and, in the issue of the very morning of our visit, their tale was set out at length.

As we drew into Sevastopol, our eyes lighted on a mob surging round the station, swarming over the platform, crowding the tracks, a mob frenzied with the blood lust and baying for our lives. I thought of Dukhonin and shuddered. It was a crowd precisely similar to that of Mohileff, and this time we were the quarry.

A villainous-looking specimen with a club-foot boarded our carriage, and behind him came two sailors with drawn revolvers. The club-footed man had come with the most belligerent intentions, and as he spoke we could see that he was full of the rumours circulated by the Germans. Then Boyle spoke, and when Boyle spoke men listened.

After two long hours of debate we succeeded in allaying the suspicions of Commissar Spiro, for such was the name of the club-footed man, and at last he was convinced that we were not the advance party of a British squadron. Meanwhile the crowd outside was getting tired of waiting. There came frenzied cries as its fury surged up once more. Spiro admitted that we were in a tight corner, as it was the popular intention to lynch us. However, Spiro was no coward. He went on the platform of our car and harangued the crowd into quiescence.

Finally a deputation of eight men came to our saloon to hear our story. We went through it all again from the beginning, and at the end of another hour we had convinced them.

It was already getting dark when Boyle and I, Spiro and the deputation stepped out of our railway carriage. Boyle made a speech in English which I translated, and at the head of the crowd we marched up to the office of the German-owned newspaper which was incontinently wrecked by the mob.

The next day we learned that after the massacre of the officers, Rakovsky and the Supreme Council had moved from Sevastopol to Odessa.

At Sevastopol this new war against Rumania was far from popular. The sailors wanted to be finished with fighting, and here they were being organised into detachments and sent by sea to Odessa to fight a new foe. At our suggestions they passed resolutions demanding that the war should be stopped and asked us to take their resolutions to the Supreme Council.

Our stay at Sevastopol was very short, but it was certainly full of achievement. Our popularity soared. From being the quarry of human bloodhounds we had suddenly become popular idols. Before we left, the sailors of the Black Sea fleet organised a special reception in our honour. In the morning we were taken over the battlefields of the Crimean War. We went over to the Malakhoff Redoubt; stood on the spot from which the charge of the Light Brigade had been made; and visited the cemetery in which the bodies of British soldiers had been buried after the Crimean War.

The Bolshevik Commander-in-Chief of the Black Sea fleet was an ex-stoker and, at the luncheon which followed, the official hostess was an ex-cook who told me that she had borrowed her mistress's best dress for the occasion. To make herself look particularly beautiful she had put on a pair of black silk mittens which were an heirloom in her mistress's family.

The whole function was naive in its simplicity, but carried out on the part of our hosts with charm and real friendliness. It was hard to believe that these people could be the wild beasts who, only a week before, had brutally murdered hundreds of unarmed men on the sole charge of having been naval officers. But even in the midst of the celebration we could not quite forget it. These were the very men who, only a day or two before, amid the jeers of the crowd, had thrown their officers, tied at the ankles with pieces of anchor chain, from the marble quay into the sea. These were the men who had thought out methods of killing even more ghastly, surpassing the brutalities practised by the pirates of former times. We were glad to leave Sevastopol for Odessa.

Chapter XXII

We found that the Soviet Commander-in-Chief operating against the Rumanians was living in Odessa station. He was a renegade Colonel, by the name of Mouravioff, and our interviews with him were rendered very distasteful when we recognised in him the man who had thrown General Dukhonin's epaulettes to the crowd and had pushed him on the platform before he was murdered. Mouravioff's troops were not actively engaged. They were preventing supplies going into Rumania, with the idea of starving the country into revolution.

When we conveyed to him the resolutions passed by the sailors at Sevastopol, Mouravioff was furious. A meeting of the Supreme Council was called and we were to attend. Dr Christian Rakovsky was the President of the Council. He was a short dark man, with intelligent eyes, and seemed to know most of the languages of the world with the exception of English. He was a Rumanian who had been born in Bulgaria and educated at the Sorbonne in Paris, and he nourished an undying hatred against the country of his origin. From his student days he had been a revolutionary and was a thorn in the flesh of both Rumania and Bulgaria. He seemed to have a personal grudge against the Royal Family and the military caste of Rumania, and was longing for the time when the Soviets would be established in that country.

Apart from Mouravioff and Rakovsky, the remainder of the Council were a shoddy collection of nonentities, one or two of whom could neither read nor write. It was strange to see Rakovsky at the head of such an assembly, and impossible then to visualise that one day, as Soviet Ambassador at the Court of St James's, he would bring off a diplomatic victory against the British Foreign Office. But that is just what he did when he engineered the Anglo-Russian trade agreement, through which fell the first British Labour government in 1924.

To Rakovsky we delivered the message that M. Bratiano had given us for Trotsky. We urged the cessation of hostilities. Rakovsky was adamant, but we gave him no rest, harrying him day after day and pointing out how completely the general situation had changed since the Bolsheviks declared war on Rumania in January. We pressed upon his notice that the Brest Litovsk negotiations had reached a complete deadlock, that the Germans were advancing on Petrograd and pushing into Ukrainia, and that the army which he was using against Rumania would be wanted for use against Germany.

At last Rakovsky agreed to hold a meeting for the discussion of the terms on which the Soviets would be prepared to cease hostilities. To make the occasion more impressive Colonel Boyle and I persuaded the British, French and American Consuls to attend. The conference commenced at ten o'clock in the evening. Boyle and I were already well aware of the general situation. Rumania, as I have shown, had temporarily to retain Bessarabia to safeguard her food supply. Rakovsky on the other hand was determined that she should not, because he had a natural prejudice against yielding any part of Russia, and behind it all he wanted Bessarabia as a base from which the Soviets could pursue their propaganda against Rumania, propaganda which incidentally would have added force in a starving country. Rakovsky's first proposals, we knew, would have no chance of acceptance by the Rumanian government, and all through that night we were urging, pressing, haggling, giving him not a moment's peace. After hours of negotiation we persuaded him to modify all the clauses but one. It was the clause dealing with Bessarabia. Rakovsky wished the Rumanians to evacuate the country immediately, and we on our side urged that they could not be expected to do so until they had been able to evacuate their stores.

Again and again we drafted that clause to suit Rakovsky's wishes as far as possible and yet safeguard the interests of Rumania.

It was not until five o'clock in the morning that he finally agreed to our wording. The document was drafted in duplicate and the signatures of the Supreme Council attached to it. It was then that I discovered that two or three of the members could neither read nor write. Only Rakovsky's signature was now required, and he could not be brought to make up his mind to sign it. He read and re-read the draft document, quarrelled with the wording, suggested alterations, procrastinated. But Boyle and I would not accept any modification. It was now six o'clock. The Consuls and the Supreme Council were all tired out. Everyone was bored. At last Rakovsky gave way, and signed the document which, when counter-signed by the Rumanian government later, constituted the first Peace Treaty made during the Great War.

The credit of getting Rakovsky's signature rests entirely with Colonel Boyle. He had been watching his man for days and knew all his habits. He knew that Rakovsky was a very hard worker, that it was his practice to work all through the night, to retire to bed somewhere about five o'clock in the morning, and to rise again at ten. He made up his mind to wear Rakovsky out and succeeded in doing so. Rakovsky signed out of sheer physical fatigue.

At once we sent by wireless to the Rumanian government the information that Colonel Boyle was bringing the treaty to Jassy and at the same time we arranged for a three days' armistice. It was impossible for 451 to go to Jassy since the railway bridge across the Dniester River had been blown up in the recent hostilities, and Colonel Mouravioff had promised to put a motor-car at Colonel Boyle's disposal on the following morning.

We waited patiently, but the promised car was not forthcoming. At half-past ten I went off to investigate, but all that I could discover was that a car had been ordered from the military garage and had left for the station. There were very few motorcars in South Russia. Perhaps there were not more than a dozen in Odessa, and all of them were in use. At last we discovered what had happened to the car ordered for us. The chauffeur had driven up to the station and left the motor in order to report his arrival. Two of Mouravioff's soldiers, seeing it unoccupied, had stepped into it and driven off to a wedding. The chauffeur had rushed off after them and, forgetting all about reporting to us, had started to search Odessa for his car. Later in the morning he came across it standing outside a house, unoccupied. He promptly jumped into the seat and started the engine. Somebody in the house where the wedding feast was in progress heard the sound and opened fire on him from the window. He returned the fire and killed two of the wedding party, was badly wounded himself but managed to reach the garage.

Another driver had to be found, and finally the car pulled up for Boyle still bearing traces of the conflict.

It was arranged that I was to remain in Odessa and, in the event of the expected German invasion taking place, to carry 451 out of harm's way. Meanwhile Boyle and the Major were to take the treaty to Jassy and return, if possible, within thirty-six hours. But I was fated not to see Boyle again until more than a year had passed, when we met at the Paris Peace Conference. The Rumanian government were unwilling to sign Rakovsky's conditions and it was days before they finally did so. It was the Bessarabian clause to which they objected. Time has shown the justice of Rakovsky's fears of Rumanian designs on Bessarabia. Many years later I met Rakovsky again at a Genoa conference, and the first words he said to me were, 'I still have the Peace Treaty with Rumania in my pocket, but the Rumanians have still got Bessarabia. You persuaded me against my will, and so it is your duty to put the matter right.' Rakovsky's words were uttered in jest, but I have a feeling that one day that Peace Treaty signed in Odessa will play a part in an International Court. Sooner or later Russia will lay a serious claim for the return of Bessarabia and Rumania will find it hard to defend her title.

At last Boyle telegraphed that the Rumanian government had signed and sealed the treaty. He added he would be delayed for some days longer over some pressing work to which he must attend before he returned.

Meantime the German forces had occupied Kieff and begun to move on Odessa. The town was doomed, and the higher officers prepared to flee.

Colonel Mouravioff had an engine with steam up attached to his train and was ready to move at a moment's notice. I demanded an engine for 451 and went to the yard to make my choice. There I found and commandeered a brand-new engine, went along to the coal depot and saw the tender stacked high with coal, and did not leave until it was attached to 451. Naturally I made friends with the engine-driver and the mechanic, gave them a nice sum of money on account and made them part of my staff.

I commandeered a motor-car, too, in case we had to take to the roads, and adding an open truck to my train had a platform made so that I could unload the motor-car anywhere I liked. Every night with great pride I used to inspect my train. The large new engine with its well-stocked coal tender, 451 with its windows intact (few Russian railway carriages had any windows left in them) and its brass beautifully polished, and behind 451 an open platform on which every night the motor-car was loaded and carefully secured.

The pass I had from Mouravioff is an interesting document and the wording of the second paragraph rather quaint, for it reads, 'Captain Hill is allowed to carry on him both cold (meaning steel) and fire-firing arms.'

Then one morning I awoke to find that Mouravioff's siding was empty and his train gone. It meant that the Germans would reach Odessa at any moment. Mouravioff had slunk away without a word to me. Furiously angry, I drove into the town to see Rakovsky. He also was prepared for flight but he had not gone very far. He was on board one of the ships in the harbour. I went down and interviewed him. Yes, the Germans were coming straight to Odessa, and he did not think that I would be able to get away by train.

There was just one chance. The Germans might not yet

have reached the junction from which the branch line ran to Sevastopol, and I climbed on the engine and we made a dash for the junction station. There was no sign of the Germans. Everything at the junction was quiet.

As a matter of fact it had been a false alarm. The Germans did not actually occupy Odessa for another week. But it was a false alarm which prevented me from joining up again with Boyle. He had, meantime, come back to Odessa with a copy of the Peace Treaty with the signature and seal of the Rumanian government, and after interviewing Rakovsky had returned to Rumania.

Before he was able to get to Odessa once more the Germans had come down and occupied the town, and Boyle and I were cut off from each other.

Meanwhile, at a station near Nikolaev, I ran into something which might have proved even more fatal than capture by the Germans. The little station was empty and there did not seem to be a soul about. Presently the station-master appeared and from him I learned that Marucia Nikiforova, who had been terrorising the countryside, was expected at the station at any moment, and everybody had taken to flight.

This Amazon had collected a band of about two hundred cut-throats and had been operating on her own account along the railways. Her custom was to come into a station, seize all the ready money and anything else that took her fancy, confiscate food, shoot anyone who protested and then move on again. Marucia lived with anyone of her band who took her fancy, for she was a lady of catholic tastes and constantly changing her lovers. She had no political views and was just a common marauder.

Suddenly the station-master took to his heels. 'Here she comes,' he said as he disappeared into a hedge.

I raised my eyes and saw an engine with three or four carriages coming down the line. In a moment my train was surrounded by a horde of savages, one of whom, a giant of a man, demanded fiercely who I was and what I was doing there. I replied in terms equally polite, and he went off to report. A few minutes later he returned and said that Marucia wanted to see me. I followed him to the carriage and found the occupant to be a good-looking girl of twenty-three or four, with dark hair, rather sensuous lips and a fine figure. She was dressed as a man in soldier's clothes and top boots and carried a revolver on each hip. Her hands were well kept and she was smoking a cigarette, and altogether looked the most unlikely person to be at the head of two hundred scoundrels.

The giant and two other armed rascals had followed me into the carriage. Marucia looked at them coldly. 'What the devil are you doing here?' she said. 'Get out,' and they slunk away.

Then she offered me a cigarette and we chatted quite informally for a few minutes. Finally she asked me my business. I told her and gave all the news from Odessa. We were getting along famously together.

After a time her eyes fell on my beautiful new engine, and a look of greed came into them. I knew at once that she was going to try and get that engine from me.

'What a beautiful engine you have,' she said.

I shook my head sadly. 'All paint. It doesn't go very well. It is always breaking down and has deceived me cruelly.'

It was a shame to slander that engine, but it had to be done.

It was getting very hot in the coupé and she unbuttoned her

Russian blouse and quite unnecessarily exposed her throat and breast. I suddenly realised that the lady was making overtures to me, and I just got scared all through. I cannot be said to be a woman-hater – far from it – but I knew too much about Marucia to want to have an affair with her.

She put it to me quite bluntly. 'I am tired of all these men and I rather like you. Let's join forces. Two engines are safer than one.'

But I wriggled out. I told her a beautiful story about my passion for one woman and one woman only, and that I was one of those unfortunate men cursed with faithfulness when they loved.

'Besides,' I said, 'I am going to join Antonov. I spoke to him on the telephone from the last station and he expects me tonight.'

That frightened the lady. She had no desire to meet Antonov. She had not known that he was anywhere in the vicinity. For that matter neither did I.

We parted company very reluctantly on her side. I have often wondered what was the end of Marucia.

Chapter XXIII

At Elisavetgrad I overtook Mouravioff. Commissar Spiro also was there with a detachment of sailors. This was the chance I wanted. If I could persuade people like Mouravioff and Spiro to throw their detachments at the advancing Austro-Germans I could not only hold up the advance and make the enemy's entry difficult, but would also be able to aggravate the bad feeling which had grown up between the Bolsheviks and the Central Powers. The more intensively guerrilla warfare could be developed the better for the cause of the Allies. By telephone I got through to Antonov, who promised to put a cavalry division at our disposal, and I began to make plans to start a guerrilla warfare against the German Army.

For a few days I had hopes that we could make the Bolsheviks stand and put up a fight against the invaders. The detachments of Mouravioff's and Antonov's troops were in touch with the enemy and fighting had actually taken place. In one skirmish, it was reported, about thirty Austrians had been killed and the remainder of the detachment had retired. This information only reached me two days after the fighting had taken place. I could get no further details and I was most anxious to identify the regiments which were making the invasion. I explained the importance of this to Antonov and we drove to the spot where the fighting had taken place. There were no wounded, the dead were already buried and the actual Soviet detachment engaged in the skirmish had moved off – no one quite knew where.

The only thing to do was to disinter the buried Austrians. Even then I did not get the required information. The Austrian soldiers had been stripped by the victors, their clothes and boots taken and the naked bodies buried.

Thereupon Antonov gave orders that all identification marks from clothes, tunics, cap badges and papers were to be sent under penalty of death to his headquarters.

But it was too late. In the next few days, on 3 March 1918, the Soviet government had accepted the peace terms dictated by Germany. Antonov was ordered to cease hostilities. Before leaving I persuaded Antonov to damage the coal mine shafts and destroy the stores which we could not move, so as to prevent the Austro-Germans getting them. I must say that the irregular detachments excelled in destruction work, and I would back them against any professional demolition gang.

I had kept in touch with Boyle by wireless, but there seemed no hope of our rejoining each other for the present. Part of his amazing adventures after we separated are told in *Light and Shadow* by Madame Pantazie; part of them appeared in his obituary notices; part of them have never been told. It is not my purpose here, nor would it be possible to write an obituary; but for an epitaph these are the words which I heard a Russian say after one of Boyle's speeches, 'Eh, brat, vot tchelovek!' – 'Eh, brother, there's a man!'

A congress of all the Russian Soviets had been called to ratify the Brest Litovsk Peace Treaty at Moscow and I decided to attend. On arrival I found that the British Aviation Mission had already returned to England via Vladivostock, but fortunately it had left behind, safely hidden, two cars; one, a grey twelve cylinder 'Pathfinder' two-seater, which had been a favourite of mine. To this car I promptly fastened a small silk Union Jack and put it into commission. The Allied Embassies had moved from Petrograd to Vologda; while the Soviet government had left Petrograd, which was menaced by the German Army, and had made Moscow the new capital.

I telegraphed to the War Office in London suggesting that there was still valuable work which I could do, and received orders to remain in Russia with a fairly free hand.

There was little difficulty in getting a permit to attend the Fourth All Russian Soviet Congress; the opening session found me in uniform among some hundreds of delegates. The sole topic of discussion was the Peace Treaty. Its ratification was almost a foregone conclusion. Lenin had won the People's Commissars and the Central Committee of the Bolshevik party over to his way of reasoning.*

The Soviet government could do nothing else, Lenin had so utterly disorganised Russia – her army, her industry, her food supply – that she lay defenceless before Germany.

Rumour had it that the Bolsheviks were bought by the German government, that what had been going on at Brest Litovsk had been merely a comedy, in which each delegate had been allotted a part.

Lenin and Trotsky and the Bolshevik party in general were regarded by the Allied Missions in Russia as traitors and agents of the German government. The press in England, France, Italy and America for the most part took the same view.

It is true that after the 1917 revolution the principal Bolshevik leaders reached Russia in a special train which the Germans had allowed to come through from Switzerland, and cross the Russian front, and it is true that the Bolshevik party received large sums of money from Germany. But it is a mistake to regard Lenin and Trotsky as ordinary agents. They only carried out the orders of Germany when it suited their particular book. They did not regard Imperial Russia as their own Motherland and felt themselves bound by no obligation towards it. They were revolutionaries whose aim was to bring ideal conditions to the proletariat. The Bolsheviks would have been just as ready to take Allied money and Allied help if it had served their purpose.

I was convinced at the time, and nothing which has happened since has gone to alter my opinion, that the Soviet delegates did not act according to instructions from the Central Powers, and that Brest Litovsk was no staged affair.

I have never been a supporter of the Bolsheviks. Their whole doctrine is repellent to my nature. I dislike them for their tyranny, for their ruthlessness, for their hatred of the British Empire. But this dislike did not blind me to their ideals, nor has it blinded me to their influence, both for good and bad, on the rest of the world.

From the moment I arrived in Moscow to attend the meeting for the ratification of the Brest Litovsk Peace, I began to wrestle with Bolshevik institutions, trying to use them as factors against Germany, as Germany was trying to use them as factors against us.

One of the clauses of the Brest Litovsk Peace Treaty stipulated that the Arctic Ocean was to remain mined and blockaded against the Allies. This meant that Germany would have a submarine base in the White Sea from which to menace shipping in the North Sea. The signing of this Peace Treaty meant that Germany could cut down her fighting forces on the eastern front to a mere skeleton formation, and throw the whole of the troops so released on the western front. It meant that Germany could penetrate into the Black Sea and get the coal, oil and petrol of which she was in such desperate need. It meant that the sorely depleted German granary would be replenished from the stores of Ukrainia for, under the separate Ukrainian treaty, Ukrainia was to give a million tons of bread stuffs per annum.

In fact the Brest Litovsk Treaty was a disaster for the Allies. The whole of my subsequent work, when I became a secret service agent and lived disguised as a Russian, was directed at the German secret service and German organisations.

There were other officers – like Sidney Reilly – who employed their energies against the Bolsheviks. They were working from a different angle; sometimes the lines on which our work ran were parallel, sometimes even linked, but it was against German activities that my work and energies were directed.

Lenin's prime object in accepting the German conditions was to preserve the Soviet government and to gain time. His great hope was that the Soviets would be able to spread Bolshevism among the German troops and people.

At the Congress, Lenin made one of the most interesting speeches I have ever heard. His facts were naked; he told the whole bitter truth with no attempt at evasion. He told the delegates that it was not easy to be a revolutionary, and gave his reasons for accepting the German peace conditions in such a simple but such a forcible way that even a child could have understood them. His opponents showered question after question upon him, each one more cunningly phrased than the last. Lenin, calm, brilliant and with almost unnoticed irony forced his opponents from their every position. For each question he had an answer. He finished up his oration with the words: 'We have signed this peace treaty, bitter as it is, and we will keep it.' He looked at his audience squarely. His left eyelid dropped slowly over his eye; it was an unmistakable wink. 'And we will keep it,' he repeated.

I left the hall feeling that all was not yet lost.

I was living in 451 and was really attached to it. But the weather had become warmer and whenever the sun came out a thaw set in. At the platform where we stood there were quite a number of other saloon carriages in which people were living, and owing to the thaw and the sanitary conditions which exist in all railway carriages, the air around them was becoming, to put it mildly, far from sweet. I therefore jumped at an invitation which I received from friends of the owners of the Haritonenko House. They asked me to take up my quarters with them in order to protect their property. For, once I made my permanent residence there, the house would automatically become property under a foreign flag, and have that small immunity which the Bolsheviks extended to the Foreign Missions.

Later Haritonenko House was to become the first Soviet guest house, where distinguished foreign visitors were housed and entertained, watched and spied upon while visiting Moscow. Later still it was rented by the British government as the home of our ambassador at Moscow. It was a beautiful building of palatial design and size and contained many priceless treasures. Two rooms were put at my disposal, one of which I used as a study. I managed to find a Union Jack, and while I lived there it was flown above the house.

Part of the family was still in residence, and I suppose some twelve or fifteen people sat down every night to dinner. My hosts, apart from being millionaires in Russia, had sufficient funds abroad to make them temporarily independent of the acts of nationalisation passed by the Bolsheviks. The meals were cooked by artists, and the cellars were freely drawn on. Many of the hated bourgeois and aristocrats, such as the people with whom I was living, were far more broad in their democratic outlook and understanding than a rabid Bolshevik could ever hope to be, and in some respects they were even more radical and revolutionary than the extremists who wanted to wipe them out. Our hostess was a delightful woman. Night after night at table and long after she would keep the conversation going brilliantly. We teased and chaffed her, we played bridge and poker, we had violent arguments until three and four o'clock in the morning, and she was always the leader in everything that was done. The surprise of the house-party, then, can be imagined when her husband came down on Easter morning and said, 'My wife presented me with a daughter during the night.' Not a single visitor in the house knew or suspected that such a happy event was even remotely possible.

The house was situated on the left bank of the River Moskva and looked right on the Kremlin on the other bank. The Kremlin fortress is surrounded by battlemented walls of pale pink with nineteen towers. Behind this palisade rise the domes of the churches, painted in gold, silver, or blue, the steep roofs of palaces and the squat tops of museums. Sunrise and sunset over the Kremlin is one of the most beautiful sights in the world and in its way equal to the grandeur of sunrise and sunset at the Grand Canyon of Arizona.

From the house one turned right to go into the centre of the town, and over a bridge into the Red Square, one of the largest squares in the world and for centuries the centre of Moscow life. It was the market-place, in the middle of which stands the tribunal, formerly the forum and place of execution. To enter the town one passed under the Ivernian Gates where, in a small chapel, the Ivernian Virgin had her shrine. The Bolsheviks were closing the churches as fast as they could and persecuting all forms of religion, but they failed to prevent the faithful from crossing themselves as they passed this sacred spot.

One morning I returned to the house to find it full of armed men, who announced that they were anarchists and had decided to make it their headquarters. Their leader was a crazy fellow, an ex-actor-manager of note (no crazier of course than some actor-managers in London), by name Mammontov-Dalski, and between us there raged a verbal battle royal for about two hours. He maintained that there was enough room in the house for all of us, and I replied that there was not. He promised that I should not be interfered with; but, during the discussion, some of the anarchists purloined my 'Pathfinder', and my man reported that a pair of my spare links had been stolen. It was a pair I prized very much, as they were left me by a friend who was killed early in the war.

These two incidents put my blood up, and I went off with a complaint to my old friend Commissar Muralov, and finished up by asking him, 'Can't you keep order in Moscow?'

That put him on his mettle. Mammontov-Dalski was summoned to Muralov's office. He came, argued, and refused to move his anarchists. 'Very well,' said Muralov, and called up the garrison Commissar. 'Send a battery of guns, four armoured cars, the second machine-gun brigade and a battalion of Lettish infantry to the Haritonenko House and surround it. If the anarchists who are occupying it at present are not out by 5 p.m. you are to open fire without further orders. I do not mind what damage you do to the house, but not one of the anarchists is to be left alive.'

After a further discussion Mammontov-Dalski decided that he would consult with his confreres. I offered him a lift in my car, which he accepted, and when we reached the house we found that it was already surrounded and the troops in position.

This fact decided the anarchists to move on, and like a swarm of bees they descended on some other unfortunate house. Some days later, however, they openly defied the Soviet authority and after a day's desperate street fighting were liquidated by Muralov. Mammontov-Dalski, however, escaped, but did not survive for long; some weeks later he was knocked down by a street car and killed.

---

* The following is a chronological table of the principal events leading up to the acceptance of the German terms by the Soviet government.

7 November 1917, the Bolsheviks captured Petrograd and established the Soviet government.

22 November 1917, the People's Commissars sued for peace and dismissed General Dukhonin for refusing to transmit a request to the German High Command for an armistice. In Dukhonin's place they appointed Krylenko who made a request for an armistice.

5 December 1917, Ten Days' Truce signed between Russia and the Central Powers (Austria, Bulgaria, Germany and Turkey).

22 December 1917, Soviet delegation headed by Kamenev (Trotsky followed later) went to Brest Litovsk, and the peace negotiations were opened, Germany being represented by Herr Von Kuhlmann and General Hoffmann, Austria by Count Czernin. The Peace Conference did not sit after 26 December, until

5 January 1918, when the sessions were resumed. Little progress was made; the Bolsheviks discovered that the Central Powers intended to impose very stiff terms.

Very cleverly the Central Empires had separated the Ukrainian Rada delegation from the Soviet delegation and thereby weakened the position of the Bolsheviks.

6 February 1918, the Central Empires signed a separate Peace Treaty with the Ukrainian Rada.

10 February 1918, Trotsky made his famous declaration 'No War, No Peace.'

This was Trotsky's statement: 'In the name of the People's Commissars, the government of the Russian federated Soviet Republics hereby informs the governments of the countries which are in a state of war with us, which are allied to us and which are neutral, that Russia while refusing to sign a peace of annexation, proclaims terminated, on her part, the state of war with Germany, Austro-Hungary, Turkey and Bulgaria. Simultaneously an order for the complete demobilisation on all lines on the front is being issued to the Russian troops.'

14 February 1918, members of the German Commission in Petrograd prepared to leave as hostilities were to be resumed.

18 February 1918, Germany declared the armistice ended at noon; immediately afterwards they captured Dvinsk and Reval and moved troops to strategic points on a wide front and against Petrograd.

19 February 1918, Lenin decided to climb down and accept the German peace conditions if Germany still agreed to them.

24 February 1918, Germany presented her new terms which were infinitely more onerous than her previous demands. Trotsky left Brest Litovsk.

3 March 1918, Commissar Chicherin accepted the German conditions and the Peace Treaty was signed.

Chapter XXIV

Soon after the anarchist incident I found it advisable to give up the Haritonenko House. For one thing its owners had decided to try and escape to Italy; for another the work I had begun against the German secret service necessitated my living in a place where it would not be quite so easy for anyone interested to keep account of my comings and goings. Moscow was terribly crowded and it was not easy to find accommodation, but by chance I heard of a suite of rooms which had just been vacated at the Union Hotel and hurried to take them.

Mr Bruce Lockhart, the unofficial British representative to the Soviet government, had taken up his residence in this hotel. He had been Consul-General in Moscow during the war, and no man could have been better fitted for the intricate work of the Mission. He knew every grade of Russian society inside out, spoke the language fluently and always had the courage of his convictions.

The revolution in Russia had brought about a collapse on the eastern front, and the Brest Litovsk Treaty had enabled the Germans to transfer large forces from East to West, thereby rendering the position of the Allies in France more difficult.

There were great stores of war material accumulated at Murmansk and Archangel which would ultimately fall into the hands of the Germans unless protected. The Allies feared that if the Germans got possession of Murmansk and Archangel they would use them as bases for submarines, and the occupation of these ports was obviously essential to the Allies. I think that one of the purposes of Mr Lockhart's Mission was to persuade the Bolsheviks that such an occupation was not to be interpreted as an unfriendly or an aggressive act.

This was no easy matter, as there was a school of thought which held that an Allied contingent landed in North Russia might hope to obtain assistance from all Russian elements dissatisfied with Soviet rule, and thus form not only an anti-German front, but also an anti-Bolshevik front throughout the northern provinces of Russia.

The British government had not made up its mind what attitude to adopt towards the Bolsheviks. By my own department I was instructed to keep in touch with them, bearing in mind that they might come in on the Allied side. I therefore took an early opportunity of calling on M. Trotsky at the War Office. Trotsky knew all about the work I had been doing and received me well.

Lev Davidovich Trotsky, whose real name was Bronsky, was a man of about forty years of age. He was tall, dark and thin. He wore pince-nez, and fidgeted alternately with these and with the little tuft of a beard which sprouted on his chin. He was the son of middle-class Jews, born in South Russia and educated in Odessa. Behind him he already had a long revolutionary record. He was first arrested in 1898 and exiled to Siberia, whence he escaped to England. In 1905 he was prominent behind the street barricades of Moscow and proved himself a good leader of men. Again he was sent to Siberia and again he escaped. He then settled in Switzerland where he became a pamphleteer, journalist, editor, author and war correspondent. During the war he was expelled from France and went to Spain, where he was arrested but allowed to proceed to America. As soon as the revolution broke out in 1917 he attempted to return to Russia but was arrested by the naval authorities in Canada. He was no ordinary man as can be seen from this very brief outline of his career. He was a brilliant orator, and though nervous and very highly strung gave remarkably little thought to the safety of his own person.

After our first talk he appointed me 'Inspector of Aviation', and I was given extensive powers in that department. This brought me into close touch with the aviation personnel, gave me access to all aerodromes, and also linked me up with the Evacuation Committees. I was to give Trotsky advice on the formation of a new air force.

Two or three times a week I would spend half an hour with him discussing matters of aviation. He had marvellous powers of concentration, and the knack of putting his finger on the weak spot of anything and of scenting when information was not being given to him freely.

Apart from myself he had lessons every day from Russian experts on the subject of one military branch or another, and they all found in him the uncanny perception which I have mentioned. For four or five months Trotsky devoted all his time to the arts of war, and became a brilliant leader and founder of the Red Army – a queer fate for a man who had been for years one of the greatest anti-militarists in Europe.

Coming in and out of Trotsky's room I always had a few words with his most trusted secretary, Mlle Eugenia Petrovna Sholopina. For brevity I will refer to Mlle Sholopina as E. P.

E. P. was a very big woman. She must have been two or three inches above six feet in her stockings. At first glance one was apt to dismiss her as a very fine-looking specimen of Russian peasant womanhood, but closer acquaintance revealed in her depths of unguessed qualities. She was methodical and intellectual, a hard worker with an enormous sense of humour. She saw things quickly and could analyse political situations with the speed and precision with which an experienced bridge player analyses a hand of cards. I do not believe she ever turned away from Trotsky anyone who was of the slightest consequence, and yet it was no easy matter to get past that maiden unless one had that something. She was a glutton for work; morning after morning she would be at the office at nine o'clock and not leave it until well past midnight. It was no easy matter to get her to take a meal. One heard rumours of Bolsheviks living on the fat of the land. I dined (I mean ate at midday and midnight) with many of the prominent Bolsheviks, and I can honestly state that during the whole time I never had a really good meal. Their rations were the same as those on which the rest of the population of Moscow existed – poor black bread, cabbage soup, potatoes and tea – lots and lots of hot tea with possibly a lump of sugar. Meals were irregular, eaten while at work or just snatched between conferences.

One of the people with whom I was constantly in touch at this time was Mr Arthur Ransome, the correspondent of the *Daily News* and the *Manchester Guardian*. Ransome the essayist, novelist and successful defendant in the trial brought by Lord Alfred Douglas on his biography of Oscar Wilde, I had heretofore met only in print.

He himself interested me even more than I expected him to

do. He had radical views which he never hesitated to express, and he was not exactly *persona grata* with British officials in Russia. This was partly due to a trick he had of entering into an argument and deliberately exciting the anger of his opponent – I suspect because he found that this was one of the easiest ways of getting at the truth, and Ransome was pre-eminently a journalist out for news. He was extremely well informed, intimate with the Bolsheviks and masterly in summing up a situation. He was a tall, lanky, bony individual with a shock of sandy hair, usually unkempt, and the eyes of a small, inquisitive and rather mischievous boy. He really was a lovable personality when you came to know him.

He lived on the same corridor as I did, but had no bathroom attached to his bedroom and so used to come in early every morning to take my suite. Our profoundest discussions and most heated arguments took place when Ransome was sitting in the bath and I wandering up and down my room dressing. Sometimes, when I had the better of an argument and his feelings were more than usually outraged, he would jump out of the water and beat himself dry like an angry gorilla. After that he would not come for his bath for two or three days, then we would meet and grin at each other, I would ask after the pet snake which lived in a large cigar box in his room, and the following morning he would come in as usual and we would begin arguing again, the best of friends.

Lectures to Trotsky, theatre and supper parties did not interfere with the work I had planned. First of all I helped the Bolshevik military headquarters to organise an Intelligence section for the purpose of identifying German units on the Russian front and for keeping the troop movements under close observation. Within a few weeks we had a complete net of agents working in all the Eastern territories occupied by the Austro-German Army. Identifications came to me every day, and a copy of them was telegraphed to the War Office in London. Time and again I was able to warn London that a German division had left the Russian for the western front.

Secondly, I organised a Bolshevik counter-espionage section to spy on the German secret service and Missions in Petrograd and Moscow. Our interception organisation worked well. We deciphered German codes, opened their letters and read most of their correspondence without even being suspected.

Thirdly, the work that I was doing with Trotsky gave me power with the Evacuation Committee which was constituted for the purpose of saving war material from the threatened areas. The Bolsheviks had given orders that from the towns lying close to the area occupied by Germany military stores were to be systematically evacuated. For they feared that the Germans might find a pretext for making a further move into Russia, and securing the stores which they needed so sorely.

At first the evacuation proceeded without organisation or judgment, and old limbers, wooden office furniture, snow-shovels took precedence over machine guns, ammunition and raw metals. However, once the Evacuation Committee was organised, we moved in three months thousands of tons of steel, aluminium, copper and other materials from under the noses of the Germans. Twenty-two aviation squadrons with machines and all spare parts were sent into the interior of Russia. The gold supply (part of which was afterwards captured at Kazan by the Czechoslovakians) was moved from Moscow to the Volga. In every one of these moves I had a finger. I cleared the Moscow

Aviation Park and personally supervised the evacuation of one hundred and eight brand-new Fiat 200-h.p. aeroplane engines.

All anti-Soviet sections of Russian society considered that the Bolsheviks had sold themselves to Germany, and those that were not pro-German became, merely out of hatred of the Bolsheviks, pro-Ally. For instance, the Social Revolutionary organisation led by Kerensky's former Minister of War, Boris Savinkov, revived the Social Revolutionary and Terrorist centre which he had formed years before to combat Tsardom by assassination, and became a pivot of patriotic and anti-Bolshevik sentiment, eager to cooperate with the Allies and to nullify the effects of the Treaty of Brest Litovsk.

I have already mentioned that I had met Savinkov at Stavka, but it was at this period that I came really to know him. He was a short, dark man, whose penetrating eyes certainly had hypnotic qualities. In the days of the Tsar he had organised the terrorist section and had personally planned and carried through nineteen successful political assassinations. He had never actually done the killing himself, not because he was afraid for his own skin, but because he recognised that he was the brain of the group and therefore should not expose himself unless it was essential. Accordingly he always took up the second position, so that in the event of failure in the first instance he would be ready to hurl the second bomb or fire the fatal shot.

His pen name was Ropshin, and when not organising assassinations he wrote many articles and a number of books of note. His best-known works are *The Pale Horse*, dealing with the assassination of a Governor-General in the Tsar's days, and *The Black Horse*, covering the period after the war when he was fighting the Bolsheviks from Poland. I had a long discussion with him on the subject of assassinations and asked him why it was that the Bolsheviks, who were so hated throughout Russia and were in such a minority, seemed to be safer from the attack of fanatics than the officials of the ancient regime? Savinkov maintained that it had always been easy to get hold of simple people and make them into fanatics. It was easy to instil the idea into their heads that they were carrying out a divine purpose by murdering representatives of the oppressors. But it was another matter to get conscientious revolutionists, however much they might dislike their political opponents, to use the weapon of assassination, for they would have tender memories of the many years during which they had worked with the Bolsheviks. Savinkov himself confessed that on two occasions he felt that it was absolutely necessary for the good of Russia to kill his colleague and leader – the Prime Minister Kerensky. But he could not bring himself to draw his revolver and do the deed, and bitterly had he regretted his weakness since. On the other hand it was very difficult to use the so-called 'White Russians', the officers of the Imperial army, who hated the Bolsheviks. From childhood they had been taught that murder was a sin and a crime; to kill anyone in cold blood was anathema to them. No matter how gallant and brave they were, men who had received decorations equivalent to our VC, men who had calmly captured machine-guns single-handed or brought in comrades under heavy fire at the risk of their lives, could not bring themselves even for the good of their country to become assassins.

I never liked Boris Savinkov. My distrust of him was a matter of frequent contention between myself and Sidney Reilly, who had a blind belief in the man and spent a fortune in helping him to fight Bolshevism.

It is impossible now to know what was going on in Savinkov's mind. After years of waging the bitterest war against the Bolsheviks, in 1924 he went into Russia by arrangement with them and treacherously betrayed his cause. A trial was staged in which Savinkov solemnly recanted. He was condemned to death but the sentence immediately was commuted to a nominal term of imprisonment, during which he enjoyed all the privileges of a free man. He died in mysterious circumstances in 1925.

Savinkov's organisation at the time of which I am writing had its own secret service, part of which was concentrated against the Germans in Russia. I was constantly in touch with this section. To be completely independent of the Allied Missions, the Bolsheviks and the Social Revolutionaries, I organised a secret organisation of my own which was divided into three sections; the first, for the identification of German and Austrian units, acted as a check on the information I obtained from the Bolshevik Military Section and the Social Revolutionaries; the second, a courier service, made me independent of the post and telegraph office. This was necessary because the Bolsheviks were controlling and watching all communications, and because I realised that it was only a matter of time before the Allied Missions and I myself would be completely cut off from Murmansk and Finland unless I had a special organisation ready. The third was a special section of patriotic Russian officers operating within the German lines, arming peasants, derailing troop and supply trains on their way to Germany and generally harrying the Germans by every means in their power; this required arms, money, passes and, most of all, direction, with all of which I supplied them.

Quite naturally it was not very long before the German secret service had a fair inkling of my activities and the first attempt to assassinate me was made at the Moscow Aviation Park.

I was in the habit of driving up alone, practically every day, to see for myself how the evacuation work was going on. I had noticed that at the place where I left my car a man was always loitering and gradually the suspicion dawned on me that he was watching me. I always stopped my car outside a large, long warehouse with doors opening its whole length. Here the Fiat aeroplane engines were stored, and here they were loaded on trucks run in from the far side of the building.

Then one morning my watcher acted. I drove up to the warehouse as usual and leaped up on the platform. At that instant I saw the watcher's arm go up and next moment a bomb had dropped at my feet. By the greatest good fortune it failed to explode, and I took to my heels down the platform with the bomber hard behind me revolver in hand.

I slipped into the shed. Alongside the door there was a large wooden cask packed with millions of match-sticks, and on the top of it was a large brick. I seized the brick and stood up against the door. As my assailant rushed into the door I smashed him full in the face, and he went down to the floor with the whole of his face a crimson mess. Into this mess with all my might I hurled the brick. By his side lay a Mauser-Parabellum revolver. I had long wanted one of these, but as they were only issued by the German Army I had been unable to obtain one. I slipped it off its lanyard, detached its wooden case and then made off to my car.

I did not report the incident to the Bolshevik authorities. It would have only meant endless cross-examinations, inquiries and fuss, and I might have even found myself charged with the murder of my assailant. I never knew whether I had killed him or not, but at the time I sincerely hoped I had.

The whole incident had rather shaken my nerve and I was feeling far from happy. I needed recreation and that evening I took my troubles to the Bat. This was Balieff's famous cellar where the *Chauve Souris* made its bow to the world.

It was a long, narrow room, a converted cellar, at the far end of which was a stage with a number of boxes around. On the floor of the hall were tables and chairs, and meals were supplied to guests throughout the performance.

I have often seen the *Chauve Souris* since, in London, and Paris and New York, but I do not think that the company has ever been as good; or the production so ambitious and artistic as it was in the Moscow cellar. Balieff was not the confrère behind the curtain, as he has since become, but the genial host who was at one moment on the stage, the next mixing with his guests on the floor of the auditorium, and a moment later making an announcement from one of the side boxes. I knew him and all his company and always had a great reception whenever I visited them. It was the custom of Balieff to announce to the hall various visitors whom he thought to be of interest, and he did this in a whimsical and peculiar way of his own. He had no fear of the Bolsheviks and was running an open house, serving food and wine to anyone who could pay for it. The place in those dark, dreary days was always gay, and members of the theatrical profession who visited it were invariably called upon to give an impromptu turn.

That evening I took four great friends of mine to the Bat. When the sun had already risen, and my depression was left behind me, we drove home.

Chapter XXV

When half a dozen secret service organisations are working simultaneously in the same country and some of them happen to be Allies, curious coincidences, overlappings, misunderstandings, intrigues and funny things generally are bound to occur. During the war this was the case in France, America and in neutral countries. This was the case in Russia.

One of the most amusing I recollect was the intrigue over what are known as the Sissons documents. These documents purport to show the close liaison existing between the Bolsheviks and the German High Command. Many of them are natural communications between the German High Command and the Bolsheviks, but some of the more startling – those indeed upon which rested the whole proof of the alleged inspiration of the Bolsheviks by the German General Staff – are undoubtedly forgeries.

They were first bought at a very high figure by one of the Allied secret service organisations. It was felt that such irrefutable proof of Bolshevik knavery would be of the greatest value, and the documents were kept locked behind the stoutest safe door and only shown to the elite.

When Sidney Reilly had just arrived from England he and I examined them and brought a friend of ours into consultation on the question of their genuineness. An expert proved that most of these documents had been written on the same typewriter, which, as they purported to have come from various places many hundreds of miles apart, was distinctly odd.

It was no good holding them, but a great deal of money had been spent on them which bade fair to be lost altogether. Accordingly they were put on the market again and eventually bought by Mr Sissons for the American secret service, at a price which repaid the other secret service organisation in full.

The genuineness or falsity of these documents are still hotly debated questions, used differently by different people to prove the most contradictory contentions. I can say at once and definitely that the more important of them are forgeries, for afterwards, with Reilly's help, I succeeded in running to earth the man who forged them.

I first heard of Sidney Reilly as a cipher: and knew of him only as 'STI', his secret service name. He had been sent out to tackle the new situation which had arisen with the advent of the Bolsheviks. Next I heard of him under one of his assumed names, and finally was introduced to him as Sidney Reilly. He was a dark, well-groomed, very foreign-looking man, who spoke English, Russian, French and German perfectly though, curiously enough, with a foreign accent in each case.

At our first meeting we took a liking to each other. I found that he had an amazing grasp of the actualities of the situation and that he was a man of action. Reilly knew of my activities. We were for all practical purposes in two separate departments, but agreed that whenever possible we would cooperate.

It had become obvious to us, after the Anglo-French troops had been landed on the Murmansk coast, in the spring of 1918, that there was practically no hope of the Allies reaching an understanding with the Bolsheviks. The campaign in the north must not be regarded as an isolated part of the world war, but as a definite part of the Allies' plan for the defeat of the Central Powers. Lenin and Trotsky, however, were convinced that the expeditions of the British to Archangel and of the Japanese to Vladivostock were actually aimed at themselves, with the purpose of driving them out of power. A few days after the landing of the Allies at Murmansk an order was published by the Bolsheviks prohibiting Allied officers from leaving the towns in which they were living, and generally restricting the freedom of their movements and stopping the sending of code telegrams, diplomatic or otherwise. It was then that I put my courier service, already prepared, into action.

Savinkov had determined to raise a counter-revolution at Yaroslav, a town some two hundred and fifty miles north of Moscow, with a special detachment of picked troops, and I was kept informed of all his plans.

By this time I was living a double life. Part of the day I would be in uniform, going about my occupation in the 'Pathfinder' and living as a British officer; the rest of the time I was dressed in mufti visiting my agents on foot. I was looking ahead, too, and beginning to organise secret quarters, which would be very necessary for me once the Bolsheviks attempted to restrict my activities.

Meantime I renewed the activities of my organisation in Ukrainia. The German Army was using the area as a sort of rest camp for their wearied divisions from the western front, a sana-torium where for five or six weeks whole brigades were turned loose on the countryside, properly fed, and well looked after. Then they would be marched back to Germany by easy stages and during the march drilled into efficient fighting troops once more. The more we could harry these men the better.

I had a splendid band of irregular troops composed of ex-Russian officers. We used to organise surprise night raids on German camps, fire volley after volley into the tents or billets and fade away before the Germans could organise a resistance.

The Germans promptly doubled their guards, and made the carrying of arms by any unauthorised person a capital offence. Gun-running forthwith became a most complicated and exciting undertaking. We armed peasants to resist the Germans when they tried to collect grain. The Germans retaliated with severe reprisals till the whole of Ukrainia became a seething cauldron of unrest. General Eichorn was assassinated in the streets of Kieff. Hundreds of patriotic Russians gave their lives as willingly and freely in the fight against Germany as did our men on the western front. On one occasion I led a band of my men into Ukrainia carrying machine guns and ammunition. When delivering our stores I heard that a raid on a German battery position had been organised and I was asked to go with them to see the fun. I was far from eager but policy demanded that I should accept the invitation. About twenty of us, dressed as peasants and taking with us two low wooden peasant carts, left our secret quarters in the forest and proceeded for about eleven miles inland. The peasant carts were covered with hay and beneath the hay were two machine guns. As soon as the raid was over the carts were to be abandoned and the band would return under the shelter of the forest.

It was early morning when we came on the German battery position. There were two or three sentries on duty, but the rest of the camp was still asleep. In two sections, each one carrying a gun, our party approached to within about seventy yards of the Germans. It seemed to me as if our guns would never come into action, but at last one burst out – rat-tat-tat-tat – and then stopped. It had jammed before the second had time to open fire, and I looked upon ourselves as lost. However, number two came into action and number one was cleared. We poured four belts into that camp, sprayed and damaged the guns and then, dragging our own machine guns away, split up into parties of four and took separate routes back to the frontier.

Soon after this raid a second attempt was made by the German secret service on my life.

For the public and uniformed part of my existence I had taken an office quite near the Grand Theatre. One afternoon a Madame Hermann was shown in, and in a very nervous state sat down opposite me at my writing-desk. After much hesitation she told me that she had come to warn me that there were plots against my life, and to beg me to give up the work I was doing and to return to England. I laughed at her fears but asked for the source of her information. This, she said, she could not tell, and if I refused to take her seriously the only thing she could do was to go. So I rose from my table and escorted her to the door. As I sat down to my work again I pondered on what lay behind her visit, and the more I thought of it the less I liked it. Suddenly my attention was drawn to a steady ticking coming from the opposite side of my writing-desk, as if a cheap alarm clock had been left on the floor. I got up, went round to the other side of the table, and peered into the well of the writing-desk. And there I saw a small attaché case from where the ticking was coming, and recollected that Madame Hermann had carried just such a thing with her when she arrived, nor did I remember that she had it when she went. I did not stop to investigate. I was pretty certain that it was some sort of an infernal machine. At the Lubianka I had a friend in the Cheka who was an expert at explosives. I ordered my assistant and my man out of the building and, jumping into the 'Pathfinder', went round to find my friend.

He was delighted to make the investigation. 'If it is a time-bomb,' he said, 'and she only left you twenty minutes ago, we ought to have anyway thirty or forty minutes to spare before it goes up.' I told him that I would rather not trust to such a chance and flatly refused to go back to my office. In marched the brave man himself, opened the case, found there was a time-bomb, disconnected the mechanism, and came out with a broad smile all over his face.

'I think I am entitled to this as a souvenir,' he said, and I was only too glad to give it to him. After that my man inspected all visitors closely before they were allowed to enter my room.

I was finding my work a constant strain on nerves and mind. At the end of each day, when tired and spiritless, I felt that the best I could hope for was imprisonment in the near future, or death in some violent form or other if I was not very careful. But a good night's sleep generally enabled me to take a more rosy view of life on the following morning.

The Bolsheviks had called the fifth All Russian Soviet Congress to assemble at the Grand Theatre of Moscow on 4 July 1918. Important policies had to be ratified by the Congress and it was an occasion for a great parade of the Bolsheviks. The Diplomatic Corps were invited. The boxes on the left of the stage were reserved for the Allied diplomats; those on the right for the diplomats of the Central Powers. The Executive

Committee of the Bolshevik party sat on the stage and speakers spoke in front of their table and came on and off from the wings. The vast auditorium was so packed that not only was there not a single vacant seat, but the gangways and all available standing room was filled. The air was electric. Everyone who entered the auditorium had his pass carefully examined and was thoroughly searched for firearms or bombs. The corridors were patrolled every few yards by Lettish guards armed to the teeth and carrying hand-grenades.

Comrade Sverdlov was chairman. I have never known a man better at the task. A small man with a tremendously deep bass voice, he was able in any meeting to command respect for the chair.

Outwardly the Social Revolutionaries were still working with the Bolsheviks and over half of the delegates in the hall were members of that party. From the very opening it was clear that the meeting was to be a battle royal between the Social Revolutionaries and the Bolsheviks. Small fry from each party made uninteresting speeches, but each representative spoke until the feelings of the opposing side were lashed into a foam of fury. Then Trotsky made a masterful if somewhat technical speech which seemed to have the support of nearly everyone in the house. He was dealing with the achievements of the revolution, the need of a Red Army and the progress which had been made during the last nine months.

Opposite my box was the German Ambassador, Count Mirbach, with whom sat the Austrian, Hungarian, Bulgarian and Turkish ministers. In the other boxes opposite us were their naval and military attachés, secretaries and other officials, among them Rudolph Bauer, head of the German secret service in

Russia. I was sitting in Mr Lockhart's box and he was surrounded by his staff. Above us was the French Ambassador, the American representative, and other representatives of the Allies, and in another box were the ministers of the neutral countries.

When Lenin took the floor a shiver of expectation ran through the packed house. He walked about during the whole time he was speaking, sometimes away from his audience, sometimes forwards, according as he wanted to make his point; sometimes he crossed from one side of the stage to the other – talking all the while – a trick which hypnotised his listeners into following every word he said. He was supremely arrogant in his attitude to his followers, contemptuous of his opponents and baited the representatives of the Allied and Central Powers alike.

One of the queer figures in that very ill-assorted assembly was Captain Sadoul, who, being a well-known socialist, had been sent at the outbreak of the revolution to join the French Military Mission. Sadoul had quarrelled with the head of the Mission, had defied his superior officer, taken off his uniform and was about to join the Bolshevik party. To attend this conference he had dressed with supreme care, and wore a silk hat, frock-coat and white kid gloves. As interpreter he had a Russian princess who was dressed as fashionably as he, and they certainly made a ludicrous sight among the poorly dressed proletarian horde in the auditorium. Sadoul became a thorough Bolshevik and at one time directed Russian troops against the French at Odessa. A year later he was tried, in absence, by a French court martial in Paris and condemned to death. For some years he kept away from Paris and then boldly returned and brought an action to set aside the verdict of the court. Naturally he was arrested, retried and condemned to death, but the sentence was commuted to banishment from Paris. Once again he defied the court and after a nine days' wonder returned to Paris and is living there to this day.

I always felt sorry for Sadoul and think he was tried beyond his strength. Nor can I understand why foreign governments feel that they are obliged to send as their representatives to countries who have gone through a revolution men of advanced views in their own country. The Bolsheviks never made that mistake; they have always sent sound Communists as their representatives abroad.

Spiridonova followed Lenin, and her speech was almost the means of overthrowing the Bolsheviks. Spiridonova was a slender, pale wisp of a little woman and looked utterly uninteresting. Yet she was the heroine of the day, one of the principal leaders of the Social Revolutionaries and a trusted spokeswoman of the Russian peasantry. As a young girl she had shot and killed a particularly brutal Governor-General. The General's bodyguard pounced upon her and for some days she was ill-treated and terribly used by her captors. This was not denied by the old regime, who held a special court of inquiry into the treatment she had received. Horribly battered, she was tried, condemned to death, but because of the way in which she had been treated the sentence was commuted and she was exiled to Siberia for life. There she fought tuberculosis and, at the outbreak of the revolution in 1917, she was still alive and made her way back to Petrograd. Her family put her to bed and thanked a merciful providence for returning their loved one to die at home. But Spiridonova had no intention of dying and within a few weeks was back on the political platform.

She opened her speech with an attack on Trotsky for having Admiral Stchastny shot after a farce of a trial in camera. Spiridonova was bitterly opposed to capital punishment and to trials in camera. Then she attacked the Brest Litovsk Peace Treaty and the terms which had been imposed on Russia by the Germans. She spoke in a low, monotonous tone without gesture or any kind of movement; she stood absolutely motionless and looked rather like a tired school-teacher addressing a class of naughty boys. After a time the toneless voice penetrated into one's very marrow and made it an agony to listen to her. I realised then why it has sometimes been found necessary to cut a woman's throat to stop her noise. Suddenly, towards the end of her speech, she turned to the boxes occupied by the Embassies of Germany and her allies and shook her fist at them, declaring that Russia would 'never submit itself to become a German colony or a State dependent on Germany'. It was an amazing sight; I was wild with joy and had the greatest difficulty in preventing myself cheering with the rest of the house, but to do so would have been a gross breach of etiquette. I must say that Count Mirbach and everyone in the boxes of the Central Empires took it remarkably well, and did not flicker an eyelid.

Spiridonova's speech really terminated the meeting for the day. On the following afternoon, when leaving his house, Count Mirbach was assassinated by a Social Revolutionary, Savinkov started the revolt at Yaroslav and there was an insurrection of the Social Revolutionaries and four days' street fighting in Moscow.

On the morning of that fateful day there was just a short session. The house was as packed as it had been on the previous day. Suddenly there was an ear-splitting explosion, followed immediately by two others. The whole house rose in panic.

Sverdlov crashed his fist with all his might on to the rostrum before him. 'Order please, order please,' boomed out his mighty voice. 'Kindly take your seats. I must have order,' and the panic was completely quenched.

It appeared that one of the Lettish guards, bored at standing in the empty corridor, had been making experiments with one of his hand-grenades. It had gone off. Two other guards, hearing the explosion and seeing pieces of the body of their friend lying about, hurled two other bombs down the corridor on the chance of someone being there.

Following this excitement the session was raised for an hour. I took the opportunity of returning to my hotel, where one of my agents told me of the assassination of Mirbach.

I jumped into a car and drove round to his house to confirm the story. All the blinds were drawn. There was ample evidence outside.

A couple of days later Arthur Ransome and I went round to see Radek, the brilliant Polish journalist. He told us with expansive glee that at last a suitable occupation had been found for Russian generals of the old regime. They would be formed into detachments and trained to shed crocodile tears and follow correctly in the wake of the assassinated ambassadors of Capitalism. Radek was a queer-looking being, with a straggling beard which grew all round the side of his face and under his chin and down his throat – his upper lip and chin were hairless though they did not look as if he ever used a razor. This hair-effect always made me think of him as a sunflower. He had the most extraordinary ideas of dress and at the time was wearing a pair of very smart riding-breeches, leather top-boots three or four sizes too large for him, and an amazing tunic which did not fit anywhere. He was a consummate actor and a very clever mimic, and amused us with representations of the various members of the German Embassy as they would behave when protesting to Lenin about the Mirbach outrage.

I had called on Radek because of an article he had written describing the execution of some Communists by the British authorities in Murmansk. The article was pure propaganda and I ascertained from Murmansk by telegraph that there had been no executions.

Radek made little of my complaint, adding that if he had time he would put the matter right by a disclaimer. He then started speculating about my fate. Obviously the British were going to land at Archangel and he foresaw a debate in the near future as to whether I should be held as a hostage and at some time or other exchanged for a worthy Communist, or clapped into prison as a dangerous enemy, or executed to show Bolshevik contempt for officers of a capitalistic power. The joke was far too near probability for me to enter into a discussion with any feeling of enjoyment.

Chapter XXVI

The Allies had originally planned to occupy Archangel and the surrounding country in the middle of July, but later had postponed the move until 2 August 1918. Savinkov felt very bitter over this postponement, for somehow or other he had learned their original intentions and had timed the revolt at Yaroslav to coincide with the coming of the Allies, with whom he then expected to join forces.

Savinkov's force put up a gallant stand against overwhelming odds and held out sixteen days before they finally capitulated, though not before Savinkov had time to escape. I felt very certain that as soon as the Allies landed at Archangel the Bolsheviks would try to intern me, as I was not a member of Mr Lockhart's diplomatic Mission, and I prepared for this eventuality. It was decided that Sidney Reilly and I should remain in Moscow after the Allied Mission's departure. He was to carry on his work against the Bolsheviks, and I was to continue my activities in Ukrainia against the German Army and also keep my courier service going. I felt quite cheerful. Provided that the Allies landed in sufficient numbers at Archangel I could give them any amount of help and possibly even the chaotic situation which had been created by the Bolsheviks could be cleared.

I had of course forgotten that it had never been the policy of the Allies to land a sufficient force. I was thinking that with twenty to thirty thousand men we should have a fair chance of carrying out what we wanted to do. I leave it to the reader's imagination what I felt when I heard that we were proposing to land for a start a force of just over a thousand men. I wanted the landing postponed until it could be effected with a sufficient force.

My sole means of communication with the Allied commander in Northern Russia was my courier chain through which it took twelve to fifteen days to get a message. My only hope of holding up the landing at Archangel was to see the General Officer in Command personally, and to reach him in time it would be necessary to go up by special train. The only person who could authorise a special was Trotsky, and I therefore decided to try to persuade him to give me the special. I explained that the business calling me to Murmansk was urgent and assumed that he would grant my request. Far from doing so he immediately suspected me of trying to escape. I undertook to give my parole to return to Moscow, and he laughed at me. I spoke of the many permits he had given me from time to time to do work for our common interest, and observed that I had never abused Soviet confidence. He looked at the passes which I held out to him, and said, 'That is all over now,' and tore them in half.

I said, 'Thank you!' turned my back on him and left the room in a fury, slamming the door hard behind me. I had no sooner returned to my room at the Union Hotel than the telephone rang, and the voice of one of my agents in the Cheka came over the wire with the Intelligence that an order had been given by the Minister of War for me to be arrested immediately and that a warrant was even then being issued.

I put down the receiver and with regret looked round my room and possessions. There were my kit and sword, my photographs and favourite books, one or two prized decorations, various small things I had bought to take back to England and souvenirs which I had picked up. The Mauser revolver so recently acquired and my own Webley-Scott – all these things had to be left behind, shed so as not to encumber me in my new life as a spy.

I had already decided that I would not risk carrying a revolver, for nine times out of ten a revolver is of no earthly use and will seldom get a man out of a tight corner. On the other hand, however small it may be, it is a bulky thing and is easily found when one's person is searched; it was illegal to carry firearms. I had decided to take, just for my own comfort, my swordstick, though I knew that under the circumstances in which I should live I would never use it.

Then I had a momentary but first-class attack of nerves; in half an hour I should be a spy outside the law with no redress if caught, just a summary trial and then up against a wall. What a fool I was … bound to be caught. Why take off my uniform? It was a crazy thing to do. What good could I do, anyway? 'Steady,' I said to myself, 'you are bound to feel like this. It is just like going over the top, quite natural. Come on, get a move on or you will never go.'

I did not risk taking the lift. The Cheka sometimes acted very quickly. Instead I ran down the staff stairs and out into a yard. A few doors away from the hotel there was a very large apartment house with three or four entrances and many small flats. For the last two months one of these flats had been mine. Nominally an elderly Russian woman lived there and kept it tidy for me. She was a dear, deaf old lady who had lost both her sons early in the war. She knew that I was doing some political work, but never asked any questions. I went to my room, changed into a suit of mufti which I had worn when going through Scandinavia, gave my kindly friend six months' rent and a sum in addition which would enable her to live for some time, and told her that she would not see me again.

I went out by a different entrance from the one I had used in entering, casually glanced round to see that I was not being followed, stepped into a cab and drove to the other end of Moscow. Here I scrambled on to a tram which was already packed to suffocation point and travelled by a roundabout way to yet another part of the town where I rented a small flat.

It was a flat which had been selected by the chief of my courier service. He was a Russian cavalry officer who had served with great distinction in the early days of the war, a patriot, fearless, a first-class judge of men and as good an organiser as I could have wished for. It was essential to have a place where the couriers could come on return from their various missions, where they would rest for two or three nights in safety and where he could visit them daily. One of his acquaintances was a lady, the wife of one of his brother officers who had been killed early in the war. For reasons best known to herself she had taken to the oldest profession in the world, and had been making quite a fair living on the Tverskaya Ulitza, the Bond Street of Moscow. But she was a patriot, and she gladly undertook to put two rooms of her four-roomed flat exclusively at my friend's disposal, for which naturally he paid her a good rent. The value of such a flat was enormous. Even under the old regime she had been registered by the local police. Later she had duly registered her calling at the district commissariat, and the House Committee knew all about her. What was more natural than that unknown men should constantly be coming and going in and out of her flat? She was absolutely reliable and our weary couriers could rest in safety in one of our rooms there.

With a beating heart I rang the bell. A rather good-looking woman in a kimono answered the door. 'I am Mr Holtzmann,' I said. This was the name I had arranged to assume when using her flat. 'Ah, yes;' she admitted me and pointed to a door at the end of the corridor, and without more ado returned to her own room. I went into the room she had indicated, a small chamber with a bed and a telephone. First of all I called up the chief of my couriers. 'I am here,' I said; 'come round at once.' Then I telephoned Reilly, warned him that in all probability a warrant for his arrest would also be shortly issued and advised him to make tracks for his secret lodgings.

Then I put my hand under the bed by the pillow, and drew out a small trunk. In it was a complete change of clothes made to fit me. There were three or four dark blue Russian shirts which buttoned at the neck, some linen underclothing, a pair of cheap ready-made black trousers, peasant-made socks such as were on sale on the stalls in the market, a second-hand pair of top-boots and a peak cap which had already been well used.

I dressed myself hastily. I put my English suit, underclothing, tie, socks and boots into the stove; I laid a match to the kindling wood and shut the stove door. Ten minutes later my London clothes were burned. Presently Z., the chief of my couriers, arrived. He brought with him my new passport made out in the name of George Bergmann, the description on which tallied with my appearance. We had prepared and forged this passport some weeks before and tried it out by sending a volunteer with it from Moscow to Petrograd and back again. Thus recent seals and visas from the Cheka gave it an appearance of authority. It had taken me long to decide on my new name. I hated giving up the name of Hill, and finally decided to get as near to it as I could in German. That is why I chose Berg, the equivalent for Hill, and tacked on the 'mann' to make it quite certain that I was of German descent. For, while my Russian was almost word-perfect, I did from time to time make mistakes, and it was much better for me to claim that I was a Russian of German extraction born in the Baltic provinces. It would be almost impossible for the Bolsheviks to verify such details even if they wanted to, for the Baltic provinces were then occupied by the German Army.

Z. had brought a cheap mackintosh, a hundred Russian cigarettes, and the latest reports from various of our agents, which I put into the bag, and then I left the flat as George Bergmann, looking very different already from the Mr Holtzmann that had entered less than an hour before.

Z. and I had agreed that it would be better and safer that he should not know my future headquarters, but we arranged two other meeting places in case our present rendezvous was raided.

Altogether I had eight secret flats or rooms in Moscow for the use of myself and my organisation, as well as a small wooden country residence forty miles away, which was to be a final retreat and refuge if Moscow grew too hot for me or any of my agents. Each one of the places had to be kept going and had to have a completely plausible and natural *raison d'être* for its existence.

Feeling rather awkward in my new clothes, but much happier within, I decided to walk to the house where my new headquarters were fixed. This house was in the Zamoskaretchye district, situated on the south bank of the Moskva River, in the poorer quarter of the town.

Weeks before, when I had first realised that I might have to go underground, I had discussed the matter with my very competent and devoted secretary, Evelyn, who was *au courant* with all the work I had been doing. Evelyn was partly English, but had been educated in Russia, and besides English and Russian she knew German, French and Italian perfectly. She was a brilliant musician and could turn her hand to anything which required skill.

We had decided that our best chance of success was to become people of the lower middle class and to live an entirely double life. She had immediately obtained a situation as a school-teacher in one of the mushroom schools which had been founded by the Bolsheviks. This gave her the necessary papers and also the very coveted ration cards from the Bolshevik organisation; coveted because, without cards or enormous sums of money, it was impossible to get food.

Then, as a spinster teacher, she had rented a small four-roomed house, which she had furnished with the barest necessities, picking up sticks of furniture in the various markets of Moscow in the guise of a poor young woman. Everyone was selling furniture in order to be able to buy food.

It was essential that the people about us should be entirely trustworthy. Evelyn and I discussed the matter and decided to ask two friends of ours, girls of English birth but Russian upbringing, to join our organisation. Sally and Annie both jumped at the chance. They had brothers, one in the machine-gun corps and the other in the tanks, fighting on the western front. Both had been wounded, but were back in France and the sisters were aching to do something. Sally was one of the most beautiful girls I have ever seen. She had raven-black hair, a peach-like complexion and the most sensitive, pale, transparent hands. Annie, her sister, was not so good-looking, but was a plump, merry, good-natured soul.

We had decided that Sally should become cook to this establishment of ours, and do all the housework, cooking and buying what was necessary. Annie was to start a dressmaking business. She was clever with her needle and could knock up blouses and re-make costumes. At a dressmaking establishment it was only natural that there would be people coming and going. We wanted another ally to run messages for me and deliver the parcels to Annie's customers. After a great deal of thought between us we decided to enrol a young Russian girl we knew, an orphan who had just reached the mature age of seventeen. Vi was a tall blonde with blue eyes, and the most appealing ways, and time proved that she was also full of pluck.

The girls had taken up their residence about a month earlier; Evelyn went to her school every morning at 8.30 and returned at four. Annie was working up quite a good little business. Vi ran the errands, and Sally stood in food queues waiting her turn, scrubbed the floors of the house and did the cooking. They all had forged Russian passports, and never spoke anything but Russian. They told me that they had to arrange to fine themselves when they first started, for they were constantly breaking into English. Whenever they broke the rule they would go without sugar for twenty-four hours.

I was to take up my residence in this house as a lodger.

I had never been inside the house, but knew exactly where it was, had passed it many times, and knew all about it. It was a low, single-storied, white-walled building, in a block containing many other houses just like it. It had two great advantages, a front door opened on the street, and a back door led out into a large yard shared by the other houses around it, through which there was a separate entrance into the road. The wall at the end of the yard was low and, if necessary, one could easily slip over it.

I had decided to go in through the back entrance. As I reached the house and turned into the yard the light was already fading. Just before I reached the back door it was opened, a woman took three steps into the yard and then pitched a bucket of dirty water into a grated drain. I gasped. It was Sally, the beautiful Sally transformed into a barefooted slut who wore a begrimed white blouse and some sort of a skirt. Her hair straggled in a plait down her back, and her hands – her beautiful transparent hands – were red and swollen and the nails caked with dirt.

'Good evening,' I said in Russian. 'I am the lodger Bergmann, may I come in?'

'Yes,' she said, blowing her nose in the way noses were blown before handkerchiefs were invented, and added, 'I have a bad cold.'

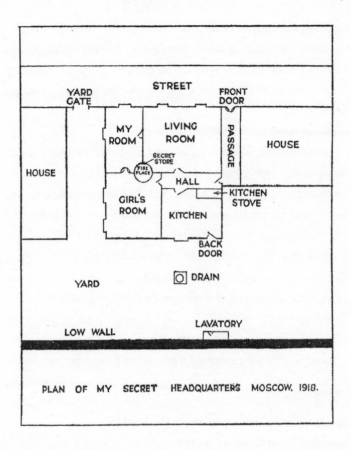

PLAN OF MY SECRET HEADQUARTERS MOSCOW, 1918.

I entered a tiny dark kitchen in which was a long typical Russian cooking-stove. The kitchen led into a tiny windowless hall with four doors, the front door being on the right-hand side. Another door led into the living-room, which had two double windows looking out on the street, and communicated with a long, narrow, one-windowed chamber in which I was to live. A communicating door led from my room into the girls' room, which was also the dressmaking establishment. From this room, too, a door led into the tiny hall.

Evelyn jumped up as I entered. 'Girls,' she called softly; 'he has come!' Annie and Vi bounded in, Sally slammed the back door and rushed into the living-room. We all looked at one another and grinned, feeling excited, unnatural and rather foolish.

I explained to them what had happened, and then they were eager to show me the rooms. These were quickly inspected, and I chuckled when I found that Sally – to keep absolutely true to character – slept as women of her class did in Russia, on the cooking-stove in the kitchen. As soon as the fire was damped down, a mattress would be thrown over the top of the stove and with a pillow and blanket Sally's bed was complete. She slept in her clothes and had got quite friendly with other cooks in the yard. My heart rather sank when I discovered that there was no bathroom and that the sanitation was outside and of the most primitive kind. Little things like that are overlooked when one is planning big adventures, but oh, the misery of having to live under those conditions!

Evelyn had very cleverly smuggled a typewriter into the house in a clothes basket, together with the secret service codes. Two short floor-boards had been taken up along the inner wall of the living-room, and there the typewriter and codes were housed. In my room they had worked loose some tiles from the heating-stove, put our reserve of money in the cavity and replaced the tiles with putty.

'Tomorrow,' said Evelyn, 'I will give your passport to the *dvornik* and tell him that you are suffering from malaria and will not be out for some days.'

Dvorniks, or yard porters, combine the functions of the French concierge, the American choreman, the English hall-porter, and act as a sort of subordinate police official. No one is allowed to stay in a house without the *dvornik* being informed and given the passport of the visitor or, as in my case, the lodger, which he takes to the local commissariat for registration. The Bolsheviks had complicated the existence of people like myself by forming House Committees which, under the guidance of the Cheka, pried into the doings and sayings of the people living in every block. The House Committees also issued the ration cards.

I partook of some food, not having eaten since a very hurried early morning breakfast, and then I analysed the reports which Z. had given me and wrote out dispatches to the War Office in London, a copy of which would also be sent to the British force at Murmansk.

Evelyn and I did the coding. The code had been invented by a genius at the secret service headquarters in London, and of the many I have seen was the easiest and safest for a secret service man to carry. It consisted of a pocket dictionary and a cipher which was on a tiny card and could be easily hidden. As soon as a message was coded the figures were typed out in duplicate. Evelyn had thought of everything. Common but heavy curtains over the windows and doors dulled the click of the typewriter. When coding messages we always observed the same ritual. The metal cover of the typewriter was turned upside down, with a large bottle of petrol at its side and the codes to hand. If the house was suddenly raided messages and codes were to be pitched into the typewriter cover, the petrol poured over them and set alight.

Our story to the *dvornik* about my malaria was framed with the purpose of giving me time to grow a beard. I was very well known in Moscow. For the last six months I had been driving in a conspicuous car, dressed in a conspicuous uniform, and although I knew that my clothes made a big difference, any one of the people I had been meeting constantly would have no difficulty in recognising me.

On the following morning, therefore, and for the first time since I started shaving, I did not use a razor. The next five days were a nightmare of torment. I could not go anywhere but was confined to the tiny house, a circumstance which almost drove me mad after the active life I had been leading. All news came to me second-hand, messages from my destruction gangs and from Z. being brought to me by Vi. I had sent my chauffeur a letter telling him that I had gone back to England, enclosing him six months' salary and asking him to hand over the 'Pathfinder' to the British Consul. And then all I could do was to sit and wait patiently for my beard to grow. The growing of a beard in itself was a torment. First of all, the beastly thing was of a brilliant red colour. Now, my hair is a darkish brown, and has no red in it, and I took an instant aversion to this red growth. Then as the hairs sprouted they turned round and bit my face and covered my skin with a sore and irritable rash. I felt dirty and miserable.

What with inaction and beard-growing I became surly and bad-tempered and nearly drove poor Evelyn to distraction. I felt ashamed of myself, for the girls had all taken up their various parts without uttering a grumble. On the fifth evening that blessed woman Evelyn returned with a large box of Havana cigars – they were Bock's Rara-Avis – and a bottle of old brandy. Never in my life have I smoked such perfect cigars or drunk such excellent brandy. At the end of a week I decided that if I kept to our part of the town it would be safe for me to venture into the streets. Luckily, quite close to our house was the Tretyakov Picture Gallery, and for hours I studied Vereshtchagin's wonderful war pictures and gloried in the portraits of Ryepin. He has a large picture depicting Cossacks of the sixteenth century preparing a defiant letter to the Sultan of Turkey. This somehow or other brought me no end of comfort. A few days later I sent Vi to one of Reilly's girls, suggesting that he and I should meet and appointing a seat in one of the parks for our rendezvous. I shall never forget my first glimpse of him. He too had grown a beard, and he did look an ugly devil. I told him so and he returned the compliment. By this time we were both completely used to our Russian clothes, and walked up and down the garden very much at our ease. He gave me some messages which he wanted sent by my couriers to Sweden for London, and as we both intended to reappear freely in the streets we arranged to meet every day in one of the cafés of the town.

I went to a barber that afternoon and had my beard trimmed and part of my face shaved. This changed my appearance much more than the actual straggling beard I had worn before. I looked utterly foreign and even did not recognise myself when I looked in the glass. My face with a goatee beard was striking.

The next day I obtained a post at a cinematograph studio as a developer of films, and within a day or so my hands were coloured a deep yellow from the developing solutions. This work at the studio entitled me to the ration cards of a worker, and moreover I joined the local Cinematograph Operators' Union. The hours suited me very well, for I came on at six o'clock in the evening and finished at eleven o'clock at night. For the rest of the day I was completely free to carry on my work.

At the end of three weeks I moved about freely all over Moscow. I used to meet people in the streets who knew me very well and not one of them recognised me. Once I collided with two members of Mr Lockhart's Mission who passed me by without a word.

But I made mistakes – mistakes which could easily have cost me my life. One day Evelyn happened to be looking out of the window when I left the house and what she saw made her chase after me. 'For goodness' sake don't walk like a British officer. You are striding along as if you were on parade. Your walk gives you away completely. No Russian of your class has ever walked like that.' I was humbled and altered my walk.

On another occasion I met in the street a lady whom I very much liked, smiled and raised my hat – in Russia it is correct for the man to make the first greeting. The moment I took my hat off I knew I had given myself away, but luckily she did not recognise me and favoured me with a haughty stare.

Perhaps the worst mistake I made was after I had been living as a Russian for two months. Things were very bad both politically and economically in Moscow. We did not have sufficient food for our needs at the house and I had been worrying a great deal about my work. Walking down the main street I passed Eliseaves, the Fortnum and Mason of Moscow. The glass windows, which used to be filled with delicacies to make your mouth water, were now empty. Just a few boxes of biscuits, some smoked fish, and some stale-looking chocolate was displayed; but my eye was caught by a notice: 'We have fresh caviare and butter today.'

'The very thing,' said my tired brain, and I marched into the shop.

'Yes,' said the attendant, 'we have caviare,' and named a price, equivalent to seven pounds per pound.

'Well, I will have two pounds please, and three pounds of butter, and a box of biscuits, and if you have any brandy I will have two bottles.'

The order was given by a shabby-looking individual who had forgotten his part. I was behaving like a customer who was in the habit of giving such an order. The attendant gave me a searching look which brought me back to realities, and with a sick feeling, I, who should not have had a penny in the world, paid for my purchase and walked out of the shop carrying a large parcel. I was terrified lest I had given myself away, lest the attendant should tell somebody, lest I should be followed. With every step I took the parcel grew heavier and heavier but I stuck to it doggedly, boarded a tram and by a circuitous route made my way home.

I must confess that all this time I was constantly haunted by the fear of being caught, and always before my mind I had a vivid picture of the spies I had seen executed in Macedonia. I maintain that however stout-hearted a spy may be, if he has any imagination at all, the idea of capital retribution does get on his nerves, and at times affects his work. That is why in time of war I would always urge death as the penalty for espionage.

Evelyn scolded me for my folly in buying the caviare, but that night all of us thoroughly enjoyed our supper which Sally, true to her role, ate by herself in the kitchen.

One day we read in the papers that two of our couriers had been caught on their way to Murmansk and executed by the local Soviet. Two days later X. reported that another of our men, making his way to Archangel, had been captured but had managed to escape. At a wayside station he had been searched and the coded messages typed on paper and sewn into the lining of his coat had rustled when the examiner's hand had been passed down his body. From then on we typed all coded messages on strips of linen. It was tedious work and took infinitely longer than typing on paper. At the same time Annie put out a notice that men's clothes could be pressed. This enabled us to take in the coats of our couriers, unstitch the collars or the shoulders and sew in the strips of linen. Some of the couriers told me that they preferred not to know where the messages were sewn for when they passed through the control stations they did not feel their hearts jump into their throats as they did when they knew the exact place where the message was.

After the Allies had landed in Archangel Mr Lockhart and his Mission were arrested. The other Allied Missions were closely watched. The French regular secret service had been caught to a man and the Cheka had made a visit to Reilly's old address and were making diligent inquiries as to his whereabouts. This made us very nervous.

With Evelyn I arranged a code signal to enable me to know on my return to the house if the coast was clear. It was a simple device, a small Russian illustrated paper known as *The Copek* (that being the price at which it was sold) being carelessly placed between the double windows in the living-room. When I entered the house the paper was always taken out of the window. One afternoon I went off to see the chief of my wrecking-gang, and when I returned there was no paper in the window. Feeling rather dizzy I walked straight on. Half an hour later I returned, but still the window was bare. For the next two hours I walked the damp and muddy streets, depressed and wildly anxious, passing the house every half hour, not daring to go in.

The last time I passed I saw Evelyn come out of the front door and walk up the street. I followed her and when we were a safe distance away stopped.

'Where have you been?' she demanded angrily. 'I have been worried out of my life about you.'

'The signal,' I said; 'the signal is not in the window.'

'But I told Vi to put it in,' said she. 'There has been no raid.'

Vi had given me three very bad hours. She had just become interested in the paper and put it down somewhere, quite forgetful of its purpose. Dear Vi, she was a darling, irresponsible, forgetful person whom we had to be reprimanding constantly. She made many a long hour pass quickly for me, and at one time we gravely discussed having a serious affair. But on account of her extreme youth and some pig-headed streak in me we decided that it should not bud. I have often smiled at that decision, as only a few months later she married an elderly man whom she divorced within a fortnight under the Soviet laws. Then for a time she lived with an operatic tenor, then married again, and then again before she finally settled down. In her fourth husband she seems to have found her true mate for from time to time I hear of her and in the last seven years she has raised a family of which she is extremely proud.

Meantime my wrecking-gang in the Ukrainia was going through a bad time and I took a trip to see what was wrong and to give them encouragement. The German secret service had grown very diligent, and had arrested and executed a number of our men. We decided on new methods of harrying the

Germans. At one of the towns in Ukrainia near to the Soviet frontier we planned to blow up a gasometer as a demonstration.

We had not the proper materials to do this but collected a bundle of cotton-waste which we soaked in paraffin and then one of us placed it against the gasometer. There were eight of us in the party, and we took up our positions about a hundred and fifty yards away. At a whistle from us one of our number put a match to the waste and then ran for his life. We gave him just enough time to get away and then put three rounds of rapid fire into the gasometer about the height of the flame. There was a blinding flash followed by a terrific explosion and then a deadly silence. We staggered away. For hours afterwards my nose bled most violently and nothing I did would stop it.

I returned to Moscow and my wrecking-gang concentrated on destroying gasometers in the towns where the German troops were quartered in any numbers.

Chapter XXVII

On my return to Moscow Z. reported that things were not going well with the courier service. Six of our men in all had now been caught and executed. It is to the credit of these White Russian officers that not one of them gave Z's address away, nor did they ever betray for whom they were working or whither they were going. Every one of them faced his end like a hero.

It took a courier a minimum of twelve and an average of twenty-two days to make the double journey from Moscow north either to Kemm on the Murmansk front or Archangel, and back to Moscow. Each message was sent in duplicate over both these routes. I originally thought that it would be possible to maintain this northern service with an average of twenty-five couriers. It was of vital importance to get the messages through, and finally we elaborated a new plan which meant that we would have to employ over a hundred men and replace casualties as they occurred.

The original courier service as I had planned it was for keeping communication with Northern Russia, and also throughout the territories occupied by the Austro-Germans in South Russia. The southern courier chain worked very well, and the Germans did not catch one of our men. Naturally these couriers also acted as observation agents and each time they returned from a trip they would put in a report as to the conditions they had met with, and what they had seen; and they kept in touch with the destruction-gangs in Ukrainia.

The map reproduced in the end-papers of this volume shows the new courier service. Our southern organisation remained unchanged, but it will be noted that the northern one now spread out in a fan-shaped formation from Moscow, with a chain service linked up to the centres. These centres are denoted on the map by ovals. At each of them was a group commander whose duty it was to organise his men, select suitable places for living, procure documents and passports, and control the funds for carrying on the work. Under this new system, instead of a courier going all the way from Moscow to the Allied lines in the north he took a short journey from Moscow – say to Vyatka – whence after a rest he would return to Moscow, while the message would be taken by another courier to Kotlas and from there be relayed by yet another messenger to the British lines. Each courier got to know his particular run, its pitfalls, dangers and dodges, and the strain was much less than would be involved in the entire journey. The chain of men near our front lines were also able to act as observers of everything which was happening along the front in the north and were of extreme value. Once this service was established all messages went in triplicate, and it took an average of five to eight days to get a message from Moscow to the Allied headquarters in the north. The experiences of these men would make an exciting story which would demand a book to itself. Every time one of them set out he did so at the risk of his life and the ways in which they overcame difficulties were miraculous.

One night the couriers' flat in Moscow was raided by the Cheka. Luckily none of my men was there at the time and the lady in residence put up a very good excuse, but thereafter we did not dare to use the place. I looked around and found a good antique shop which was filled with all sorts of junk and treasures, as the better-class people were selling their possessions for ready money. I bought this shop from its Armenian owner and put in as the owner one of my own agents whom I thought I could trust. Thereafter the couriers reported there and, if necessary, spent the night in the shop. It served as an excellent cover, for I could go in and see the agents there under the guise of having something to sell or wanting to buy something. I spent a lot of money in acquiring this business, but to my surprise it showed a very excellent return, and before I had finished it almost wiped off the purchase price. We bought things cheaply from the rich who had become poor and sold them at a high price to the poor who had become rich, the profiteers and dishonest Commissars, of whom there were many.

One day four of my wrecking-gang arrived from Ukrainia. The Germans had made things too hot for them and for a time they had to lie low in Moscow. They were thirsting for revenge and so I gave them the address of one of the important German secret service centres in Moscow. One night my friends visited the place, popped a couple of incendiary bombs through the windows, and burned it to the ground.

The courier service, although working well, was not getting messages to the north quickly enough to suit me. I knew that the men were doing their best and that I could not in any way accelerate the service, and my mind began to cast around for other means of communication. The obvious thing to do was to get hold of someone in the Moscow wireless station who would be prepared to send Marconigrams direct to England for the

War Office, who could then, when necessary, relay them to the Allies in Northern Russia.

The wireless station was at the far end of the Field of Mars and some little way from Moscow, but it was possible to get there by tram. I knew the district well, for the Air Park at which I had worked was adjacent to it. Taking a tram, I went out to examine the station. I found that a screen of barbed wire had been erected all round it and that at the gates there was an armed Lettish guard. For two or three days I watched that entrance carefully and noted everyone who came in and out of the wireless station between the hours of seven in the morning and midday. I used my imagination and separated probable transmitters from the rest of the personnel. Then I weighed up in my mind all the men I had marked and selected the one whom I felt was the most likely to entertain my proposition.

I did not choose the weakest, but went for the strongest and smartest-looking man of the lot. We travelled back two or three times on the same tram to Moscow, and each time I made a point of nodding to him and passing the time of day. When I had established myself I asked him if I could have a talk somewhere privately with him. He looked at me suspiciously and said that he did not know me or where we could talk. I knew it was a big risk, but suggested that he should come to one of my flats which was empty at the time. Rather reluctantly he agreed. At first he would have nothing to do with my proposition. All his business life he had been a telegraph transmitter and had never done anything underhand, and although he was anti-Bolshevik he did not propose to undertake anything underhand, even in the difficult conditions under which he was living. He had not the least idea that I was an Englishman, but of course suspected that I was working as an English agent. In any case, he said he could not do the work as he was not transmitter during the hours when it would be possible to get a wireless message from the Moscow station to an English one.

'Well, then,' I said, 'introduce me to the man who is on duty,' and paid him for his trouble. The man he sent to me was nowhere near such a good specimen or so highly principled as the man I had picked out, but he undertook to transmit messages secretly to England. I managed to get about ten messages through that way and then the German counter-espionage gave the show away. Their wireless service had detected that messages were being sent from Moscow to England. They asked their own secret service to inquire into the matter. Instead of doing so the German secret service went straight to the Bolsheviks and told them what was happening. The Germans scored certainly, for I was not able to send any further messages, but had they waited they could have easily caught me. The Bolsheviks promptly held an inquiry at the wireless station, but my operator was warned in time and in great fear came to me. I gave him sufficient money and directions for escape into Ukrainia. I had thought of sending him to the Allies in the north, but did not consider him sufficiently trustworthy.

I was seeing Reilly daily, and he kept me informed of what he was doing and of his plans for a *coup d'état* against the Bolsheviks. Reilly's plan was bold and masterfully conceived, its purpose being no less than to have the whole of the Bolshevik Executive Committee – including Lenin and Trotsky – arrested by the Letts, their own bodyguard. Had his plan succeeded it is impossible even to visualise how different would have been the history of the world since those fatal days of 1918. Bolshevism would have been wiped out, the directing machinery of the Communist party would have been destroyed, Russia would have been saved from civil war and famine, the world would not have been harried by the gadfly of Bolshevism, and the history of the last two decades might have developed on evolutionary rather than revolutionary lines.

The position of the Letts was peculiar. In the early days of the war special divisions composed of Letts were raised by the Russian Army and sent as far away from the Baltic provinces as was possible. By their thought, religion, upbringing and language these men were entirely alien to the Russians; but having – for centuries before the cession of the province to Russia – been under the domination of German Baltic barons they disliked everything German infinitely more than they did anything Russian.

The personnel of the regiments which composed the Lettish divisions were men of splendid physique, well-trained fighters and disciplined by their own officers. When the Brest Litovsk Peace Treaty was signed the whole of the Baltic provinces were occupied by Germany. The Letts could not return to Latvia and would not if they could – and there they were stranded in Russia.

Lenin saw his chance. He made the Letts the backbone of Bolshevik power. To serve the Bolsheviks was the only resource left to the Letts. They were given good food and pay and housed in excellent barracks. Everything was done to make them contented with their lot. They guarded the Kremlin and the government offices; a Lett was at the head of the Cheka; Letts were at the heads of the prisons and banks and railways; and whenever there was serious street fighting it was put down by Letts. At one time the sailors of the Baltic and Black Sea fleets were the predominant military power in Russia, but now they had been supplanted by Letts, and, indeed, Russian troops could only be relied upon to fight if they were coerced from behind by Lettish battalions. When at last the Letts fell from power they were replaced by Chinese mercenaries who, in their turn, gave way to the Red Army and the organised troops of the OGPU.

As a people the Letts were smallholders. The ideas of Bolshevism were entirely alien to them, and it is to be noted that while the Lettish soldiers carried out the orders of the Bolsheviks, the majority of them never became members of the Communist party. After a time the rank and file of these divisions became dissatisfied with being used as policemen and executioners by the Bolsheviks, and it was not surprising therefore that their leaders should approach the Allied diplomatic representatives in the hope of being transferred to the northern front or otherwise used for the purposes of the Allies in Russia.

While these negotiations were going on the political situation in Russia had changed so rapidly that Mr Lockhart's sojourn in Moscow obviously might come to an end at any moment; he therefore put Reilly into communication with the Lettish leaders.

Reilly conceived the notion of arresting the Executive Committee of the Bolshevik party by the help of the Letts, during one of its sessions in the Kremlin. As soon as this was achieved a provisional government was to be formed, whose first object would be to summon the Constitutional Assembly which had been dissolved by force early in the year by the Bolsheviks.

Reilly's idea was that none of the Bolsheviks were to be killed if possible. He proposed to march them through the streets of Moscow bereft of their lower garments in order to kill them by ridicule, and then to intern them in a prison in Moscow from which they could not escape. The plan for the *coup d'état*, the establishment of the provisional government and a hundred and one other things for the change-over were worked out to the minutest detail. I was kept informed of all this so that if anything happened to Reilly it would be possible for me to carry on the work.

The chief representative of the Letts was Colonel Berzin. I never met Colonel Berzin or any of the Lettish representatives. Before I could do so the plot was given away by certain agents of the French secret service. When the blow did come my section was not affected, as Reilly and I worked in absolutely water-tight compartments and had quite separate organisations.

Early in August the British and most of the other Allied Missions had been arrested and imprisoned by the Cheka. Mr Lockhart himself was confined in the Kremlin, but released after a few days, and negotiations were now proceeding to enable him and the other members of his staff to return to England.

On 28 August, Reilly told me that he was leaving that night for Petrograd, where he wished to discuss certain matters with Commander Cromie, RN, the senior British naval officer at our Embassy there, and to make arrangements with other people in Petrograd. Reilly had no difficulty in travelling between Moscow and Petrograd, as he had obtained a position with the Cheka and had a Cheka pass.

The following day the first blow fell. The house of Colonel de Vertement, the head of the French secret service in Moscow, was raided by the Cheka. The raid was made with a view to obtaining evidence of the conspiracy, which the traitors in the French service had revealed to the Cheka. The Colonel himself managed to escape by way of the roof and across other house-tops into another street, but the Cheka found explosives and other material at his flat and managed to arrest half a dozen of his agents. This information was given to me by one of my agents closely connected with the Cheka. My informant further told me that the reason for the raid was the discovery by the Cheka of a gigantic plot to be brought off by the Letts at the instigation of the Allies. I at once instructed my go-betweens to keep absolutely clear of any of the French secret service agents and sent a courier to Petrograd to warn Reilly, but this man was arrested in the train.

On the following morning a Social Revolutionary, Dora Kaplan, attempted to kill Lenin as he was addressing a meeting at one of the larger factories in Moscow. She managed to wound him seriously with two shots, one of which lodged in the tissue of a lung. Dora Kaplan was nearly torn in pieces by the factory workers and executed two days later by the Cheka. Lenin was not expected to live and had it not been for his superb constitution he certainly would not have recovered. On the same day Uritsky, head of the Cheka in Petrograd, was shot down and killed by another Social Revolutionary.

That evening and the following morning the Bolshevik press gave full details of these terrorist acts. In revenge for the shooting of Lenin the Cheka took five hundred of the most prominent figures of the old regime and shot them that night in Moscow, and they took the same number of citizens in Petrograd and shot them in revenge for the assassination of Uritsky. Next morning they published a list of the people whom they had executed. I do not think that I have ever read anything quite so terrible. The people they had seized were entirely innocent and came from every class. Imagine a similar situation in London. The death-roll would include all the prominent politicians of the opposition, commercial magnates like Gordon Selfridge and Sir Herbert Morris, newspaper men like Lord Beaverbrook and Lord Rothermere, the editors of most of the London daily papers, men of the theatre like Charles B. Cochran and Henry Ainley, women like Ellen Wilkinson and Lady Astor, prominent writers and many more humble folk.

The relatives of these unfortunate victims were allowed to take away the bodies for burial – the Bolsheviks wanted Moscow to see the actual funerals, *pour encourager les autres*. Then they published in Moscow and Petrograd a further list of seven hundred and fifty prominent members of each city who had been arrested as hostages and would be shot if the life of a single Commissar were attempted, whether the attempt was fatal or not.

A high official of the Cheka defined the principles of the Red Terror in two phrases: 'Strike Quick' and 'Strike Hard'; he might have added a third: 'Strike Secretly', for arrests were carried out at night and the families of prisoners rarely had news until the unfortunate was either condemned or freed. Summary arrest, judgment and execution was the order of the day. The Cheka began to search Moscow systematically by day and night. Raids were made throughout the town. Whole blocks would be surrounded by the Cheka troops, and everybody systematically examined. Numbers of people were arrested at each of these raids, some simply because of their names or their positions, ex-officers, bankers and merchants being taken even if their documents were perfectly in order. Other people they would arrest on suspicion and woe betide him who had no documents or papers of identification.

On the afternoon of Saturday 31 August, the Cheka, in violation of all international usage, raided the British Embassy in Petrograd and murdered Commander Cromie. The remaining members of the British Embassy were thrown into prison. On 1 September Mr Lockhart and his Mission at Moscow were re-arrested, and the Bolshevik Press stated that they were to be executed if Lenin died.

On the same morning the Bolshevik papers printed a full account of the Lettish conspiracy, which quite falsely and from political motives they attributed to Mr Lockhart. They called it 'The Lockhart Conspiracy', and cited Sidney George Reilly, Lieutenant of the Royal Air Force, as his chief spy, printing the aliases under which Reilly had been working, together with his photograph. It was a horrible morning, for the newspapers gave publicity to a rumour that Reilly had been arrested in Petrograd, and I felt that I had lost a great friend and a brilliant colleague.

I sent Vi along to one of Reilly's girls with a verbal message to the effect that I would take over his organisation. I expected her to be absent less than an hour; she did not return until seven p.m., and when she did she brought me most disquieting news. She had arrived about eleven o'clock in the morning at the house of Reilly's chief girl agent. It is still impossible for me to give her name and so I will call her E. E. Vi was carrying, as usual, a blouse wrapped in paper and she rang the bell of E. E's flat.

The door was opened and Vi found herself covered with

the revolver of a Cheka agent. 'Come in,' he said. 'Whom do you want?'

Vi was terrified. She gave E. E's name, but kept her presence of mind and added, 'I have come to deliver a blouse. Is the lady in, and will she please pay for it?'

Vi was marched through into the living-room, where she saw E. E. being examined and put through what amounted to the third degree by three expert examiners. The two girls pretended not to know each other. Vi played up, burst into tears, and said that she had simply brought a blouse for the lady which she had made herself. This was a clever lie on Vi's part, for she realised that if she said it had been made by Annie they might come to our house for confirmation. As it was she gave an address where she had been living before she joined us. She was the only one of us who was living under her own name and passport. Vi was thoroughly cross-examined, but the Chekists failed to break down her story, though one of them, holding a revolver to her head, said she was lying and urged her to tell the truth. After two or three hours the examining officers, having searched the flat from top to bottom, had found nothing incriminating, but decided to arrest E. E. nevertheless. Vi, they said, could go home.

E. E. burst into tears, and one of the examining officials told her kindly that she need not worry, for they had come to the conclusion that she was only one of Reilly's lady friends and most probably would be allowed to go. But alas! How unkind is Fate! As Vi reached the door to leave the flat the bell rang and a go-between called Marie, of the American secret service, walked in. She was bringing messages and documents to E. E. for transmission to Reilly. On seeing the Chekists she completely lost her head and began to scream. The officials seized her and after a moment's search had the documents in their possession. Vi kept her head and walked out of the flat, down the stairs and into the street.

Although she was trembling all over and feeling sick and dizzy her first thought was for the safety of our house. It occurred to her that she might be followed and therefore she walked all the way to her old house, but for the sake of the occupants did not go in, turning instead into a shop where she bought some cotton and trimmings, just as if she were a dressmaker. Then, still fearing that she might be followed, she went to one of the public baths, bought a ticket for the third-class section and spent two hours in the women's bath-house. Only then did she venture back to our house.

If Marie had not lost her head E. E. would not have had to spend months in prison and stand her trial with many others of the secret service agents who were caught. It was owing to Marie that Kalamatiano, the head of the American secret service, was arrested that afternoon.

In the meantime, no arrests had been made in my organisation and we carried on our work as usual. I visited the couriers, conferred with the head of my wrecking-gangs, coded messages and sent them off. The four girls were splendid, and were examples of the devoted bravery women will show in the most trying circumstances.

It was not until two days later that a girl came to my flat from Reilly, with the news that he was safe in Moscow. He had been temporarily put up by this agent, but the house he was in was liable to be raided at any moment. I immediately went to see him.

His experiences are set out in detail in a book recently published under the title of *Sidney Reilly*, which to a certain extent recounts the days he spent during this time in Moscow.

Reilly's bearing when I met him was splendid. He was a hunted man, his photograph with a full description and a reward was placarded throughout the town; he had been through a terrible time in getting away from Petrograd and yet he was absolutely cool, calm and collected, not in the least down-hearted and only concerned in gathering together the broken threads and starting afresh. He discussed with me the advisability of surrendering himself to the Cheka in the hope that by doing so he would be able to clear Mr Lockhart and his Mission from the charges which the Bolsheviks were making against them. I advised him not to do so, maintaining that it could be of no help to Mr Lockhart, that the Cheka would only detain both of them and that, if he could get away, it was in the interest of the service that he should do so. I urged that he should go into Ukrainia, where my organisation could help him, on to Baku which had been recently occupied by the Dunster Force from Persia. However, Reilly decided that he would take the more dangerous route through Petrograd and the Baltic Provinces in order to get his reports to London as early as possible. It was necessary to get him new identification papers. As the matter was of great urgency I gave him my Bergmann passport. At the same time I managed to get a blank passport which I filled in for myself, and the chief of my couriers forged various visas on it.

Our great difficulty was to find a place for Reilly to stay during the next few days. Members of his own organisation managed to put him up for three days, and on the fourth night I found him a place. It was in the room of a friend of the lady who kept our courier flat. This girl was in the last stages of the disease which so often curses members of her profession. I will never forget Reilly's reaction when I told him, for he was the most fastidious of men and while being caught by the Bolsheviks had little terror for him, he could hardly bring himself to spend the night on the couch in her room. It was a good thing that he did, for the place where he had spent the previous night was raided by the Cheka the next evening.

Reilly had a mane of jet-black hair and once or twice when he had been in my room before I went underground he had used my hair brushes. These brushes had particularly long and strong bristles and Reilly had always admired them. One day when we had been discussing his plans for the overthrow of the Bolsheviks he said to me, 'Hill, the morning I turn the Bolsheviks out you will give me as a present your brushes.' 'Done,' said I, 'providing the provisional government give me the Rolls Royce used by Dzerjhinsky, the head of the Cheka.' 'Done,' said Reilly, and we left it at that.

All arrangements were made for Reilly's journey to Petrograd. I made up a parcel of food for him, put in a bottle of wine and also one of my brushes, and went along to bid him farewell.

I told him that I thought he had come so near to achieving his purpose that he deserved, anyway, one of the brushes. It was the only time during these four days that he showed any emotion. We grinned at each other, shook hands, and he went off to the Nicolai station. After many adventures he got safely out of Russia; but I did not see him again for many weeks, when we met in the Savoy Hotel in London. A few days after this meeting I received a case with two silver brushes engraved with my regimental crest and the words: 'In memory of Moscow, from S. T. I.', which was Reilly's secret service name.

Chapter XXVIII

During all this time I was regularly working at the film studio. Near the studio I used to pass a shop which had been a big confectionery establishment in the old days, when it was noted for its homemade sweetmeats. For many months the well-known brand had been no longer made and the shop window displayed instead some very unpleasant grey sweetmeats, made of flour and honey. Whenever I passed I would see the proprietor's daughter, a pretty, jolly girl, sitting in the doorway of the shop reading a novel and waiting to serve anyone who was tempted to buy the grey sweets.

One afternoon, making my way to the studio, I met a peasant who had come from the country with a large basket of apples. Fruit was hard to get in Moscow and I promptly bought a bag of them, and took them with me. I am very fond of apples and did not care to wait, so I took one out of the bag and munched it as I walked along. As I passed the sweet-shop the pretty girl looked up and smiled, partly, I suppose, because there is something about a good rosy apple and a juicy one to wit which makes one smile, and partly because she liked apples. For my part I had long wanted to speak to her and this was an excellent means of introduction. 'Have an apple,' I said, and she gladly accepted. Thereafter we always nodded to each other and sometimes I would stop and chat with her.

One evening when I passed I found her sobbing as if her heart would break. What was the matter? She told me that her father had been arrested that day by the Cheka and imprisoned in the Butirsky prison because he had been hoarding sugar and selling it at a high price to his old customers. Her father was the only relative she had; she was left all alone with the shop and did not know what to do. Nor had she any money with which to buy food for herself or make up parcels for her father in prison. Food was so scarce that, even if they had wanted to, the Bolsheviks would not have been able to give their prisoners sufficient to keep body and soul together, and in consequence they allowed relatives to send in food-parcels. As a rule, no matter how bad the famine was, by going without themselves the relatives managed to scrape together some sort of a food-parcel to take to their dear ones in prison.

I asked whether her father had any other parcels of sugar concealed, and she told me that he had.

'Well, give them to me and I will sell them for you and give you the money.' She trusted me and without a moment's hesitation accepted my proposition, and that night I picked up a bag of about ten pounds of sugar. This the head of my couriers sold at a huge price the next day, and I handed the proceeds over to my friend.

Some days later, as I was on my way to the studio, a Cheka raiding party put a chain at each end of the block and began a systematic search of everyone in the street and in the houses which bordered it. Luckily for me the block was that which included the confectioner's shop, where the pretty girl was in the doorway as usual. There was not a moment to be lost. I went up to her.

'Hide me,' I said; 'I must not be caught.'

She was very pale. 'Come in,' she said.

At the back of the shop was a large cauldron in which the sweets were made.

'Get in there! It is deep and I will hide you with sacking,' and she took off the wooden lid. I jumped in and crouched down at the bottom; she put some old sacking over me and replaced the wooden top.

After a time I could hear the searchers approaching and examining the people in the street, and then an examining party came into the shop. The pretty girl told them that her father was in the Butirsky prison and that she was there alone. The examiners searched the shop, walked round the cauldron, took some sweets without paying for them, and went away. For another hour I remained in that miserable cauldron suffering untold agonies from cramp, and finally I ventured forth. The girl beamed on me as I came out. 'Now I have repaid you for that nice apple,' she said; but that was only the beginning of her payment, for she became one of my most trusted agents.

Some days later I had another shock. I was walking through the great square outside the Grand Theatre when a motor-car pulled up alongside the kerb and Dzerjhinsky himself alighted. I had to step back to let him pass, and he gave me a searching look. I had had two or three interviews with him before I grew my beard but happily he did not recognise me. Feeling thoroughly frightened I went on my way up to the Kuznetski Most and was only a little way up the hill when a perfect stranger greeted me with:

'Mr Hill – Mr Hill, how are you?'

'You have made a mistake,' I said, while icy fingers gripped my spine. 'My name is Bergmann.'

The stranger looked at me in astonishment then shook his head and said: 'Forgive me, I have made a mistake. You could not be the man I thought you were; he was an Englishman I have not seen since we last met in Persia, thirty years ago.' I bowed coldly and walked on. I realised that he had mistaken me for my father who, thirty years before, had worn a beard.

I went to the flat occupied by the head of my destruction-gang where some of the Ukrainian organisation were waiting for me. They reported that it was becoming more and more difficult to carry on the campaign against the German Army, but that they thought a great deal could be done by way of sabotage and deliberate destruction of machinery in the Donetz coal mines. The trouble was that the coal mines were being watched carefully by German engineers and that they had not got the technical knowledge requisite for putting machinery and pumps out of action undetected. Now I knew that there were still in Ukrainia quite a number of Belgian miners who, prior to the German occupation, had been the technical advisers in the Russian coal mines, and I decided to make a hurried visit to Kharkov and try to put some of these Belgians in touch with my organisation. That evening I left Moscow in a goods truck of a pattern which was calculated to carry forty soldiers in time of war. There were more like seventy men and women in the truck into which I fought my way, and there I spent two days squatting on my haunches in a stifling atmosphere.

The crossing of the Soviet frontier was no common ordeal. I pretended that I was going to get flour for my relatives in Moscow. As evidence I had three empty flour sacks with me; and also a tin kettle. A tin kettle with a double bottom. Inside the kettle I had US dollar notes and German marks to pay for the work I wanted done. The soldering had been done by Annie most skilfully: it was quite safe to put tea leaves into the kettle and pour boiling water on them and get a good brew of tea without in the least damaging the notes.

Getting through the German control was still more difficult, as they were very thorough and extremely suspicious. Luckily my German was almost word perfect and I told the examining officer that I was a native of Riga, that my family were literally starving in Moscow, and that I had come to buy some flour to take back to them. The officer was sympathetic and promised to help me on the train on the return journey.

Kharkov presented a very different spectacle from that I had seen when I had last been there. Then it had been first under the control of a homicidal maniac and then of Antonov.

Now the station was clean, the streets policed by German soldiers, order everywhere, telephone and postal communication direct with Berlin and an air of freedom in the town. The civil population were going about their business, shops were open and trade re-established.

Within two days I had found my Belgian experts and had put my organisation in touch with them. The Belgians were only too pleased to instruct my men in the art of doing the maximum of damage to the mines in the easiest way. In many cases it was simply a matter of putting certain pumps out of action by means of a handful of sand in the bearings. Once the main pumps were out of action mines in many places would automatically flood, and many weeks of pumping would be necessary before work could be resumed.

My mission accomplished I filled two of my bags with flour. Into the third went six pounds of sugar and with these I made my way back to the frontier. The German control sergeant was as good as his word, securing me a corner in a third-class compartment on a train leaving for Moscow, and for his kindness I paid him well. Little did the poor man know the damage I had done to his cause. At the Soviet frontier I had to part with all my sugar as a bribe to the station Commissar that I might be allowed to proceed to Moscow. When the train finally pulled into the Kursk station in Moscow all the passengers were carrying bags of flour with a good proportion of which they had to part to the Cheka guards before being allowed to leave the station.

The tramway system had apparently broken down and I had to stagger back under the load of the two sacks to the flat. Sally was overjoyed at receiving the flour. A little of it she gave away to our neighbours, while Evelyn presented five or six pounds to the *dvornik*, saying: 'Our lodger has been to Kharkov and you must share in our good fortune.' It must be remembered that we were living as the poorest of poor people. We appeared to have no money and never attempted to bribe people like the *dvornik*, but the poor help the poor the whole world over, and so it was natural for us to share our good fortune with him. He, for his part, was delighted and grateful, and in gratitude for Evelyn's kindness was the unknowing means of saving our lives a few days later.

Chapter XXIX

The Red Terror was at its height. The horrors of the Inquisition were surpassed by the Bolsheviks. Arrested people gave their friends away in the hope of saving their own lives. Weak characters sold information for a few pence to the Cheka. A man wishing to wreak his vengeance on some poor fellow against whom he had a grudge had only to whisper a few words to one of the Chekist officials on the ground floor of the Lubianka and a whole household was thrown into turmoil and misery.

It was getting more difficult every day to keep my courier service going. A further twelve of my men had been executed during the Red Terror. Some of these men knew my headquarters and could undoubtedly have saved their lives by betraying me, but because they held the cause of the Allies dear, because they were White officers and gentlemen, they preferred death at the hands of a firing squad to treachery. Whenever I hear those inspiring words: 'At the going down of the sun and in the morning we will remember them,' each of my eighteen couriers stands out vividly in my mind.

It was almost impossible to raise funds to carry on the work, as the Bolsheviks had made it illegal to sell foreign exchange and were rapidly devaluating their own currency. I knew that before long it would be necessary for me to leave Russia to get fresh instructions from England, and that alternatively it was only a matter of time before I should be caught by the German secret service, who were now hand in glove with the Bolshevik counter-espionage section. In the meantime, however, I carried on the work, destruction-gangs were doing their best, and my couriers left regularly.

One night the day's dispatches had been coded, typed on linen and sewn up in the courier's jacket. The courier in question had stayed late with me making a report and it was dangerous to let him return to the courier headquarters by night. I therefore made up a bed for him on the couch in the living-room. We put away the typewriter and the codes and turned in for the night.

I was just dropping off to sleep when I heard motor-cars draw up outside the house. Now the only people who used motor-cars were either the more prominent Bolsheviks or the Cheka, and I was immediately alarmed. Presently I heard the tramp of soldiers and a few seconds later knew that a sentry had been posted outside our house. I crept out of bed to the window and peered out, but from my bedroom window could see nothing. I went through to the living-room, and saw that there was an armed sentry standing by our front door. I returned to my room and looking through the gap by the blind on the left, observed two or three armed men standing at the gate. Then I knew that the house was surrounded.

At once I took out the key to our code with the intention of chewing and swallowing it as soon as arrest was imminent.

Then I stole through to the girls' room and woke Evelyn, and the two of us decided that the girls should be told but instructed to remain in their beds. The courier was tired out and fast asleep. Not being certain how he would behave in the present predicament – for panic is a terrible thing – we decided to allow him to go on sleeping.

Evelyn then went out to reconnoitre. Barefooted and in her night attire she stole into the yard and pretended to cross to the lavatory. She saw enough to know that the whole block was surrounded by the Cheka, that it was one of their flying raids, and that they would be going through all the houses in the block. This was a great relief. It meant that they were not making a particular raid on our house, and things would not have looked so black against us if it were not for the fact that we had that courier staying with us unregistered. Nor were his documents in too good order.

After what seemed an eternity and was in fact two hours we could hear the examiners coming closer. Next door to us on the left a woman started to scream, 'Don't take him, don't take him, he is innocent, I implore you don't take him.' We heard the tramp of men and through my window saw a man led off into one of the waiting motor-cars.

Our house was in complete darkness. Our nerves were strung up to breaking-point and, cold as it was in my night attire, I felt beads of perspiration running down my body and collecting in little pools around my feet.

Presently Evelyn and I crept through to Sally. She was lying on the stove, quite calm and collected.

'I am afraid we are for it,' she whispered. It was the first word of English that had been spoken in our house since my arrival.

At last we heard an examining party come to the back door. Evelyn and I were standing in the little windowless hall, but as the kitchen door was open we could hear everything outside. I could hear not only my own heart pounding with the regularity of a steam pump, but strangely enough the beating of Evelyn's as well. 'I am glad you let me do this work,' she whispered to me. 'It has been a wonderful experience. We have done good, and no matter what happens now it has been well worth it. Remember that, and don't have any regrets.'

I wish I could describe the quality of her voice, quite steady and natural as it was. And I suddenly realised that she had spoken the truth and that it *was* worth it. At once my heart stopped its pounding and I knew in an instant the line I was going to take with the examining Chekists.

Then we heard the *dvornik*'s voice say, 'There is no need to go into this house. It is only occupied by a poor school-teacher and a dressmaker. They are ordinary people, just like us.'

The examining squad hesitated. In the silence I could hear the steady snoring of the courier which suddenly seemed as loud as a fog-horn. I automatically pulled to the door of the sitting-room.

At last came the answer.

'All right, papa – if you say so,' and the examining squad moved to the back door of the house on the right.

Twenty minutes later from that house came a commotion. An extra squad was marched up and somebody was brought out. We heard voices crying, 'For God's sake, for the Lord's sake, in the name of mercy be compassionate – he is innocent – wait and we will prove it – I will pay you anything,' all mingled up, disjointed and together.

'Stand back,' called a commanding voice, then – 'Put him against the wall.'

For the first time we heard the terrified voice of a man, 'For the sake of Christ! For the love of Christ, what are you doing?'

There was an irregular volley and the night air was immediately rent with the wailing of women bemoaning their dead. We had just listened to one of the Cheka's summary executions.

The guards remained outside our front door and surrounded the block until the grey streaks of dawn had made their appearance in the clouds. It was a night of horror and terror for us, and but for the *dvornik*, both myself and the courier who was now awake owing to the shooting and thoroughly frightened, might have been executed just as summarily. As it grew lighter the guards were withdrawn and four motor-cars filled with Chekists and the prisoners they had taken drove back to their headquarters – the Lubianka – the Lubianka where people were taken down into the grisly execution cellar every night and where the engines of motor-cars and lorries were set going in order to drown the noise of the firing-parties.

Kalamatiano, the American secret service agent who had been captured, was taken nightly to the place of execution, but always at the last moment put through another cross-examination in an endeavour to make him give away his own confederates and the whereabouts of Sidney Reilly and the other Allied secret service agents. Kalamatiano lived through it, stood his trial, was condemned to death, and never opened his mouth.

I carried on for a further fortnight in conditions which grew more and more difficult. The German and Bolshevik secret services were hot on the scent of my organisation. I would have to break it up entirely and start afresh with a new personnel and new headquarters. I withdrew my couriers to Moscow and paid them off, and made arrangements for Sally, Annie and Evelyn to go to England.

It was essential for me to escape from Russia, get new instructions from London, and make arrangements which would enable me to have at my command sufficient funds to finance the fresh work.

The British Consul quite rightly did not feel himself justified in including me in any of the lists of English people to be evacuated to England from Moscow, as he was afraid that I might jeopardise the safety of others. For a time it looked as if I should have to spend weeks in escaping, and resort to the dangerous method of secretly crossing one of the frontiers. However, Captain Hicks, a member of Mr Lockhart's staff, who was acting for Mr Lockhart during the latter's imprisonment in the Kremlin, knew how important it was for me to get out quickly, and included me – with Lockhart's approval – on the list of the Mission which was now due to leave Moscow any day. While awaiting departure I took the opportunity of getting in touch with my wrecking-gangs in Ukrainia. On my return all the girls, with the exception of Evelyn, had left Moscow. But, on arrival at our headquarters, I learned from Evelyn that the man whom I had installed as the owner of my antique shop had started a gentle form of blackmail. He had sent desperate messages to Evelyn demanding sums of money under veiled threats, and in the circumstances she had thought it best to comply with his demand and pay the money.

A few days after my return another demand came. My agent pretended that he was being blackmailed by someone who knew of our organisation and that he required money to keep his mouth shut. When this second demand arrived I was in a position to take steps against him. For I had been included in Mr Lockhart's Mission, and it was necessary for me to have a respectable suit made. The first thing I did therefore was to get rid of my hateful beard; then I went to the best Moscow tailor, where I picked up one of the few remaining pieces of English cloth and had a new suit made. I bought boots, a hat and a pair of white spats and reappeared dressed once again as an Englishman.

Some Norwegian friends who knew the truth offered to put me up until the Lockhart Mission left. My first task was to settle my account with the blackmailer. Early one afternoon, white spats and all, looking like a thorough bourgeois, I boldly walked into *my* antique shop. 'Well, Mr K., how are you?'

'You, Captain Hill – what are you doing out, and in those clothes?'

'What do you mean?' I said. 'I have always worn these clothes. I am on Mr Lockhart's Mission, and I am shortly leaving for England. But before doing so I want an account of your stewardship.'

He went scarlet and said, 'You think I have been blackmailing you?'

'I know you have,' was my reply. 'And now you will kindly disgorge.'

I put the matter on a business footing without any anger or recrimination. First of all I took back the money he had extorted from Evelyn, then I made him pay me a sum which was equivalent to about 70 per cent of the purchase price of the antique business. But as I feared that some of my couriers might turn up and that he would try to wreak his vengeance on them, in order to 'keep him sweet' I handed the business over to him as a going concern so that he might make a living.

The head of my couriers invited me and two of his most brilliant assistants to a farewell dinner in his own tiny flat. That afternoon I had been having tea with some English friends at whose country house I had stayed before my disappearance. The last visit had been a twenty-first birthday party and I had taken down my mess kit to their house and changed there. The following morning I had gone off in my khaki uniform meaning to pick up my mess dress later, but before I had the opportunity of doing so I had gone underground. My friends had brought this uniform to their Moscow house and showed it to me that evening.

Suddenly a most foolhardy idea occurred to me. I would honour my Russian friends by wearing uniform tonight. A more idiotic thing I could not have thought of.

Over the uniform I put my civilian coat and walked through the streets to my couriers' flat.

They gasped when I took off my coat and they saw my uniform, but immediately realised it was a token of appreciation for all they had done. They took it as an enormous honour and we had a really delightful evening. I think the gods must have approved of my gesture, for they saw to it that I returned safely to my Norwegian friends in the early hours of the morning.

A few days later I joined Mr Lockhart's Mission at the Nicolai station and we were taken up by special train from which after many days we disembarked in Finland. I was safely out of Russia. My first job was to telegraph to London for fresh instructions and somewhat to my dismay received an order to slip back into Russia for a few weeks. So one dark and frosty night I waded into the ice-cold water and swam across the stream which forms the frontier between Finland and the Russian town of Beloostrov.

It took me three weeks to carry out my instructions, and I landed back in London on the early morning of Armistice Day, 11 November 1918.

Chapter XXX

A few days after my arrival in London I was summoned to the secret service headquarters for an interview with The Chief. His offices were at the top of a London building overlooking the Thames; the various rooms, corridors, entrances and exits were so like a rabbit warren that it was some time before I really knew the geography of the place. Before being admitted to The Chief I was shown into Colonel Freddie Browning's room. Colonel Browning was one of the largest-hearted and most generous men I have ever met, and a director of many companies including the Savoy Hotel. His loss was keenly felt by many of his friends when he died some years ago, and to the under-dog of London a friend in need had untimely passed on. I had not the least idea that Colonel Browning, an old acquaintance of mine, was in the secret service, and our meeting was a most happy one.

A few minutes later he took me upstairs, through bewildering passages, into the presence of The Chief. The Chief, a short, white-haired, square man, with penetrating eyes and lips which looked stern, but could in a second take on a humorous curve, was in naval uniform.

He was sitting at a desk on which were three or four telephones. Other telephones were attached to automatic brackets on the wall. For half a minute he leisurely surveyed me and I have never been so thoroughly looked over before or since in my life.

Then he came forward, shook me by the hand and asked me to make a verbal report on my last work.

It was curious to think that I had come into the secret service by chance and not by design, that, until that morning, although I had worked for the last year on nothing but secret service work, I did not know The Chief or have any official existence in his department. I think one of the most pleasing recollections of that meeting was The Chief's approval and unqualified admiration and praise for the work I had done. At the end of the interview I asked for leave and was given a month in order to have a good rest.

Alas, less than a week had passed before I was summoned to his office once again. In the meantime I had met Reilly, who had safely returned from Russia and I was not surprised, when I reported, to see him in the room. Certain important information about the Black Sea coast and South Russia was wanted for the Peace Conference which was to assemble in Paris at the end of the year, and I was asked to volunteer to go with Reilly to obtain it. We had to leave London that afternoon, but as the war was over I was not very anxious to continue in the secret service. I should have preferred to go back to the Royal Air Force, and I hesitated before replying. The Chief, who saw my hesitation, was most kindly and sympathetic and discussed the matter with me much more like a friend than a senior officer. It was this kindness and understanding on his part that finally decided me to go.

In the two short hours that were left before the Southampton train was due to depart I had a great deal to do, farewells, packing, putting off appointments, cancelling the longed-for holiday. Reilly was exceedingly keen on the trip and simply could not bear the leisurely way in which I left the building with him. We were to dash via Paris to Marseilles, whence a cruiser would take us to Athens. There we were to pick up a Greek destroyer in command of a British naval officer who was a member of The Chief's organisation seconded to the Greek Navy, and be whisked into the Black Sea as two English merchants. If we missed our train we should miss the whole connection and, most important of all, the Greek destroyer.

'Hill,' said Reilly, 'I don't believe you want to catch that train. I bet you fifty pounds you won't be on it.'

'My dear fellow, it would be betting on a certainty. I wouldn't dream of taking you on,' was my reply.

'I still make my bet.'

'Nonsense,' said I.

We were now being driven in a taxi-cab along the Strand to the Savoy. Reilly became insistent, and at last I said, 'Damn you, I will take your bet.'

The next hour was one of ordered pandemonium in my room. I must confess that it was touch and go. Various friends helped me rush my bags down to the hall as we could not wait for the porters to fetch them. I offered the taxi-driver a small fortune to get me to Waterloo Station in record time, and arrived on the platform just as the guard was about to signal the train out.

'Wait a second,' I said, dropping half a crown into the palm of his hand. 'I have to reach a first-class compartment reserved for me by the Foreign Office.'

Halfway up the train I saw Reilly hanging out of the window.

'That's my compartment,' I said, indicating him to the porter, who rushed off to put my bags aboard. I followed at a leisurely pace to be greeted by Reilly with, 'You devil, you have done this purposely!' Anyway, I had won my bet and Reilly paid up like the sportsman he was.

When we disembarked at Southampton a very queer tall figure went aboard in front of us. He had the oddest long sandy plaid coat which looked like a converted blanket. From under his hat a mass of long yellow hair straggled down over his collar and almost reached his shoulders. He was such a comical figure that I laughed aloud.

'Just look at the creature,' I said to Reilly.

'Why, that is Paderewski,' was Reilly's reply; and then I, too, recognised the famous musician.

The boat was overcrowded. We had left at such short notice that it had been impossible for The Chief's organisation to reserve us a cabin. However, Reilly, who knew Paderewski, was certain that he had a cabin and went along to see him. Presently he came back, his eyes dancing with excitement. Paderewski had a cabin and would put us up if we cared to sleep on his sofa, but, most important of all, Paderewski the musician was on his way to Warsaw to be the first post-war Prime Minister of Poland.

This fact was as yet known to only a very few, and the three of us sat up most of that night discussing European politics and the menace of Bolshevism not only to Poland, but to all the civilised world. We did not reach Paris until the following evening and before catching the Marseilles train at the Gare de Lyon we dined at La Rue in the Boulevard de la Madeleine.

We had chosen the restaurant because we had both known

the proprietor when he was the most famous chef in St Petersburg, some years before the war. We had a great welcome and a great dinner, with marvellous wine and the oldest of brandies served as brandy should be served, in deep crystal goblets. This dinner sustained us through a most uncomfortable night when we were packed like sardines in a first-class carriage with people sitting on the floor and along the entire length of the corridor outside the coupés.

We picked up our connection and, in spite of a terribly rough passage from Athens to the Black Sea, were made very comfortable by the English commander who sailed a Greek destroyer as if it were a British man-of-war.

We called in at every port along the Asiatic coast of the Black Sea, then up into the Russian ports and finally to Galatz, the Rumanian port at the mouth of the Danube. We went everywhere as two British merchants. It did not seem strange to people that we were travelling on a Greek destroyer, for they often carry traders. In three weeks we had collected the information for which we had been sent and were able to make our report before the Peace Conference opened.

Thereafter, for the next two or three years I was constantly employed on various political or secret service missions.

In the early part of 1920, just before Odessa was finally captured by the Bolsheviks from the White Russians, I was British Political Officer and representative of Sir Halford McKinder, the High Commissioner of South Russia at Novorosisk.

At the head of the White Russian Intelligence organisation at Odessa was a certain renegade colonel whom, for his family's sake, we will call Colonel R. For a long time he had been under suspicion, and at last proof had been obtained that he was betraying his trust and selling information about the White Russians' plans to the Bolsheviks. For various reasons, mainly political, it was impossible for the Russian Command to remove him openly from his post.

One day, my secretary ushered four men into my room at the Hotel London. They were Cossack officers, dressed in long Caucasian sheepskin capes which came down to their ankles. I asked them their business. My astonishment may be imagined when they asked me to supply them with dynamite.

'What on earth do you want with dynamite?'

'To kill Colonel R.,' replied the leader. 'We intend to mine the road on the way to his office and when he passes over it to blow him up. That is what the dog deserves.'

I rose from my chair in great wrath and let them have the full benefit of my anger. First of all I told them it was not the custom of British political officers to lend themselves to assassination; secondly that if they wanted dynamite they could get it from their own people; and thirdly that they would probably kill a dozen innocent people and not harm Colonel R., and that if that was the best method they could think of, then I was sorry for the brains of the White Russians.

Rather ashamed of themselves they said that they would think of some other plan and left me.

The plan they finally adopted was a clever one. The Governor-General of the town, General Shilling, was holding a reception at the palace at nine o'clock one evening. The palace was reached by a long circular drive. There was one gate for sledges entering and another for those leaving.

As the guests began to arrive a detachment of ten Cossacks took up their position a few yards away from the entrance gate.

Every sledge that drove up to the palace was stopped by a red light and the occupants were asked their names and had to produce their documents. I myself was stopped in this manner and as soon as I showed my papers was allowed to proceed to the palace.

Then came the sledge in which was Colonel R.

'Who are you, please?' demanded the examining Cossack.

'Colonel R. Head of the Second Section of the General Staff.'

'Your documents, please.' Colonel R. produced them. 'Yes, this is our bird,' said the Cossack officer stepping back. 'Fire!' and the detachment riddled Colonel R. with bullets.

A few weeks later I was back in Constantinople, for Odessa had been evacuated by the Whites and captured by the Bolsheviks. I was soon to discover that language is no bar to a trained secret service agent. The Allies particularly wanted to know what the Greeks were doing in Thrace and whether it was true that they had designs on Constantinople, and I, who hardly knew a word of Greek or Turkish, was asked to investigate the situation.

To start with I went to Athens, then to Salonica, and then through every town and village of Thrace. Everywhere I went I found the clearest of proofs that it was the intention of the Greeks to try and occupy Constantinople. Time and again I warned Greek politicians, officers and bankers that if they did so it would be fatal. My warnings fell on deaf ears.

I knew that Adrianople was the centre where the plans were being made. Moreover, I wanted to know which of the forts of that city the Greeks had reconditioned. It would be natural enough for them to concentrate their attention on the western forts, for that would be a protective action against the Bulgarians – whose frontier was only a matter of a dozen miles away. On the other hand, if they were reconditioning the eastern forts it would point to the fact that they were arming against a possible retreat should their advance on Constantinople meet with a reverse.

My task was difficult. I had to reckon with three factions. Adrianople was practically a Turkish town, and 70 per cent of its population were Turks, from whom I might reasonably expect information. But the Turks were cowed. The Greeks themselves were not a united camp. There were the Royalists and the Venizelists. The Royalists were in power and the Venizelists hated them more than they did the Turks. It was their mutual suspicions and animosities that made my task supremely difficult.

By the time I had reached Adrianople I was very much suspected by the Greek General Staff, and the Commandant of the town – who rather fancied himself as a sleuth – was put on to watch me.

I was living at the only European hotel. It was kept by a woman who had the blood of pretty well every nationality in Europe in her; but German blood for cleanliness and Greek blood for driving a hard bargain were uppermost, and her hostel was habitable.

Every day when I went out my room was subjected to a systematic search by the Commandant. This I knew after my first morning. It is simply a matter of habit and training to arrange one's room and effects in such a way that after the room has once been cleaned by the maid in the morning one instantly knows if anything has been touched.

My room, when I returned, always looked to my trained eye as if the whole place had been spring-cleaned – including my bed, writing-table and clothes. The sleuth even went so far as to slip a knife into the soles of my shoes; and forgot to sew them up again. Papers were replaced in their wrong order, and my mattress was always turned. As for my trunk, which I always made a habit of leaving open, it was thoroughly searched every day.

The only place the Commandant did not search was the nickel bar hinged on the trunk. This bar was a hollow tube which was pulled out whenever one wished to get at the suits hanging on the clothes hangers. It was in this bar that I put any papers that were important and of a nature that I could not memorise.

I arranged to be given the plans of the forts at a Dervish meeting which I was attending the day before I left Adrianople. The sect I was going to visit were Whirling Dervishes, who had their own mosque at the far end of the town. It was quite the usual thing for a foreigner visiting Adrianople to be invited by the Mullah to visit their service, and as a rule there were quite a number of visitors; moreover I knew that Greek officers were always present, and that it would be safest to receive the fort plans under their very noses.

That morning I went into the French bank where all my letters were addressed. The manager of the bank was a Frenchman whose wife was English. He was very pro-English and one of the best-informed men I met in the Near East, and it was not until years later that I knew that he was a French secret service agent. In my mail I found very distressing news. Someone very dear to me in England had had a serious operation which might easily prove fatal. The crisis, however, so the letter told me, would not be reached for ten days, and the letter had been posted ten days before. Before I left the bank I received a telegram which told me that there was practically no hope. I felt absolutely crushed. My private grief came up and choked me and almost put all thought of work out of my mind.

But I was powerless to do anything. I was six days from England, and the only thing for me was to go and get the plans.

The Mullah of the sect received me, and we went into a mosque where devotions were in progress. Then we walked across to a large stone building not unlike the interior of a mosque except that it had a very fine polished wooden floor which was railed off by a low railing.

Guests to the number of about twenty were seated on wooden platforms covered with piles of precious Persian carpets. Behind this rostrum, along the wall, were windows latticed in wood through which the Turkish women and ladies of the harem watched the ceremony, for the women of Turkey were then still veiled and secluded from the eye of any male but their husbands.

The rite began. About twenty male dancers of all ages and shapes, dressed in long flowing robes, barefooted and befezed, entered in single file. When their leader reached the Mullah he bowed low before him and then moved off, slowly gyrating in a circle at a speed rather like that of a top at the end of its spin. One by one the dancers who followed him did the same thing, and within a few minutes twenty men were whirling round and round the room in their own orbit, each keeping an equal distance from his neighbour and the whole of them moving round in an oval formation. And round and round they went until my eyes became dizzy; until all consciousness had faded from their faces and they were like lifeless bodies obeying some unknown law which kept them spinning round and round without any reason known to the human mind. The air became heavy with the sweat of bodies, and beads of perspiration trickled off the dancers' feet until the entire floor was slippery with human dampness. Sometimes the whirlers increased their pace and their gowns whirled round above their waists. Some of them spun with their hands above their heads and at times their bodies seemed to be almost parallel with the floor.

I forgot the purpose for which I had come to the meeting. Half of my brain was hypnotised by the dance and the other half was going through agony at the thought of the person in England whom I would see no more. I was living in a mad, senseless, cruel world – watching an unnatural phenomenon of unearthly creatures – and I wondered whether the person I was thinking of was perhaps even then passing through unknown worlds and experiencing strange, frightening things as I was doing.

Some of the dancers had commenced to froth at the mouth. Suddenly one of them collapsed and lay inert upon the floor, but the rest of the dancers whirled round the body and never touched it. This went on for over an hour until there were not more than a dozen dancers left dancing. Then suddenly they stopped and formed single file and, passing before the Mullah, bowed low and walked out of the building. On the floor remained the eight insensible forms. The ghastly performance was over.

In another room coffee was served to the guests. The man I was expecting came up to me. As we shook hands he slipped a tightly rolled paper about a foot long and the thickness of a pencil up my sleeve between my shirt and my arm. They were the latest plans of the forts of Adrianople.

No one had seen the transaction. I walked back into the town with the Greek officers and took my leave. The plans joined the other papers in my hiding-place in the trunk. That night I had my evening meal in my room, and on the following morning I took the Orient Express to Constantinople.

Chapter XXXI

I can look back now on my perilous time of espionage and, collating my experiences with those of men whom I am proud to call my friends, compare our service with the services of foreign countries.

In pre-war days Russia was supposed to have the finest secret service and undoubtedly for a time she had, but her organisation did not stand the test of a world war and a revolution.

Germany spent huge sums before the war on her espionage department, and yet when I read the memoirs of her foremost secret service organisers I come to the conclusion that they used spies in the mass and not men picked for their quality. From this generalisation I particularly want to exclude Karl Lody, who would not cringe for mercy, and, early one autumn morning in 1915, was shot in the Tower of London. He met his end like a man.

The best method seems to have been that used by the British, who selected men of a resourceful kind and allowed them to work out for themselves the methods by which they found they could best achieve their individual tasks.

I endeavoured to follow the same principle in selecting my own agents, and while I always tried to keep them separate from each other, at the same time I endeavoured to give them a corporate sense that they were working for a definite end. I never tried to bribe them; I paid them in order that they might have the means to live in comparative comfort, and most of them worked for the joy of the task or for love of their country. I do not think I ever callously sent a man into danger, and certainly not without that man knowing exactly into what danger he was going.

Secret inks, tiny cameras the size of half a crown and not much thicker, photographs reduced so that their films can be concealed in a cigarette, coding messages on linen, concealing them in bread, soap, or the soles of boots, secret wireless stations, the payment of huge rewards are all useless unless one has the essentials – will, wit and determination to carry out the task which is set.

A man like Sir Paul Dukes is one of the finest examples of those whom The Chief selected. His book – *Red Dusk and the Morrow* – gives just a peep into the life he led in Russia for two years – during which time he served both in the Cheka and the Red Army – yet managed to keep London informed of what was going on in Soviet Russia.

Then there is Sidney Reilly, who, when he left the secret service after the war, continued to fight Bolshevism with his own private fortune. With the tenacity of a bulldog he went after his quarry and finally lost his life in the cause he had espoused.

I mention Sir Paul Dukes and Sidney Reilly because their stories are known, but there are a score of other names in this silent service to which I once belonged, who could tell of tasks done and obstacles overcome which would read like fairy stories and yet contain not a syllable of exaggeration.

The secret services of all countries are functioning more

actively today than they have ever done before in the history of the world. The Bolsheviks, together with the Third International, have built up a new powerful secret service organisation which employs an entirely new technique, which plays a prominent part in international intrigues, and which calls for the most brilliant counter-espionage work on the part of the countries they attack.

While armaments exist, secret service funds will be available no matter what the economic position of a country, and recruits will be easily found among men and women who will risk their lives for the need of money, for adventure, and in time of national danger for the love of their country.

Appendix

Report to the War Office from the National Archives

From:-

Captain G. A. Hill,   London
    4th Manch. Regt., & RAF   Nov. 26th, 1918

To:-

DMI
    War Office,
        London.

Sir,

I have the honour to enclose herewith a report showing work done for DMI from February 24th until October 2nd 1918.

DMI work directly reported on is on page, 7, 8, 10, 12 to 26.

    I have the honour to be,

        Sir,

        Your obedient servant,

        (Sgd.) George Alfred Hill, Capt.

        4th Manch. & RAF.

Copies to Lt-Gen S. C. Poole, CB, CMG, DSO.
Lt-Col. Thornhill, DSO.
R. H. B. Lockhart, Esq.
MI1c

Report of Work Done in Russia to End of 1917

September 1917
28th Reported to Lt-Col. Maund RFC and worked under him in Moscow for some weeks.

October 1917
Was ordered by Lt-Col. Maund RFC to Stavka at the summons of General Barter to attend the Russian Aviation conference to which the French specialists were also invited. This conference sat for about five weeks and was composed of officers from every aviation and artillery branch of the armies of the field, and its technical problem was to introduce western methods into its very badly organised services. Underlying this conference, which was attended by Kerensky, was a strong political movement, which however, came to nothing.

November 1917
End of November, I returned to Moscow under Lt-Col. Maund RFC.

December 1917
Early December, I was lent by General Poole to Lt-Col. J. W. Boyle of the Canadian service.

At this time, Colonel Boyle had been working for some weeks with the Soviet government that had just come into power. Previously under the provisional government he was employed in the Russian General Staff on railroad construction and organisation of traffic. The work consisted in clearing the congestion caused by internal affairs (October Revolution) at the Moscow knot.

By virtue of this congestion, the South Western and Western Armies were cut off from their supplies, and starvation was felt causing mass desertion, which was further blocking the sorely tried traffic. With Colonel Boyle on this work was Major du Castelle of the French Army, and some Americans.

The knot was successfully cleared and supplies were got through to the starving armies.

Middle December
In connection with the Russian Roumanian Protocol, Colonel Boyle left for Jasi, taking with the Roumanian Foreign Office archives, which had been deposited in the Kremlin during the evacuation of Roumania in 1916, the Roumanian Crown Jewels, and some millions of Lei for the Treasury. Permission to transport these had to be wrung from the Bolshevik, and the task was by no means then accomplished as our route lay directly through the armed and fighting parties of the white and Bolshevik Guards of south Russia.

Situation in Roumania

The Roumanian government, faced by starvation that was being accentuated by the non-fulfilment of the Russo-Roumanian Protocol on the part of the Russians, was being pressed by the Germans to follow the lead of the Soviet government in signing the Armistice. Internally, while still feeding their army and civil population with great difficulty, they were able to maintain an excellent discipline. Their ally, however, the Russians, were causing every kind of trouble, and had just taken to demobilising themselves. In doing so they disorganised the railroads, used up reserve supply rations, and finally, when retreating by road, pillaged, and plundered, to say nothing of often destroying villages they passed through on their way. The Roumanian government at once took measures to protect their people from the Russian marauders, being ably assisted in doing this by the loyal troops of General Tcherbatchoff.

In restoring order very much friction arose between the Roumanian officials and Russians with Bolshevik leanings, and on a number of occasions fighting took place. This fighting caused trouble on the railways, especially at those points where the Russian removing gangs met, and the transference of stores was held up, causing a shortage of stores in the front. Added to this the Bolshevik had agents on all stations deliberately spending their efforts on sabotage. The first effort therefore was to get improved conditions on the railroads. Accompanied by Russian and Roumanian transport officers, the Sokola Kischinev and other knots were visited. All local disputes were settled on the spot, and friction allayed between the Russian and Roumanian knot controllers. In places where much labour was needed, and wholesale desertion had taken place from the railroad battalions, Roumanian labour companies supplemented by Austrian prisoners were sent to fill up the gaps and thus a great improvement followed. The 4th Russian Army (General Andreanoff?) had been giving much trouble, and at the direct request of General Tcherbatchoff it was visited. For some time past this Army had been under the full control of its Committee, which was Bolshevik. They had been deliberately starving the Army with a view to producing revolution and had brought their horse transport to a standstill, owing to cutting off the fodder. This sabotage was easily stopped. We had half the Army horses shot, and the meat frozen, and the civil and military population rationed on it. The hides were used at once, while the remaining horses were quickly got into a fit condition, owing to their [*sic*] being sufficient fodder.

Communications

The construction on the Binderi–Unghany, Bielzi–Unghany and Bessarabakoj lines, had practically ceased owing to constant labour trouble. As the rationing of these gangs was a great difficulty, and the funds for payment had run dry, it was decided to completely shut down construction.

End of December 1917

The political situation between the Soviet and Roumania was becoming more critical every day. The Bolsheviks, with Dr Rakovski (the Roumanian) (Bulgarian?) (socialist) at their head, were financing and running a strong agitation against the government and with their large mass of more or less uncontrolled Russians, were putting a very strong lever on the Roumanian Army. The Soviet wanted to force an issue quickly with Roumania, as they greatly feared an arrangement with Ukrainia, who was throwing off the Soviet yoke.

M. Bratiano, the Roumanian Prime Minister, wishing to avoid trouble with the Soviet, requested Colonel Boyle, in the name of the Roumanian government, to visit Petrograd and explain Roumania's position to Trotsky, and her great desire to avoid all friction and misunderstanding. M. Bratiano, in his message, enumerated the following four points:-

1) That they could not and would not allow the Russian troops to leave their positions on the front, march through Roumania armed and pillage as they had done. All Russian troops would be allowed to leave Roumania as soon as transport was available for systematic evacuation. They would leave their arms behind which would be returned as soon as transport could be arranged.

2) The Roumanian government had not arrested any of the Soviet delegates or Committees, and any arrests of Russian subjects had been carried out by the order of General Tcherbatchoff.

3) They could not, however, in future, allow any agitation against themselves to pass without taking steps to check it.

4) That it was imperative for Roumania to negotiate with Ukrainia, as geographically, the former depended for supplies upon the latter.

January 1918

On the 1st January Colonel Boyle and staff left for Petrograd via Kieff. While in Roumania Colonel Boyle was in close touch with the Allied Diplomatic Corps and conferred, before leaving, with General Ballard of the British Mission and General Berthelot of the French Mission. On our journey North the condition of the southern railheads was beyond description. The civil war that had raged in the Donnets Basin had stopped the export of coal supplies, the meagre stores were fast being used up, and the disorderly evacuation of the Armies from the south-western fronts had brought the traffic to a standstill.

On arrival in Petrograd Colonel Boyle saw the Diplomatic Corps, who informed him that their colleague M. Diamandi, the Roumanian Ambassador, had that day been arrested and thrown into the fortress of St Peter and St Paul, with all his staff.

As a result of a strong protest on the part of the Diplomatic Corps M. Diamandi and his staff were set free on the day following the outrage. On the Ministers [*sic*] release, Colonel Boyle went to deliver M. Bratiano's message to the Soviet Foreign Office. This, however, was too late, as their policy was to make war on Roumania at any price, and M. Zalkind, the then acting Minister for Foreign Affairs, made no disguise of their plans. 'Starve Roumania into revolution' was the motto.

A few days later a plot was hatched to murder M. Diamandi with one or two members of the Constitutional assembly. This we heard from an Agent, and M. Diamandi was warned. It is interesting to note that Messers Chingareff and Kokoshin were murdered the day after in the hospital they were in.

Shortly afterwards war was declared on Roumania by the Soviet government.

A new staff was formed to take charge of the Roumanian front, at the head of which was placed Dr Rakowski. He had for his Chief of Staff a Colonel Muravieff (SR) and M. Spiro (SR) with a Doctor Bronshavon. This staff left at once for the south.

Political Situation at end of January 1918

Everything was extremely critical for the Bolsheviks, and they were daily becoming more unpopular.

Starvation and anarchy reigned in the Capital and the extremely unpopular negotiations of the Brest-Litovsk meeting were in progress. Added to this came a new war with Roumania.

With a view to relieving Roumania from her isolated position, Colonel Boyle determined to go down and effect a peace between the Roumanian and Soviet governments.

Permission for Allied Couriers to go south had been withheld for some time, and heavy bags had accumulated at all the Embassies. A direct offer to go as mediator between Russia and Roumania would certainly not have met with any success, and would have caused suspicion. However, knowing the great chaos that was reigning in the Donnets Basin, Colonel Boyle offered his services to Nevski, Commissar of Ways of Communication, to go down to do what he could. This offer was not only gladly accepted, but Podvoiski and the Food Controller gave us carte blanche for all work we undertook in the Donnets Basin.

Leaving Petrograd with the Jassey and the Odessa bags, and two officers being sent to the Caucasus by General Poole (Lts Nash and Crutchley), we took to the Moscow–Kursk–Harkoff route. Our journey was delayed some time, as our train ran into a railroad smash, and much damage was done to our car.

Kharkoff was the Headquarters of the Bolshevik Army, operating against Korniloff and Kaledin. The Commander in Chief was a powerful revolutionary named Antonoff.

Heavy fighting was still going on south of Kharkoff and the whole district was in disorder. Antonoff proved friendly and passed and executed Colonel Boyle's suggestions. At our recommendation he also had many of the old traffic experts reinstated and Superintendants [sic] and railroad managers given a freer hand in technical matters, and freed them from their ever-suspicious, insolent and very ignorant Committees. In twelve days the food supplies going to the northern and western fronts, and the cities of Petrograd and Moscow were increased by 47%.

Measures were also passed which dealt with the movements of troops, and these measures to a certain extent relieved the railroads.

From Antonoff we heard that part of the Supreme Council for the anti-Roumanian campaign was in Sebastopol, and that trouble was expected there, as recruiting among the sailors for the Roumanian front was unpopular. Antonoff had been more or less convinced by Colonel Boyle of the mistaken policy of the Soviet leaders in declaring war on Roumania.

This, and the great need for crude oils for railroads and Mechanical Transport (rumours of vast quantities purported to be stored at Sevastopol), finally induced him to give us permission to go to Sevastopol.

Sevastopol

Owing to German circulated news that 79 British pennants had forced the Dardanelles and a Squadron was on its way to smash up the Bolshevik fleet, we were extremely badly received on our arrival at Sevastopol. Agitation was rife to murder the British party. Unpleasantness everywhere we went. The Black Sea Congress was sitting, and after a lot of trouble, our party and Captain Le Page RN (who was stationed here) managed to get in touch with the leaders.

It did not take us long to allay their suspicions and win over their goodwill, and then to run the anti-intervention Roumanian propaganda. Recruiting was stopped in the Black Sea fleet. M. Spiro (Internationalist and SR) requested us to go and see Dr Rakovski at Odessa, and to do what was possible to stop the Roumanian war. Rumour already had it (early February) that the Germans were advancing in the North, and Spiro with a few others who feared the Germans, were keen to turn their Southern force, with the Roumanian Army, against the invader.

Before leaving Sevastopol it was arranged that Lts Nash and Crutchley should leave in a special transport for Batum.

Odessa

The Supreme Council consisted of Dr Rakovski (the leader), Colonel Murovioff, Commander of the operating armies, and Messers Spiro, Bronchevan and Workman's and Soldiers Council. This Council's motto seemed to be to down Roumania at any price, and therefore force her into the hands of Germany. On arrival at Odessa, Colonel Boyle called a Conference of the allied officers French – Colonel Arquier and staff; American – the Consul General; British – Captain Pitts, General Service, the British Consul Mr Lowden. This Conference opened negotiations with the Supreme Council, with a view to their sending a note, the foundation of which might be the basis of a peace between Russia and Roumania.

After five days' discussion, the Supreme Council, thoroughly discouraged by lack of recruits and general unpopularity of their war, sent a reasonable Note to Roumania, and transferred their attention to their new enemy, the Germans marching on Kieff. Their Note was carried by aeroplane and car to Jassey and except for a few alterations was accepted by the Roumanian government.

Colonel Boyle was flown back to Odessa and the Treaty was signed by the Council, then in great fear of the German advance.

Colonel Boyle returned to Jassey to make final preparations for the carrying out of the Treaty and the exchange of prisoners.

My orders from Colonel Boyle were to take charge of his train, staff and baggage, and that I was to carry on to the best of my judgment. I was also to evacuate north and eastwards on [*sic*] the event of the Germans coming to Odessa.

End of February
I waited at Odessa as long as I could, and then moved on to Nicolaievsk and Kherson to evade the rush of Germans. I took two of MIic people with me from Odessa as they had orders to leave there.

At Nicolaievsk the Mission joined up with Colonel Muravieff (the Bolshevik leader) and fostered his desire to offend Germany. During the first week in March his army did make a stand, but was hopelessly outnumbered in guns and men, and his rabble came back in great disorder.

However a fair amount of destruction was indulged in and one or two small bridges destroyed.

At Kherson and Nicolaievsk the British Consuls were most active and seemed to realise the importance of agitating the destruction of military material; Hon. Vice Consul — of Nicolaievsk and Hon. Vice Consul Curouana of Kherson.

It is interesting to note that the Red Guards did take a few prisoners, but killed them all, stole their clothes before interrogating them so that their staff had no idea what troops were against them. We got orders issued that all prisoners should be brought to Headquarters, but after that prisoners were not taken.

Travelled with Muravieff to join Antonoff, at Kharkoff who were getting ready to put up a defence of the Donnetz Basin. Antonoff's forces were a hopeless proposition, as half of them had turned from Bolshevik to Anarchist and were in favour of allowing their 'German brothers' to come and take what they wanted as there was enough for everyone!

M. Spiro had in the meantime elected himself Commissar of the Black Sea Fleet, and Dictator (or Minister) of the new Taurida Republic, and were [*sic*] feverishly organising sailors into a fighting unit for use against the Germans. M. Spiro formed the backbone of the Muravieff–Antonoff Army, and it was hoped that something might be done, if not in checking the German advance, then in the destruction of material – an art in which the Red Guards excel.

Mr Blakey, the British Consul at Kharkoff, and his assistant Mr Gillespie (now MIIc) were working hard and introduced me to some of the prominent French miners, with a view to arranging destruction of property and mines.

I also got into contact with the District Mine Owners Union and with one of their representatives, Engineer X, of the Donnetz District Miners Federation, arranged the destruction and sabotage of certain mines.

Arranged for the clear passage of five echelons of Allied Military Missions evacuating from Roumania.

Middle of March

Hearing that the 4th All-Russian Assembly of Soviets was about to meet in Moscow, to vote on the Brest-Litovsk Peace Treaty, I decided to leave with my Mission in order to attend same, and arrived on the eve of the opening of the Congress.

On arrival at Moscow I found that our Aviation Mission had already left with the Embassy Staff and Petrograd Military Mission and MIIc officers. A few went to Vologda and Archangel, the others returned to England.

I then got into touch with M. Fritcher, Commissar of Foreign Affairs, and M. Muraloff, the Bolshevik Commander of the Moscow Area, and from them I obtained permits to attend the Congress.

Before attending the Assembly I called on the Consul General M. Wardrop, who concurred that it was advisable to attend the Congress, and he introduced me to Lt Reid (MIIc) who had decided to remain behind and was also attending the Congress. This Conference which opened on the 14th March lasted five days, and the Assembly after very stormy sittings ratified the Brest-Litovsk Peace Treaty.

Mr Lockhart and his Mission arrived about the 20th of March.

At the conclusion of the Assembly I got into close touch with Mr Lockhart, Colonel Robbins, of the American Red Cross, the American and French Military Missions. Also with the following Soviet Departments:-

War:- M. Trotsky (new Minister of War), M. M. Muraloff, Podvoisky, Analoff, and their respective Military Staffs;

Foreign Affairs:- Messers Tchetcherin, Karakhan, and Rodak (for Central Empires), and later M. Voznisneski (for Eastern Affairs), and M. Vorovski (now Ambassador at Stockholm), and a large number of their Secretaries.

Evacuation:- M. Mechonoshin and others;

Trade & Commerce:- M. Bronsky and members of the Central Executive
    Committee.

I also kept in touch with the Railroad Controllers and Technical
Institutions.

End of March

The Austro-German advance into South Russia and Ukrainia seemed complete;
Kieff, Odessa, Kherson and Nicolaievsk had fallen, and the road to Roumania
was cut off. Despite the difficulties of communication I had kept more or less
in touch with Colonel Boyle, though it would naturally be a long time before
he could return to the north, so I telegraphed to General Poole and to the War
Office for permission to carry on the work in hand in Russia as long as possible.

General Poole gave me permission to stay in Russia and instructed me
that, until his return, I would be under Captain McAlpine, then in Archangel,
who would shortly be coming to Moscow.

After conversations with Mr Lockhart and Colonel Robbins, of the
American Red Cross, I gathered that it was just possible that the Allies would
recognise the Soviet government. I therefore decided that my Mission would
make its policy to be a special study of all secondary Bolshevik leaders, and to
those who would very likely incline naturally towards Great Britain.

April

The general situation was, however, so uncertain, and enemy agents were so
active, that drastic action in evacuation matters was imperative.

Lt Pinder, of the British supply Mission to Russia, was working on a
commercial scheme of evacuation in conjunction with French and British
interests, which were preventing the buying up of certain materials by the
agents of the 'Alliance'.

At that time the Bolsheviks were evacuating some of their towns and
stations to the west of Moscow, without any order or judgment, but with such
activity that they blocked the lines, not only to the west, but also to the east
of Moscow, with the rubbish they were saving.

It therefore seemed that a great deal of material in the Moscow Aviation parks
might be saved if only the government could be made to start and prevented from
blocking the lines by carting away old limbers and wooden furniture.

The chief difficulties in front of the Evacuation Committees were:-

1) Lack of order and direction
2) Lack of fuel and transport.
3) Lack of organisation between the Evacuation Committees and the rail-
    road controllers.

To facilitate our effect on evacuation I got into very close touch with Trotsky and was appointed by him as 'Inspector of Aviation' and given extensive powers in that Department. This brought me into close touch with the Aviation personnel, and gave me an entrée into Aviation Parks and Evacuation Committees.

Identifications (DMI)

This work commenced during the last days of March and developed during April.

Propaganda

Towards the end of April propaganda was started.

End of April

I got into touch with Captain McAlpine and [was] instructed to carry on.

May

1) Evacuation continued with great difficulty.
2) Identification (DMI) continued. Amalgamated with MIIc Department for Identifications and they sent their material to DMI.
3) Aviation. Much work among Corps who were getting restless.
4) Instructed during the month to look into motor and other trades, by Captain McAlpine, this was done.
5) Propaganda.
6) Captain McAlpine visited Moscow.

June

1) Evacuation continued.
2) Identifications end of the month sent to MIIc instead of DMI.
3) Aviation General work continued. Request for hydroplanes and personnel. Personnel sent; hydroplanes unobtainable.
4) Got into touch with Tcheko-Slovaks and sent messages to them.
5) Russian invention section organised, and worked in conjunction with Propaganda.
6) Recruiting started.

July

1) Evacuation continued, but towards end of the month with very little effect.
2) Identifications continued and linked up with the south and Tcheko-Slovak fronts.
3) Aviation Sabotage and judicious evacuation fostered.

4) Systematic Recruiting started.
5) Courier service started.
6) Station control in Moscow organised.
7) Attended Congress of All-Russian Assembly of Soviets.
8) Preparations for remaining behind.
9) Passports, etc.

August

1) Evacuation. Wound up early part of work.
2) Identifications. Official channels closed, opened my own.
3) Aviation Sabotage.
4) Recruiting discontinued.
5) DMI and MIıc work.

September

DMI and MIıc work.

October

Left Moscow 2nd October 1918.

Evacuation

By the beginning of April good progress had been made and the first truck-loads of metal were shipped east.

Our work consisted in:-

1) Showing the Evacuation Committee what material should be evacuated first; and to get them to pass stringent rules against unnecessary evacuation.
2) Allaying the friction arising between the Evacuation Committees and the transport controllers. Cases were constantly arising where the sectional engineers, in their efforts to sabotage, refused cars despite Bolshevik Evacuation Committees. In all this sort of strife the Mission stepped in and took over control as a neutral.
3) Constantly keeping all hands up to their work.

During April we also took over the sorting of material coming from Smolensk, and west of there, as this was blocking our lines.

All material from Moscow went east, and the following places were selected from the main dumps:- Kotelnitch, Viatka, Nishni-Novogorod, Kazan, Sarapol and Penza.

It was decided that there should be a rush, the new line, Kazan–Sarapol, would be filled with rolling stock, and lines destroyed west of Kazan.

‡

During April. Flax transport was taken up, but later this was turned back to the Commercial Agent of NBM Consulate at Moscow.

‡

Escaped Prisoners of War
During May, July and August three British prisoners escaped from German hands into Russia, and were taken charge of and forwarded on to England.

‡

The Aviation people were persuaded to send a small group of men to Kharkoff, and nearly all the aviation material was saved or destroyed here before the Germans took possession. The first Japanese descent at Vladivostok, however, brought all our work to a standstill and evacuation to the east was forbidden. Later this was counteracted by the arrival of Count Mirbach (of Germany) and the German occupation of Finland, and our work was recommenced.

The month of May opened disastrously, as what with Socialist Day, and the three days holiday that followed it, Church holidays and a small strike, very little was got away until the middle of the month. June evacuation opened under the dampening effect of the Tcheko-Slovak affair, but proved to be the best month for material evacuated. Besides metal, a great deal was done to move out aviation units from Moscow and get them well scattered over the country, north-east and south-east of Moscow.

July
Much sabotage done by Bolshevik Committees and agents and also by German agents, and little material was got away, although many aviation units were sent out to the Tcheko-Slovak fronts. As most of the units commanders were of our orientation, and in league with myself, this was very much encouraged, as we hoped to get whole squadrons deserting to the Tcheko-Slovaks.

August
Very little done, but continued to take an interest in squadrons that were being sent to the front. Closed all connection with the various Departments on the 5th August.

The following are the approximate material evacuated:-

- 84,000 poods of Aluminium
- 29,000 poods of Steel
- 10,000 poods of Other metallic materials.
- 62 Fiat 200 h.p. engines,
- And about 22 squadrons, all complete with spares, to the east.

It should be clearly understood that this evacuation was done by the Bolsheviks and their Committees and that apart from entertaining and feasting certain dignitaries of theirs, our part was to bully them and to constantly be on the spot, exhorting, arranging and persuading them into notion [*sic*].

The Mission owes great thanks to Messers Utchenko, Chief of the Railway Department, and their staff, for their constant support and willingness to concur in our suggestions and requirements. Muraloff, the Commander of Moscow, a true hater of Germany, did all he could to aid us until the Tcheko-Slovak affair started in full. Great thanks are also due to many loyal aviation officers, and members of the aerial staffs and Commissar of the Aviation Park.

Aviation

During the whole of the time we were in Moscow very close relations were kept with the Air Forces. This was partly due to the necessity of my working under Trotsky's cover as 'Inspector', and partly that I had good connections with them through Colonel Maund.

It proved very advantageous, and later nearly all my confidential men were from the ranks.

When the recruits were wanted, about 450 were sent to the north; the first party, under Colonel Kazakoff, consisted of six or seven officers. It was also through the Aviation that close relations were maintained with the Cadets and their organisations.

Commercial

In June I received instructions to gain information and details on the Moscow industries. The large motor, aeroplane and electric manufactures were visited, and much general information obtained.

Propaganda

I tried to do publicity and general information work. Sent out war news (when obtainable) to various departments. Kept closely in touch with those of Allied orientations, and spent much spare time with Bolsheviks, all of which meant some sort of entertaining. Considering the very limited material at our disposal fair results were obtained.

Russian Inventions Section

In conjunction with propaganda this section was started in the hope that some useful inventions might be picked up, and to prevent Russians hawking their inventions to the Germans.

Most of these inventions were for 'Anti-Aircraft Fire Control' and sighting systems for same.

Next in order, aeroplanes, new machines, ideas and gadgets.

Then followed hosts of automatic rifles, protector shields etc. of all the things examined nothing of great interest was discovered, and one felt that all exhibits had long been out on the retired list at home.

DMI Work

It was found at the end of March that very little enemy identifications were going to London. This was due to the departure of the British Embassy and Military Mission from Petrograd, and the Mission in the north, owing to the disorganisation caused by the rapid evacuation from Petrograd, were unable to pick up the old threads of information. At the time there were great possibilities of picking up information and having done this work in Salonica, I started a small section for DMI in Moscow:-

1) To start with sent three men to the Russo-German front for direct identifications.
2) Got the Moscow District Military Commander to organise a Bolshevik identifications section, and promised them every assistance from England.

The reason for forming this section was that the MI Section of the Russian General Staff had been completely thrown out of action by the Bolsheviks and although still existing, were practically unable to do any work, owing to the lack of support from the Bolshevik.

After the Bolshevik identification section in Moscow had been fairly established, the Bolsheviks realised at once the importance of the information they were getting, and re-established the MI Section of the General Staff, and then brought them from Petrograd to Moscow so that one received a very good summary every few days.

During the demobilisation of all the Armies and Staffs all the German handbooks were lost, the Russian General Headquarters had one copy dated 1915, and the M. A. of the United States had a copy dated 1916, and although constantly asking for them from London these valuable books never reached us.

From April on, every few days identifications were sent to London, and I was instructed to carry on this work. At the end of the month Lt Boyce MI1c sent Lieutenants Urmston and Small to get in touch with the old General Staff 'I' Section. This at first resulted in the overlapping of our work, as they

sent all information to MI1c London. To prevent this it was agreed between
Lts Boyce and Urmston and myself that we should amalgamate, and thereby
syphering [sic] would become simplified, and the very heavy expense on
duplicate telegrams would be saved. From then on all cables went to DMI.
We pooled our staff and officers, and continued to get good information.

Besides matter coming from the old General Staff 'I' Section, and the
Bolshevik Section Lt Urmston had naval and personal agents, and I had free
lances on the fronts. At the end of June we had some excellent information
through Lt Riley [Reilly]'s channels. In July MI1c insisted that Lt Urmston
(being MI1c) should cable direct to them. I informed London of this, and
asked if they would be willing for my information to go through the same
channel, as if not I would have to increase my staff to cope with the extra
work; it also meant needless telegraphing. DMI agreed to this change, and
from July onwards my information went to MI1c.

Hydroplanes

Early in June I received messages from General Poole asking that hydroplanes
and personnel might be obtained from the Soviet government for the protection of the ports from German submarines. After consulting with Mr Lockhart
it was decided that it would be extremely difficult to obtain anything from
Mr Trotsky (Minister of War), as relations were then very strained owing to
our occupation of Murmansk. The only chance of getting hydroplanes was
to find them, buy them from the owners, and send them by rail or ship them,
through the connivance of one of the Railroad Control Boards. To achieve
this I went to Petrograd, but found that all hydroplanes had been evacuated
from there, and even the schools had left for the Volga district. It therefore
seemed extremely unlikely that we could arrange for transport of the planes,
with any hope of success, from there.

I communicated with General Poole and informed him that I was sending
up Russian personnel who were experienced enough to acquaint themselves
quickly with the British machines.

Recruits

Early in July it had become evident that recruits would be wanted very shortly
for the north, and therefore a new sub-section to deal with this work was formed.

A number of officers of all services were selected and given advances to
enable them to reach the north.

It was realised that all recruiting would have to be on a very limited scale
until we had established a front, but it seemed that once that were done a large
number of recruits could be dispatched.

Experience had shown that Russian organisations (benefiting from our
funds) had entailed great wastage with small results, therefore preparations

were commenced to enable one or two British officers to stay behind 'after hostilities had commenced' in order to organise the recruiting.

The idea of course was to combine identifications with destruction and recruiting. I found MIıc were also making preparations to leave an officer behind (S. T.). However, at a conference with Lt Boyce RNVR (MIıc) and S. T., they pointed out how likely it was the recruiting and organisations would be traced soon after it commenced to function and that this should, despite past experience, be handled by a Russian organisation, but they suggested that the courier service already organised by myself should be developed, and that I should remain behind. Recruiting went on, but it was intended to drop it as soon as we went underground.

Courier Service

About 7th July an order was published prohibiting Allied officers from

1) Leaving the towns they occupied and freedom of movement;
2) Wearing their uniforms;
3) Stoppage of code telegrams, consular or otherwise (about the 12th) to the north.

The Courier Service, already started to meet this eventuality, was put into motion and the first couriers left on the 8th July for the north by two routes:-

1) Moscow–Nishni Novgorod–Viatka–Kotlass
2) By the canal route via Petrograd, Petrosarodsk and the north.

I estimated that 20 to 25 couriers would be sufficient to carry on constant communications with our Army in the north. Results proved that more would be required.

Courier 1 returned after 12 days; he reported a difficult passage north, was twice arrested and searched, He returned by trickery direct from Archangel by train and so cut the journey in half. He said the nervous strain was very great and a good rest would be needed after every journey.

Courier 2 went out on the Petrosavodsk route; he was away 20 days, and had similar experiences to No. 1. His journey was however more expensive, as he had to use horses in certain places.

The service was therefore increased on the 1st of August.

Station Control

As much movement of troops was expected in the Moscow knot, it was decided, in addition to the information got from various sources, to put special agents on all the stations for control.

Destruction Gangs

A small destruction gang was organised in July.

Passes

A small section for obtaining false passports, passes and documents was started in July.

August 1918

At a conference with Lieutenants Boyce and Riley I agreed to stay behind and arrange:-

the Courier Service; take charge of coding; continue to use my own channels of information; run a small destruction gang; continue to keep in touch with the Air Force; and work in with 2nd Lt S. Riley (RAF), who was receiving very excellent information from all possible sources. I considered that Lt Riley knew the situation better than any other British officer in Russia, and as he also had the more delicate threads in his hand, I therefore agreed to co-operate with him, and leave the political control and our policy in his hands.

I had some misgivings about staying on after the Missions left, as I had no instructions from General Poole to do so. However, the obvious necessity for someone to do this coupled with the information I received from Lt Boyce MIic, that he had applied to General Poole through Mr Lindley (our Charge d'Affaires) for my services, determined me to remain.

1st, 2nd and 3rd August

Conferences with Lts Boyce, Webster and Riley and attending to details for remaining behind. I arranged to keep some of my people and to send the rest of the Mission home with Mr Lockhart's Mission.

4th August

We had our 1st conferences for arranging affairs and Lt Riley RAF and myself gave Lt Boyce MIic our plans, the proposed work of organisations and our estimate, approximately, of the amount of money we should require to carry on. Our proposals were accepted and authorised by Lt Boyce MIic.

The following were my centres:-

1) House on Pjatnitzkaia where I lived, stored money, kept papers and documents, coded, directed operations, and where I had my go-between and secretary.
2) Flat on Degtjaranija where the chief courier received all messages for dispatch, interviewed his couriers and housed them when necessary.
3) Rooms on the Karatni Rjad for recruiting and meetings.

4) Rooms on the Bolshaia Dimitrovka, for meetings and destruction organisation.
5) Flat at Yamskos Polys, for Station Control and passes, etc.
6) Rooms on Bolshaia Poljanka for agents and money store.
7) Flat on Manonovskai, for agents and money store.
8) House 16 versts from Moscow, for indirect couriers and odds and ends (Kuskovo).
9) House 60 versts from Moscow as retreat and refuge (Kudkovo).

August 5th

We had been informed some weeks past, from very reliable sources, that the British Mission and official representatives would be asked to leave, and probably even be arrested before leaving.

The situation for some days had been very critical and the Allies were not received by any of the Soviet officials and our agents informed us that the Soviet was divided into two very strong parties:-

1) The arrest of all British and French officers, pending their enforced departure from the country.
2) Our public execution as reprisals for the supposed shooting of some Soviet Commissars at Kem. This by some of the Extremists including Radek.

Therefore I was not surprised when, early on the morning of the 5th, Captain Alfred Hill of Mr Lockhart's Mission was arrested. This arrest was followed by the general arrests of French and British officers, and civilians all through the town. I immediately left my flat and went to Lt Riley's flat. He knew nothing about the events in the town, but immediately got ready to leave his flat, packed up a few remaining things he had, destroyed his papers and a report he was writing, in my presence, and with me, after sending a warning to the American Consulate, left his flat for our secret quarters.

It had been previously arranged that our go-betweens would be women, and each of us had a member on our staff who had been selected for this work. I sent for my assistant, who had not yet been arrested, and gave him his final instructions about the departure to England, instructing him to pay off all the people who had been working for us, to sell what was possible of our stores, destroy all papers and records and put himself under the orders of Mr Lockhart, whom we supposed would be leaving very shortly for England.

On arrival at our new quarters S. T. and I went through our organisations, arranged passports, and then sent H1 to Lt Webster asking him to send us all the money stored by MI1c, as we considered it no longer safe with them. He returned with the news that the money would be sent to us, and one of Riley's girls came with the news that Riley's old flat had been raided, with the object of arresting him 'as an allied official'.

Later in the day we heard that Mr Lockhart with the members of His Mission and the Consulate together with Lts Boyce and Webster, had been arrested.

1st Week in August

Mr Lockhart, Consuls and Lt Boyce were all set free, and the latter informed us that the money had been safely hidden in the American Consulate previous to their arrest.

At this time we had great difficulty with our documents, which were not in order and hampered our movements. These papers were legalised early in the second week of August, and another great difficulty was to find a suitable cover to work under. This was no easy task as the Soviet was busy preparing to exclude all non-government and manual workers from the City.

Lt Riley got a job in a technical department while I received papers as a film actor and had an interest in a curio and fancy goods store.

Our go-betweens had commenced their service and things seemed to be running very smoothly. Meetings took place as a rule in the public gardens. Lt Webster was liberated on the 7th August.

Aviation

As soon as Allied troops had landed at Archangel great unrest commenced among the Air Forces and desertion to our and Tcheko-Slovak Lines was contemplated by many. This had to be stopped as punishments were being visited on the deserters' squadron commander and members of his squadron who had remained behind; the unit was put under very strong supervision, and the petrol supply as a rule confiscated. The only form of desertion of pilots with machines justifiable at that time would have been the desertion of whole squadrons. To this end we stopped all individual desertions and worked for simultaneous squadrons' flights.

2nd Week in August

Our documents were put in order. Lt Riley's naval connections reported and much information was obtained in regard to the morale, movements and plans of the naval circle. Sabotage and destruction plans in the event of Germany occupying Kronstadt and Petrograd were discussed, and the German activities on the Finnish Coast examined.

A courier arrived from my destruction gang at Saratov with news of their plan; pro tem all destruction of naptha and oils was ordered to be stopped, but I suggested sabotage and systematic propaganda against the proposed movement of the Saratov division to the northern front, and if necessary, the destruction of the line over which they would have to be transported.

(Note. This division never went north.)

In the middle of the week, an order published by the Bolsheviks ordered all former officers, whether employed in any government branch, private business, or those out of work to report for examination and to receive new documents from the Soviet authorities. About 8,000 of the officers stationed in Moscow complied with this order, which broke up any hope of the White Guard organisation being effectively used against the Bolsheviks, as most of the officers examined were promptly arrested, put into barracks outside the town and disarmed. A similar movement had taken place in Petrograd, with the result that a great number of officers found themselves in Kronstadt and the White organisations were broken up by the Bolsheviks with equal success. In Moscow, the scattered remnants of these organisations came to me requesting that their men might be sent to Archangel, but owing to the shortage of funds, and the small likelihood of any real attempt being made by these officers to get through to the North, I informed them that it was impossible to help them.

As a set off, however, of the white Guards' fiasco at Moscow, Kazan fell to the white Guards, and the Bolsheviks' position on the fronts was very critical, especially as the Allies seemed to be pressing from the North, and the mysterious disappearance of Trotsky, Commissar of war, caused much unrest in official circles. Many of the Commissars of the various departments were procuring passports and money, and making general personal arrangements for safe departure.

Despite this victory we were constantly receiving more or less disquieting news as to the state of the Tcheko-Slovak and white Armies. Lack of order, supplies, ammunition, material were constantly being reported, and internal strife was rumoured, and we felt that some desperate effort had to be made if this was to be rectified.

It was during this week that Mr Lockhart sent for Lt Riley for a special interview. On his return from this visit he informed me that the Letts could probably be won over to our side, as a section of them considered that the time had come when it would be to their interest to come under our protection. At this interview Lt Riley had been introduced to Colonel Bersin, the leader of the movement, and it had been arranged that the proposition should be handled by Lt Riley.

Courier Service

We had had no messenger return from Archangel since the arrival of No. 3 without any reply (he having left the day before the Allied landing). News from other sources was disquieting, conditions were awkward, and one realised how great the chances were against a man getting through the lines, who did not know the conditions.

Until the middle of August the courier routes set out on page 24 were being used.

Each courier that set out received a larger advance to increase the chances of getting through, and this naturally led to some small leakages. Had the service been satisfactory, we should have continued the original plan, but as results were so poor, I decided to discontinue the direct messenger service and attempt to organise a large chain service, which though requiring a very much larger personnel and costing considerably more to maintain, would not only make the likelihood of the delivery of messages more sure, but would also fulfil the twofold object of messenger service and scout organisation for supplying information as to local conditions and all the minute details to the commanders of the allied troops operating from North to South [see map pages x and xi].

The new scheme was to provide a centre in Moscow. From Moscow there would be a relay of messengers to the three following points:

1) Moscow to Tschudowo (about 100 versts south of Petrograd)
2) Moscow to Vologda (not in town but district)
3) Moscow to Viatka – three men.

From these points the messages would be taken by the Tzchudowo – Vologda – Viatka groups, who consisted of five men and a group commander at each station.

The group commander's duties here would be to organise his men, select suitable places for living in, procure documents and passports, control the funds for carrying on the work, and meet all local needs and conditions as they arose. The commander and his group would, if necessary, work under the Bolsheviks, and in any case live and dress in keeping with the local inhabitants.

Messages would be taken by these groups to the next set of stations consisting of

1) Petrozovodsk
2) A Station north of Vologda
3) A place in Kotlass.

At these stations the organisations consisted of a group commander and eight men.

The duty of these groups would be to receive the messages from the southern stations and pass them on through into our lines. The group commanders here, in addition to fulfilling the work done at the last stations, would be provided with funds to enable them to get into touch with all local authorities. They also had to find out the best roads, know of all the troops, take stock of the disposition of the Soviet troops, guns, food stores, dumps, and morale of the army, and send these reports verbally to the Allied advanced detachments and scouts, also carry out, if desired, reconnaissance work required by these advance units. If necessary they were to occupy themselves with gentle sabotage. They should also know all those who were pro- or anti-Ally reliable and unreliable, for our use during subsequent occupation of villages by us.

It was extremely difficult to find suitable men to volunteer for this work, but by the 22 August, an extremely fine batch of men were got together under experienced and very keen leaders. All these men had suffered and lost everything they possessed owing to the Bolsheviks. They proved themselves from the very start, and had we continued the work, it would have been entirely satisfactory. The parties left Moscow on the 22nd August and the whole chain was expected to be in operation by the first days of September.

On the departure of these groups we immediately set about procuring a further 20 men to replace the casualties that were bound to occur (Note. Nine of the original number were executed by 'Extraordinary Commissions' in Vologda District).

Lettish Affairs

Mr Lockhart had arranged that Lt Riley should take charge of all questions dealing with the Letts, and from the first the Allies desired to leave the policy to him. After the first meeting, Lt Riley put me 'au courant' with all that had taken place and arranged that I should be fully posted in all matters so that should Lt Riley for any cause be prevented from bringing the work to a finish I should at once be able to pick up the threads and carry on.

To make the following quite clear, it should be borne in mind that Lt Riley conducted all the negotiations, and that at no time did I see the commander or his staff, but at the conclusion of each meeting Lt Riley fully explained to me all that had been done.

Situation of Letts

It should be remembered that the Letts were a people away from their own country, and the civil population of them were refugees in Russia, with all their interests in the hands of the enemy – that the Germans – whom they had always hated.

The Lettish battalion had retreated into Russia and on the signing of the Brest-Litovsk Treaty were a united force without an occupation. They were a people who, by their thought, religion and upbringing, were absolutely strange and foreign to the Russians, and yet had absolutely nothing to lose in serving the Soviet, but rather everything to gain, as it was their temporary means of existence.

The personnel of these regiments was composed of splendid and well tried fighters, and who in their way were well disciplined.

The Soviet government, relying upon what one might term the insularity of the Letts, decided to use them as their main forces, and by giving them special facilities (good food and pay), kept them in their services. From June 1918 on, the Letts were the cornerstone and foundation of the Soviet government. They guarded the Kremlin, gold stock and the munitions. At the head of the 'Extraordinary Commissions' the prisons, the banks and the railroads were Letts. The nucleus of strength on the fronts consisted of Letts, and wherever fighting was to be done the Letts were sent. Russian troops could only be relied upon to act if backed up and coerced by the Letts.

It was realised that if the Letts could be drawn away from the Soviet, the government would have to go. At the end of July the main weak spot was in the civil Lettish population, who were absolutely opposed to the government. As a people they had the principle of co-operation developed to a remarkable extent and most of them had landed property interests in Latvia, and the crushing of all financial and social stability made them fear and hate the Soviet.

By August the Lettish troops felt themselves to be pure executioners; they did not like the Allies coming in from the North, nor did they see what good they could hope for from the future, and the discontent of their civil population had commenced a very great impression on them. It was therefore in keeping with the time that leaders amongst them should have made an effort to stop the headlong flight they had launched themselves into, and approach the allied representative for aid and protection.

At the first meeting Colonel Bersin made a very favourable impression on Mr Lockhart, M. Grenard, the French Consul General, and Lt Riley. Certain sums of money for propaganda and work were promised, and it was arranged that, if on the departure of the Diplomatic Corps all the money had not been handed over, drafts would be left with Lt Riley to enable us to carry out the scheme.

The scheme which the Allied Diplomatic representatives worked for was: a definite relief on our Northern and Tcheko-Slovak fronts, which was to be brought about by certain Lettish units turning over to our side and thereby weakening the main force against our 'troops'.

The Allies, the Tcheko-Slovak and White Guard troops were straining their utmost to join up with each other and to form a united front. The staged Yaroslavl affair had worn itself into a disastrous failure; the confidence of the White Guard organisation was shaken in the Allies and it was impossible to rely on any mob of theirs for support of the Allied troops; especially was it the case after the arrest of the Moscow Petrograd officers by the Bolsheviks, as already mentioned.

The only sound scheme left was to back the Letts. This had been conceded as sound by most people who knew the conditions in Russia, but a few have had doubts as to the rights of staging a revolution internally in Moscow and Petrograd.

The proposed turning of the Lettish troops to our cause on the fronts could not be achieved without very seriously affecting the Moscow and Petrograd centres. The simultaneous change on the fronts and at Moscow and Petrograd would have destroyed the Soviet government, and automatically the White Guards would have come into power, and the ammunition, arms and supplies would have been at the disposal of this new force.

Destruction gangs organised by us for a time would have prevented any possible attempt at interference from the Germans until the Allied forces had linked up, and a national White Guard Army formed.

Supplies from the North, corn from the East and produce from the Volga, with a White Guard force, and there would have been no fear of any trouble from the people. This was the possibility of success. In the event of failure and our being found in any plot, Lt Riley and myself should have simply been private individuals and responsible to no one. As we hourly expected the departure of the Allied representatives, the whole brunt would have been borne by us.

Colonel Bersin considered that everything could be arranged in the space of about five to six weeks. It was proposed to use, among others, the Lettish civil population for propaganda.

Later a Committee of Letts was formed, chosen from the friends of Colonel Bersin, who organised and made arrangements for detail.

Telegrams from Mr Lockhart and ourselves were dispatched to General Poole, informing him of what had been done, and what we proposed to do.

All along we realised that in any plot so large the risks were very great, but that any success would be so great that we were justified in carrying on the arrangements.

About the 22nd of August Lt Riley informed me of a conversation that he had had with Commander Bersin (at the time I was under the impression 'with Bersin's Committee') but this impression has since been corrected. The gist of it was that it was considered advisable that men like Trotsky and Lenin should be assassinated for the following reasons:-

1) Their marvellous oratorical powers would so act on the psychology of the men who went to arrest them that it was not advisable to risk it.
2) The assassination of two of the leaders would create a panic so that there would be no resistance.

Lt Reilly also told me that he had been very firm in dissuading them from such a course, and that in no way would he support it. He impressed upon the Colonel that the policy should be 'not to make martyrs of the leaders but to hold them up to ridicule before the world'.

About 20th August, the Letts had obtained a good secret flat where Lt Reilly used to visit them.

August 12th

About this time, from independent agents, information came in that a great deal of unrest prevailed among many of the Lettish battalions, that the troops were generally dissatisfied and that a lot of anti-Soviet propaganda was going on. This was undoubtedly due to the funds we had put into circulation.

At the end of August Lt Reilly considered it was necessary for him to go to Petrograd to see the Lettish organisations there and to get a personal impression of the existing conditions. He left Moscow for Petrograd on August 28th. Before leaving he gave me the complete list of his agents, places that his money was stored, passwords to his agents, and all works he had in hand. In exchange I gave him the same information about my organisations. Colonel Bersin left a day in advance of Lt Reilly to make arrangements to meet the Lettish Committee without any loss of time.

Lt Reilly also intended to see Commander Cromie (RN) and Lt Boyce (RNVR).

I have not given any detailed reports as to what stage the arrangements with the Letts had been brought as this will be reported fully by Lt Reilly.

Thursday 29th August

The man in charge of the Saratoff organisations came to Moscow. His report for the month was extremely satisfactory, and sabotage and deliberate frustration of the Bolshevik military plans had gone very well. Stores, ammunition and equipment trains were derailed without doing any serious damage to the line, but causing three or four days' blockage. (Removing one line etc.)

Friday 30th August

Lenin's life was attempted at a mill where he was holding a lecture, and the papers which announced this fact on the Saturday morning also gave a description of the death of Uritzky, the chief for combating the counter-revolutionary in Petrograd. The papers at once did all they could to connect the British and French officials with these two outrages. (Note. Later transpired attempt had been instigated by SRs and the evidence cleared the Allies completely, though this was not published.)

We later heard that on Saturday afternoon the 31st the British Embassy had been raided, Commander Cromie killed, all the members of the British Mission and Consulate in the building arrested and those who escaped arrest were being hunted. At midnight on Saturday August 31st-September 1st, Mr Lockhart's flat in Moscow was raided, Mr Lockhart and Mr Hicks were taken off to the Extraordinary Commission for Combating Counter-Revolution, but a few hours later were released. At the same time, Commandant Devertement however escaped.

Sunday 1st September

About midday Lt Reilly's chief girl E. E. was arrested. Her House was thoroughly searched, and she was repeatedly asked whether she had not got some friend who was likely to give her away. She posed as innocent, though showing much nervousness. Through two friends in the house the money she had in her possession was saved – she carried no documents. Just as the search party was about to leave the house with E. E., whom they assured would be allowed her freedom within a few hours, as nothing had been found against her, a girl by the name of Marie Frede, of the American H. S. appeared. This woman was carrying messages, and on seeing the armed guards seemed to lose her head and gave away that she was carrying documents for E. E. This girl was likewise arrested, as a few hours later were her two brothers who also belonged to the American service.

Monday 2nd September

This was the first day of the Red Terror, and it looked like the Bolsheviks were prepared for massacre on a very large scale.

The papers were extremely bitter again at the supposed attempt on Lenin on the part of the Allies, and openly accused them of having been mixed up with the killing of Uritzky. No news was to be obtained as to why E. E. had been arrested. Mr Lockhart had been allowed his liberty after three hours' arrest, while the British and Allied Consulates had in no way been violated.

Tuesday 3rd September

Leading articles in the papers exposed the so-called Lockhart conspiracy, stating that he was the originator of the Lettish plot that was intended to raise the Letts against the Bolsheviks, murder the leaders of the Soviets and restore a monarchy in Russia. They cited Lt Reilly as Lockhart's spy and admitted the arrest of E. E. and Frede. They also gave an account of the raiding of Commandant Devertement's flat, and a full account of the raid at the British Embassy in Petrograd, and Captain Cromie's death. From the Press one gathered that Lt Reilly had been caught in Petrograd during the raid. Later on Tuesday afternoon I sent the message to Mr Lockhart that 'I had been over the network of our organisation and found everything intact, but that there was undoubtedly a fair amount of nervousness among some of the agents. That I had got all Lt Reilly's affairs under my own control, and provided I could get money it would be possible to carry on.' That we had the greatest difficulty in getting up our messages to the north, and unless the new chain organisation produced a better result than single messenger service had done it would be useless to carry on. However, I thought a lot might yet be done in destruction. My messenger arrived at Mr

Lockhart's flat just after he had been arrested for the second time. Captain Hicks received my message and said that he considered that it would be imperative for us to lie low for some days to come, and that as far as he knew there would be no money available for the purposes that I required it, as our source for obtaining same had completely dried since the crash. He also had no news about Lt Reilly and supposed that he had been arrested. Sent off a message through the now chain service informing General Poole of what had taken place at Moscow.

Wednesday 4th September

It was evident that the Bolsheviks were in a panic and were purging themselves of bourgeois and officers employed by them in the various governmental departments and it looked as if our large source of information from these channels would be no longer available for us. Mr Lockhart was re-arrested, and his flat had been searched from 'top to bottom' and things stolen from it. Some French and Allies had been arrested. Arrest had taken place in the streets, and general panic prevailed. In the morning a girl of Lt Reilly's came to say that he was safe and in Moscow, having travelled in a first class compartment from Petrograd. He had arrived on Thursday the 3rd September, but beyond the fact of knowing that Commander Cromie had been killed and the Embassy raided, he had no suspicion that the Bolsheviks knew of the plans or attempt that was being made to use the Letts against the Soviet. On arrival at the Nicolai Station he had been informed that his chief girl had been arrested, but beyond knowing this he was in entire ignorance of what the morning papers were printing. He received his paper on the Tuesday morning and saw that the Lettish affair was known, and his name cited as Mr Lockhart's spy. For want of a better place he slept at his own flat on the night of Tuesday the 3rd. His message reached me at midday on Wednesday, and I went off to see him at two rooms his agent had found for him at the back end of the town. He had changed his name but had the same disguise and was not going out during the day or night, not having any documents to prove his identity. He made the following statement about his visit to Petrograd.

He had left Moscow according to plan on Wednesday the 5th August and had arrived at Petrograd without any hitch (the passes he had being excellent), although his train was extremely late in arriving at Petrograd. He drove direct from the station to his flat and on his way there met Colonel Bersin of the Letts, who had been to his flat by appointment, having arrived in Petrograd 24 hours previous to the arrival of Lt Reilly. He returned with Lt Reilly and reported to him, telling him all that he had done and arranging another meeting at the flat. Lt Reilly then sent a messenger to Lt Boyce informing him of his arrival, and requesting him to let him know where they could meet. He then went about openly doing the work he had decided to do there when in Moscow.

A hitch occurred in the transmission of his message to Lt Boyce, and therefore he did not see him on Thursday, but owing to a misunderstanding they did not meet. However, about midday on the 31st August he got into touch with Lt Boyce, and they had a conference together. Lt Reilly explained to him the whole of the Lettish plan, and Lt Boyce said he considered the whole thing was extremely risky but agreed that it was worth trying, and that failure of the plan would drop entirely on the neck of Lt Reilly. He considered that it was extremely important for Lt Reilly to meet Captain Cromie as Captain Cromie had had a great deal to do with the Letts. He left Lt Reilly at his flat to go to the British Embassy with the intention of returning by three o'clock with Commander Cromie. Lt Reilly waited in his flat until after six o'clock, but no one turned up. He afterwards heard of Captain Cromie's death, but in no way connected it with the Letts affair. On Monday Lt Reilly booked a sleeper for Moscow. He used the same passes that he had done on his journey north and arrived in Moscow as already described and only then got the first news of the crash.

At this meeting Lt Reilly said that his mind was entirely open, and that if it was thought better for him to come forward and be openly arrested he was willing to do so. I told him I did not consider this at all necessary, and would in no way clear up the affair, and suggested that it would be the safest thing for him to try and work through to the East via Ukrainia. He strongly objected to taking this step, saying he would lose a lot of time on that trip and bring no one any good, and that if he had to go he should make for the north, either via Finland and out to a neutral port, or direct through a courier line. He wanted passports, some new clothing and as the place he was staying in was entirely unsuitable, a fresh lodging. He had already sent to Mr Lockhart his official report and what he considered had happened. He also told him that there had been no documents or anything of our work found by the Bolsheviks. However, Mr Lockhart had been arrested before he received this message, though I believe Captain Hicks had it.

Thursday 5th September

Moved Lt Reilly into new quarters at a Soviet office. Owing to the visible shortage of funds in the near future, and as our expenses were going up daily we felt that the work could not be carried on, and that I was in no way suspected, it would be best to come to life and try to get out of Russia as an official. Lt Reilly's position being different he decided to go to Petrograd and travel by the best available route.

I had a conference on this day with the chief of my couriers, and we considered that at least six or seven of our couriers had been executed by the Soviet Commissions of the North. I informed him that I should probably discontinue that service, but would want all the men for other work.

Friday 6th September

The British Consul General, Mr Wardrop, found that it was impossible for me to be included on his official staff, as he said he did not dare risk having my name on the paper, and thereby endanger the whole of his party. This was after I had explained to him that to the best of my knowledge I was in no way under suspicion, that none of my acts could be traced back to me. Captain Hicks, however, took up the matter, and it was thanks to him after a consultation with his American colleagues, that I was put on Mr Lockhart's list as an official member. I took off my disguise on the Friday afternoon and appeared again under my own name and papers. I had meanwhile given my original GB paper to Lt Reilly, and it was with these papers that he finally got out from Russia and into Finland.

Friday Evening

H.1 received a letter from one of our agents saying that he was being blackmailed by a man called G., in the employ of Lt Webster, and that unless he paid the sum of R10,000, he would notify the Soviet authorities of our address, and also that he had been asked by Lt Boyce if he was prepared to do away with one or two prominent members of the Soviet government. As this agent and the agent through whom it came, belonged to the former MI1c, the matter was forwarded on to Lt Webster for his consideration. Under the existing conditions, and not knowing the fate of our mission in Petrograd, of whom we were receiving most disquieting news, he felt it was advisable to pay up rather than have anything fresh brought up against us. He sent by return messenger the sum required and nothing more was heard.

On Saturday the 7th, on arrival at the American Consulate, I discovered that the place was under siege, but owing to a friendly warning of a chauffeur, I managed to get away without being arrested, I later heard that Lt Tamplin, 2nd Lt Tomling, Lt Pinder and Mr Higgs had been arrested outside the consulate.

Final preparations were made for Lt Reilly to leave. We had up to this date only lost one girl, E. E., the rest of our organisations being intact.

Sunday the 8th

Lt Reilly left for Petrograd, travelling in a sleeper with new documents to conform with the papers I had given him. I spent that night at the British Consulate.

Monday the 9th

I saw the chief of the couriers, and gave him instructions to withdraw the whole of his work on Moscow.

Tuesday the 10th

I sent off H.1 to Sweden as I considered it was no longer safe for her to remain behind. However, I continued to use one of my old lodgings as it had not been raided.

Second Week of September

Kalematiano, Chief of the American SS, was arrested. All his documents were found. Lt Reilly's last flat was raided and his agent 'O' arrested at the Kremlin. Nothing was found in his flat, nor any information or papers obtained from 'O'.

It was extremely difficult at this period to judge how deep the Lettish affair had gone, and whether there was any truth in the Bolshevik statements that they had staged the plot themselves. There was a feeling that the Lettish troops had bitter feelings against the Soviet.

By the end of the week I had a series of conflicting reports, but the tend of them made me decide that as we had already spent so much money, it was worth spending some more to save something of wreck, I therefore collected half a dozen Letts personally known to me, and sent them off on an anti-Bolshevik campaign showing what possibilities there had been for the Letts and the harm Latvia had done for herself in the supposed treachery and double dealing with the Allies, I sent a small section of pro-Ally Letts to work in Riga, Mitau, Pernau, and also made attempts to get into touch with the Pastor of the Lettish church, one or two of the prominent Letts in Moscow, and a Captain Dzegus, who did excellent work.

From September 3rd all British officers with the exception of one or two panic-stricken Consuls, were either imprisoned or besieged in the American Consulate so that it was impossible to get any advice or to confer with anyone, I followed general principles.

Destruction

I instructed the destruction gangs at Saratoff to commence operations. About four trains of material were derailed a week, preparations were made for the destruction of fuel and oil supplies here, and a section was sent to work on the Varonish line.

Third Week in September

The courier chain organisation was back in Moscow. It was reported to me that 12 of our couriers had been shot, as had also one or two of my independent agents. Great credit is due to this body of men and to those shot, who could all have saved their lives by giving away the HQ address in Moscow. This address was never given away, and every man shot showed the spirit of the 1914 Russian officers. I employed them collectively on one or two jobs in Moscow. As two of them came from the Baltic provinces, they were sent there, and finally the remainder were paid two months' money and sent to the East where I hope to pick them up again and resume work.

I tried to clear up the arrest of Lt Reilly's agent E. E., and had carefully discussed the matter with him, and all other matters connected with the Lettish affair.

1) The reason for E. E.'s arrest:-

Lt Reilly remembered that on the 22nd August at the American Consulate he met the SS agents of France and USA for the purpose of establishing contact. In giving the address of E. E. as a connecting link to Commandant Devertement (alias Henry), the Commandant had taken the name down in his note-book as a French name, and Lt Reilly pointed out that it was a Russian name and should be spelt in a different way. The Commandant said he would put that right when he got home and transferred it into code. Now on making enquiries, it was found that the 'warrant for arrest' was made out in the name of 'Elisabeth' and not 'Elisaveta'. We supposed that the Commandant had failed to transfer the address into code or that his notebook had been found when his house had been searched (we were under the impression that Com. Devertement had been arrested).

When the Bolsheviks arrested any person all addresses found on him were followed up by arresting the addressees. However, later I met Com. Devertement in Finland, and he assured me nothing of his had been found, and produced his note-book with the address fully obliterated.

The Commandant's theory was that it had been given away by the treachery of a Frenchman who had attended the meeting on August 22nd. This Frenchman a M. Marchand who had left a most incriminating letter addressed to President Poincare on his table (found after his arrest) giving a full description of the meeting of the 22nd August at the American Consulate, and probably giving the commandant's address away, as prior to this absolutely no suspicion of any kind had been attached to him. I discussed the matter with the Commandant in the presence of Col. Corbeille, who, though admitting that Marchand had written a very indiscreet letter, held that it was more a foolish than a criminal one, and did not think that M. Marchand would give us away to that extent. However, M. Marchand's letter written twelve days after his presence at the allied meeting, and three days after the Lettish plot had been printed in the papers, cannot produce a good impression on being read, and one feels that it was likely that he was responsible for E. E's arrest, and the raid upon Devertement's rooms.

2) As to whether Colonel Bersin was a traitor or not, this will be dealt with by Lt Reilly, though I gather he considered him guiltless.

3) The Church. When the Lettish affair burst, the Press alleged that we had been attempting to buy the Church, and that we had made statements to that effect. Lt Reilly denied ever mentioning the Church, and considers it a pure 'try on' on their part, and that treachery within the ecclesiastical circle may have given the Bolsheviks the required clue.

Difficulties and general work in Russia

I. Communications

All ordinary and modern means of communication no longer existed in the interior of Russia. Telegraph and postal services only operated in a few instances. Trains took days instead of hours to travel, and the telephone systems of Moscow and Petrograd were not open for the general public to use. All messages had therefore to be sent by trusted messengers. Owing to the suspension of the telephone system, it was quite impossible to give warnings, or to ring up to find if the coast was clear when making visits.

II. Lodgings and Cover

The new system of House Committees made it almost impossible to get into any lodgings, and certainly not without reference from your old house with Soviet papers, passes, registration and employment documents (infringement of any House Rules being visited upon the offender and the Committee itself). This overcome, however, another great difficulty arose from the constant spying of the Dvornik and Servants' League. The union of this latter, at all their meetings, were exhorting the members to spy upon their employers, and the extraordinary Commission for Combating Counter-Revolution offered Rs.10,000.- to any servant who would give evidence that would impeach their employers as enemies of the 'people'.

At one time in Russia I found it necessary to employ an English girl as a servant in order to safeguard the house.

Even if one could have found neutral cover to work under, the security would have been slight as ex-territoriality was no longer to be expected. Anyone's house might be searched without writ or order, and all houses were constantly being pryed into on all sorts of pretexts.

In August decrees were issued that everyone had to have an approved occupation if they wished to remain within the City boundaries.

Agents who had taken fictitious jobs, or opened a shop, found themselves in the position of outlaws as the result of some new by-law, which put their industry or trade in the Black List.

For instance a druggist and antique store (combination only possible in Russia) taken by myself, received two fatal blows in one month.

1) It was declared illegal to sell any druggist's goods without a special (prohibitive) licence, and all goods with fats in them were confiscated by the food controllers. (Soaps, etc.)
2) It was forbidden to serve antiques, and all such articles in shops were sealed and declared to be 'National Treasure', although no mention of recompense appeared at the end of the order.

Agents

The accounts will show the cost of agents to have been very high. This is explained by the very high cost of living, of transport, and high expense incurred by any man who uses sub-agents or has local bribings and expenses in connection with his work. Today it is more necessary that agents in Russia should be overpaid, than it is in any other country. To employ men who are reliable, one must pay them well, and allow them to live as they had been in the habit of living. If one resorts to employing a cheap form of agent, it is so very much more expedient for him to sell you than to work for you, that in eight cases out of ten he does so, and in the ninth case blackmails you. It is necessary in towns like Moscow and Petrograd to free agents from standing in provision queues, etc., as this occupation takes the members of the entire family out every day for some hours. The cost of flour is six hundred Rbs. per pood (36 English lbs.) in Petrograd, if bought without a ration card; and one cannot get work out of a man on one eighth of a lb of bread per day.

It should be noticed that today in Russia not a single agent will put his name to any piece of paper or receipt, so that if in future agents are to be employed by us in Russia, any hope of establishing control by the old system of voucher must be abandoned.

Russians on the whole have been so disgracefully treated, and have paid with their lives as the result of their employers' carelessness with receipts and notes that one cannot blame them for refusing to sign papers.

I cannot point out too clearly that our agents should have sufficient funds to be always able to employ the best men, men of standing or army men with a clean record. It is fatal to deal with the smaller bourgeoisi or the junior commercial men.

Money

This is one of the greatest difficulties of the Russian SS and the procuring of money is extremely difficult and dangerous work. To start with trading in Valuta is illegal and punishable by death. To obtain money against drafts is almost impossible. So few wealthy people now have any money at their disposal, for despite their large credit at the bank, they are only allowed to draw a few hundred roubles a month.

Once the money has been obtained, the storing of it is the next great problem. There are no banks, even the Peoples' Savings Bank cannot be used. No place that is practical is safe, and to us it was a constant worry and trouble.

(signed) *George A. Hill. Capt.*
4th Manch. Regt. & RAF.

This document is held at the National Archives, Public Record Office, file reference FO 371/3350

Index

ESPIONAGE CLASSICS